PEAK EXPERIENCES

EDITED BY
CAROL STONE WHITE

Peak Experiences
Danger, Death, and Daring in the Mountains of the Northeast

University Press of New England
Hanover and London

University Press of New England

www.upne.com

© 2012 University Press of New England

All rights reserved

Manufactured in the United States of America

Designed by Mindy Basinger Hill

Typeset in 10.5/14 pt. Minion Pro

University Press of New England is a member
of the Green Press Initiative. The paper used in this book
meets their minimum requirement for recycled paper.

For permission to reproduce any of the material in this book,
contact Permissions, University Press of New England,
One Court Street, Suite 250, Lebanon NH 03766; or visit
www.upne.com

Library of Congress Cataloging-in-Publication Data

White, Carol Stone, 1962–
Peak experiences: danger, death, and daring in the mountains
of the Northeast / edited by Carol Stone White.
    p.   cm.
Includes bibliographical references.
ISBN 978-1-61168-254-0 (pbk.: alk. paper)—
ISBN 978-1-61168-368-4 (ebook)
1. Hiking—Northeastern States. I. Title.
GV199.42. N68W45 2012
917.4—dc23   2012017360

5   4   3   2   1

This book is dedicated to all those who venture into the backcountry—day and night, in all seasons, under the most extreme conditions—to find and rescue lost and injured hikers, many times putting themselves at personal risk. Search and rescue organizations and their volunteers are truly heroic: they put their own lives on hold in order to help someone in need, sometimes persisting through deep snow, extreme cold, and hurricane-force winds.

CONTENTS

PREFACE

The stories in this volume describe peril, triumph, wonder, terror, and exhilaration. In spite of the risks of life-threatening conditions, injuries, and myriad difficulties, why do we keep going back to the mountains? Not long before he disappeared on Everest, George Mallory was asked why he climbed mountains. "Because they're there," he quipped. Those three words might well describe the culture of peakbagging that exploded in New England and New York after World War II.

The Adirondack Forty-Sixers organization began in 1948, based on the intrepid explorations of Bob and George Marshall, who climbed all forty-six of the High Peaks over 4,000 feet in elevation (as measured at the time). Bob Marshall went on to found the Wilderness Society. In the White Mountains, peakbagging began in 1957, when a list of the forty-eight peaks above 4,000 feet was created as an enticement to explore lesser-known mountains. Hikers who climb these and the other 4,000-footers in our region become "Northeast 111ers." (Thanks to more recent measurements, the number of such peaks has now reached 115.) In 1962, the Catskill 3500 Club was established, requiring climbs of the Catskills' thirty-five peaks over 3,500 feet, and four winter climbs. People discover to their delight that winter is an exquisite and exciting season to be in the peaks.

There is great satisfaction in pushing limits and achieving goals, but the mountain experience is much more than bagging peaks. Adventuring in the mountains is found to be recreation of a higher order, literal "re-creation" that nourishes the soul. After a period in the mountains, our batteries are recharged and our spirits given sustenance. In wildness we experience some of our greatest joys. "I have a thousand memories of amazing places, success, failure, pure effort and exertion, shared experiences, and scenes of beauty on this earth that will be with me all of my life," writes Ben Potter, one of this volume's authors. "I find happiness and peace in situations where my skills, fortitude, and ability to make decisions correctly under pressure will be tested. Someone once said that nothing worth doing was easy (and it may not always be safe either), but if we all practice our skills, sharpen our talents and wit, and exercise a good measure of honest judgment, the possibilities are endless and the risks manageable. No one wants to end up over their head having to make hard decisions, but how you act in those situations can define you as a person. Here's hoping that our resolve may be tested, but not broken; our strength pushed, but not exhausted; our experiences invaluable, and not forgotten. Let us respect the hills and learn from those that have suffered in pursuit of their majesty, and strive to one day look back upon the risks that we have taken with a smile and never a regret."

Beginning climbers are often surprised by extreme weather, especially above tree line—they might begin at the base on a warm, pleasant day, only to climb unprepared into wintry blasts. They might be confronted by the terrifying power of a swollen river, or find themselves in dangerous terrain, unsure of how to proceed and perhaps lacking proper gear. Our human tendency to believe that misfortune "can't happen to me" sometimes makes us resistant to turning back. In pursuit of a summit, a peakbagger may abandon prudence—as a few of these stories show. Reading such up-close-and-personal experiences can augment the comprehensive study of ice, wind, rock, and water required to safely venture into the mountains. The Cliff Notes scattered throughout the book provide additional advice, analysis, and asides.

As search and rescue specialist Peter Crane writes, "A hiker must constantly ask: Do I have the patience, skill, and strength to manage difficulties, the knowledge and intelligence to recognize and avoid dangers, and the wisdom to know the difference between what is unpleasant and what may be damaging or deadly, such as lightning, avalanche, and super-hurricane winds? Potentially fatal changes can occur with uncommon suddenness. The difference between an exciting trip and a disastrous one can be as simple as a turned ankle or a broken snowshoe."

Safe hiking is much like safe driving—both require our best judgments and a continual awareness of the immediate environment. In the mountains, as on the highways, even a brief moment of inattention can lead to serious trouble. By discerning the patterns of peril in this volume's personal stories, we can learn how to remain in the proverbial driver's seat. This can decrease our reliance on Lady Luck—and help us take responsibility for our own good fortune.

ACKNOWLEDGMENTS

I am indebted to the talented writers who have shared parts of their lives with us—along with the lessons they have learned on the great mountains of the northeast United States. Their stories will increase awareness about the hazards of this activity we all love and become a fine addition to the hiking literature.

I especially thank Peter Crane, curator of the Gladys Brooks Memorial Library, Mount Washington Observatory, for providing information about search and rescue organizations and the hikeSafe program, which educates the public about appropriate and prudent practices in the wild areas of New Hampshire. Peter shared his firsthand knowledge about the unique conditions on Mount Washington and provided important sources of information. Thanks as well to Al Sochard for sharing his insights about a successful search and rescue operation.

Great thanks to Steve Smith, owner of The Mountain Wanderer Map and Book Store, Lincoln, New Hampshire, for suggesting the names of many friends who write eloquently about their experiences in the mountains.

I'm also deeply appreciative of Laura Waterman's ready advice, assistance, and inspiration. After decades of mountaineering—and co-authoring books with Guy Waterman—Laura established The Waterman Fund to foster stewardship of the mountains of the Northeast. Such stewardship is vitally needed as ever more people seek out physical challenge, beauty, and spiritual inspiration in our wild and spectacular region. Special thanks to Doug Hunt for locating hike leaders to tell the important story of why the Wildcat Slide is called Hal's Slide; to James Goss and Marianne Lederman for permission to share hikeSafe website information; to Doug Mayer for contacting search and rescue leaders; to Mike Hansen for information about the Fabyan Path, and to David Hooke and David Kotz for contacting Dartmouth Outing Club alumni/ae.

Thank you to Steve Boheim, Douglas Hunt, Paul Misko, Alex Potter, Benjamin Potter, Scott Rimm-Hewitt, Mats Roing, Arlene Heer Stefanko, Dan Stone, and David Scott White for contributing stunning photographs to illustrate this book. It has been a pleasure to work with Richard Pult, Susan Abel, and Peter Fong to produce this contribution to the hiking literature, which we hope will enhance the enjoyment and safety of mountain hiking.

Most of all, I am grateful for my husband David's good humor, encouragement, and guidance on the many trails of our lives. Dave's ready wit and true grit have made the ups and downs of our splendid adventures into peak experiences.

PART I

Weatherwise or Otherwise?

Presidential Range Perils and Other Tales above Tree Line

The higher you go, the colder, windier, and wetter the weather is likely to be. Weather changes quickly in the mountains, and full preparation for unexpected conditions is essential, including being prepared to turn back. Local forecasts may require postponing a long-planned hike, if you know that conditions above tree line can be dangerous or deadly. Let us begin with lessons learned in the mountains by two experienced veterans:

Peter Crane and Guy Waterman.

PETER CRANE

Nature Is Unforgiving
Case Studies

Hikers in the Granite State have been exposed to a new motto that's simple and to the point: hikeSafe. The hikeSafe program is the first of its kind in the country and its keystone is the Hiker Responsibility Code, which distills much knowledge into critical advice to foster responsible hiker behavior. Jointly established by the White Mountain National Forest and the New Hampshire Fish and Game Department, hikeSafe was developed by people with experience in the backcountry, including those with search and rescue experience, to make mishaps less likely and help ensure enjoyable trips. The Hiker Responsibility Code provides core principles based on one vital fact: You are responsible for yourself.

Be prepared with knowledge and gear. Become self-reliant by learning about the terrain, conditions, local weather, and your equipment before you start. A man from Boston visited the White Mountains in the autumn of 1855, having read about the spectacular mountains, but he knew little of the terrain and came unprepared for wintry conditions. He barely survived two nights above tree line, sheltered by his overcoat and umbrella. He was aware that only a month earlier, a young woman from Maine had died on the upper slopes of the mountain—part of a party similarly ignorant of the mountain's fierce potential, and ill-equipped for an unsheltered night out.

Leave your plans with responsible persons. Tell someone where you are going, what trails you will be hiking, when you will return, and your emergency plans. The message should be: "If I am not home by "X" o'clock, come looking for me *here.*" This is both a safeguard for the hiker and a critical courtesy for those who respond when someone does not return home as scheduled. Case in point: in June 2009, a lone man hiked up Mount Washington in typically poor weather—breezy, cold, foggy, and wet. No one knew of his specific plans, and so no alarm was raised when he failed to return to Pinkham Notch later that day. A week passed before his sister, accustomed to regular communication with him, alerted authorities that something must have gone wrong. With no knowledge of his intended route, a wide net was cast to look for him; his remains were not found until July 6. With the details of this hiker's final hours unknown, one can only speculate on the possibilities for rescue. But if someone had known his plans and his expected return time, a more focused search might have resulted in a happier ending.

Stay together. If you start a hike as a group, then continue hiking as a group and end as a group, adjusting your pace to the slowest person. Should problems arise, it can be important to have access to all of the group's equipment and knowledge. In addition, splitting up a group can lead to miscommunication or worse. Case in point: on December 29, 1997, a group of three hikers were climbing on the west slope of Mount Washington. Although fog and blowing snow should have encouraged them to stick very close together, the front and rear hikers were surprised to notice that their companion was no longer between them. Circumstances delayed a definitive search for the missing hiker until December 31, when he was finally located by two searchers. In the ensuing rescue operation, both of those searchers were injured. The entire incident could have been avoided—with much happier results for all—if the hikers had recognized the singular importance of staying together in such conditions.

Be prepared to turn back. If you've been anticipating a hiking trip for weeks, it can be difficult to squelch your plans even in the face of cold, wind, and fog. The mountains will still be there another day but, if circumstances turn adverse, you might not be. Thrilling accounts of desperate mountaineering feats might fuel one's enthusiasm to struggle to the top, but remember that only the survivors write about their escapes—the victims' stories often go untold. Know your limitations, realize that unexpected weather conditions and your own fatigue will affect your hike, and you will be better able to decide when to postpone it. Case in point: J.O. and a friend attempted a traverse of the Franconia Ridge in February 2008. The forecast called for severe weather, with cold winds, snow, and limited visibility. Ignoring the ominous significance of such a forecast for a winter trip above tree line, the two started anyway. Although a passing hiker advised them that the ridgeline was socked in, and despite noticing an abrupt drop in temperature, they continued on to the ridge, where the suddenly increasing winds buffeted them. They were pinned down in a whiteout, forced to bivouac overnight in extreme conditions. J.O. suffered serious frostbite and loss of limbs; his friend had succumbed to hypothermia by the time searchers located them.

Be prepared for emergencies. Even if you are headed out for just an hour, an injury, a change in the weather, or a wrong turn could transform a pleasant hike into a life-threatening situation. Don't assume you will be rescued; know how to rescue yourself. Preparation demands thoughtful planning. It also adds weight to your pack, but that weight can become essential for survival. Case in point: a couple was climbing Mount Lafayette in late March 2004, with poor visibility above tree line. From the summit, they missed a turn on the route back to the valley. Continued poor visibility and high winds led them to bivouac on the mountain. Although they were reasonably prepared for a day hike, they did not have the extra clothing and equipment required for an extended stay. When adverse conditions the following day prolonged their ordeal to two nights, the subzero cold eventually took its toll; one of the pair succumbed to hypothermia.

Share the Hiker Responsibility Code with others. The more we are touched by the failure to hike with prudence and caution, the more likely we become to urge safe practices. As one of several persons who carried the remains of P.S. on his final ascent of Mount Washington—as someone who has visited a frostbitten searcher in the hospital, heard J.O.'s heart-rending description of his tragic excursion with his lost friend, been involved in the search for the lost couple on Mount Lafayette, and witnessed the sad spectacle of that unfortunate woman's helicopter lift from her icy bivouac—I have learned that hikeSafe is not just a motto, but a way of life. Spread the word.

GUY WATERMAN

Winter above Tree Line

November 1968's snowfall, as measured on the summit of Mount Washington, was already 87 inches. December added another whopping 104 inches to the pile. . . . That amazing winter, the total snow accumulation very nearly reached 50 feet! On the trails that led to and connected the Appalachian Mountain Club (AMC) huts, a party of four chose to divide their resources to facilitate a winter traverse: one pair would start from Lonesome Lake and work eastward toward the Presidentials. The other pair would start at the Presidentials, do a standard Presidentials traverse, and then keep going. The two parties would meet roughly halfway. From then on the going would be easier for both groups—because their trails would be packed. Or such was the elegantly worked-out theory.

On December 24, 1968, the first pair, Dave Ingalls and Roy Kligfield, started from Franconia Notch. With huge packs laden for the lengthy journey, they snowshoed up to tree line on the Franconia Ridge, crossed over the alpine zone and Mount Lafayette, and camped at Garfield Pond on that first night. Bitterly cold temperatures and high winds greeted their efforts next morning, but they laboriously chugged on over Garfield and the ups and downs of that ridge, reaching Galehead Hut for a cold Christmas night. Ingalls had partially frozen a few toes the year before, and that night he noted ominous signs of recurring frostbite. Still determined, they took off from Galehead Hut and climbed South Twin. On the high wind-racked ridge beyond South Twin, the snow had drifted so deep among the stunted trees that it was hopeless to find the trail. Repeatedly they sunk in spruce traps and had to struggle out of their enormous packs to extricate themselves. Ingalls realized his feet had lost all feeling. In desperation they opted to return to the lower and more sheltered elevation of Galehead Hut, where the temperature that night sunk to −24 degrees Fahrenheit.

The next morning, December 27, the two climbers began a desperate flight for survival. They headed down and out of the mountains, constantly losing and re-finding the trail along the Gale River, physically worn and defeated, and with the certain knowledge that Ingalls's feet were in bad shape. By late afternoon they slid down the last snowbank to the plowed road. They didn't try to hitch a ride; instead, they walked out in front of the next car and forced it to stop. Ingalls elected to be driven to Massachusetts General Hospital, in hopes of receiving more knowledgeable medical care than might be available at a smaller facility. After a long recuperation, he walked back into the world with several toes lost forever, victims of frostbite.

The other pair included the author of this account and his then sixteen-year-old son, Johnny. Their attempt to complete the traverse was just as fruitless as the Ingalls-Kligfield fiasco. . . . The raw power, the malign destructive force of a mountain winter fully impressed both father and son. Their tale—which almost became a tragedy—is worth retelling for the lessons it teaches about the hazards of winter camping and climbing in New England's mountains. On the day after Christmas, 1968, the father and son duo struggled into huge packs, donned snowshoes, and began slowly plodding through a couple of feet of fresh snow up a mountain trail called the Valley Way. Whoever named this trail had his terminology backward: "Valley" Way climbs nearly 4,000 vertical feet in less than 4 miles, up into the northern end of the Presidential Range. The hikers' objective was to traverse the peaks of the Presidentials and, if possible, to continue across other mountain ranges to the west. They never got near those western ranges.

They covered about three miles that first day. Their packs were jammed full of enough winter equipment and food to last ten days. As this was before the days of lightweight gear, the packs weighed more than 80 pounds each. The fresh, unconsolidated December snow, plus the weight of those packs, meant that at every step the lead man sank in about 2 feet. It was absurdly slow going. And they got a late start.

Lesson 1—Don't count on moving rapidly in winter. Trail conditions can make half a mile per hour an exhausting speed. The Appalachian Mountain Club suggests, "Guidebook travel times should be doubled in winter." Under some conditions, that advice is not nearly conservative enough.

That night, they camped on one of the few level spots in the trail and watched the temperature sink to –12 degrees Fahrenheit. In the morning it was –18 degrees, but so far they were doing all right. They continued until emerging above tree line in the Presidential Range, in the high col between Mount Adams and Mount Madison. Here the full fury of the notorious Presidentials' winter was tuning up. Winds shrieked and howled, buffeting the two climbers at every step. Temperatures below zero in a still valley feel

View from Mount Madison to Mount Adams and Mount Washington.
Photo by David White

darn cold; those same temperatures on an exposed, wind-racked ridge are of an entirely new order of cold.

A curious feature of the Presidentials in winter is that much of the alpine zone has relatively little snow on the ground. That is because those ferocious winds blow most of it off the treeless heights, leaving a frozen terrain of rock and ice. Where the wind permits snow to collect, vast snowfields can occasionally build up to considerable depth, covering every feature of the mountain and every trace of the trail. Aside from those great snowfields, however, New England's most wintry spot paradoxically does not have very deep snow.

Father and son came prepared for this environment. They exchanged snowshoes for crampons, pulled windproof nylon pants over their wool pants, and donned face masks. They pulled their parka hoods tight around the masks, and wore "monster mitts" that extended up to their elbows. No exposed skin must be left to that punishing wind.

Lesson 2—Bring clothing suitable for full-scale arctic conditions. Especially important are adequate headgear (as much heat loss occurs through the top of the head), genuine winter boots (not summer-weight hiking boots), and a good mitten-glove combination.

Our two climbers managed to reach the two nearest summits, Madison and Adams, by leaving their heavy packs lower down on the ridge and dashing up with ice axes in hand. The air was crystal clear and the sky an unbelievably deep blue, so they had no difficulty finding their packs when they descended, a fact they'd recall with grim irony 24 hours later. That night they reached the col between Mounts Adams and Jefferson, where they huddled into a small emergency shelter that was maintained by the Forest Service.

In the morning, the temperature had risen to 12 degrees. The mountains were socked in and light snow was falling but, since the wind wasn't knocking them off their feet, they made the decision to proceed. The trail would cut across the broad shoulder of Mount Jefferson, then continue toward Mount Washington, the highest peak in the Northeast. The decision to move on under those conditions proved to be a dangerous mistake. Visibility was soon no more than 50 feet and they had underestimated how much wind they would be dealing with as they moved out of the col. They had scarcely started when it became evident that a full-blown winter storm was underway.

Climbing out of the col onto the side of Jefferson proved to be hard work. Laboring under heavy packs, they became quite warm and shed their wool shirts from under their wind parkas. The father decided that uncovering his pack to stow the shirt inside would risk frostbite to his fingers, so he just tucked the shirt securely under the top flap and resumed the arduous climb. As they rounded the shoulder of Jefferson, they began to traverse one of those huge snowfields that collect on the Presidentials, visible from the highway well into July most years. It covered almost every cairn or other trace of the trail.

With the low visibility, it became difficult for the two climbers to stay on the trail. As they came out of the lee of the summit, the full fury of the wind slammed into them, blowing a steady torrent of ice crystals into their faces. Progress became painfully slow. To guard against losing their way, which could have been disastrous, the son would go out from the last identified cairn as far as he could—and still see it. Then the father would go out from there, as far as he could without losing sight of the son, and stand waiting for some brief lapse in the wind to try to squint forward, into the fury of the storm, in a forlorn effort to find another cairn. In all that snow, however, only the tops of the tallest cairns showed, and often many minutes passed before they could spot the next one and move on.

To one who has not been there, it's difficult to convey the full import of a winter storm above tree line. The myriad unfamiliar sensations include:

- barely being able to stand on your feet, braced always by your ice ax, and moving forward fitfully, only between gusts of wind

- the unrelenting din and tumult of the wind, so loud that you must shout into your companion's ear to be heard
- the featureless enigmatic whiteness created by the unrelieved snow, ice crystals, and clouds that surround you on all sides, up and down
- the sense of every little procedure being enormously difficult and time-consuming; even looking at your watch, for example, involves uncovering that wrist from the monster mitt, parka, and shirt, then painstakingly getting them all snugly back together; it seems like it shouldn't take so long to do so, but up there it does.

All these sensations are exciting enough if you step into them for half an hour. If you're out in them for several hours, they'll wear you down. If you're out in them all day long with no prospect of escaping them at night, save for a tiny tent somehow staked down, you have to learn to accept the conditions as part of life. Eventually the father and son did get across the snowfield and out onto the southern slopes of Mount Jefferson, where once again they could stumble on rocks and ice, and where cairns were at least visible from time to time, when the wind-driven snow would subside enough to permit them to steal a look ahead.

Lesson 3—Never try to move in a full-scale storm above tree line. These two should have stayed put in their shelter for a day, as they were to do in an even greater storm later. No one should risk becoming exhausted or lost in a snowfield in the incredible and relentless fury of a White Mountain storm.

When they got to the far side of Jefferson, the cloud cover momentarily lifted, revealing a gentle slope angling upwards. As climbers, they could not

CLIFF NOTE As you near tree line on the Valley Way Trail (and many other White Mountain trails), you will see a prominent sign with the words: "STOP. The area ahead has the worst weather in America. Many have died there from exposure even in the summer. Turn back now if the weather is bad. White Mountain National Forest." A local weather report might have advised postponing this traverse, perhaps until later in the winter when daylight is longer and temperatures are milder.

resist the lure of the summit. They had already bagged Madison and Adams; they had to grab Jefferson while they had the chance. Dropping their packs, they decided on a quick rush up to the nearly visible peak. The climb went easily and they delighted in the freedom of an easy uphill, without packs, and with the wind at their backs. But after they landed on the summit and congratulated each other, the Mountain King stopped smiling.

The clouds came down again, and the wind picked up. Father and son suddenly realized that they could not see more than a few feet. The wind-driven snow had completely obliterated all trace of their tracks in a matter of minutes; each rocky outcropping on the mountain looked like all the others and they lost all sense of direction. Then came the crushing blow: the father's compass, which he always carried handily in the pocket of his wool shirt, was still in that shirt—carefully tucked under the top flap of his pack, which now lay on the trail, somewhere below.

How can you be lost when you know precisely where you are: at the very summit of 5,715-foot Mount Jefferson, in a howling, screaming, swirling thicket of fog and driven ice crystals? The two tried to remain calm, moving slowly about the summit, trying vainly to get some sense of which way anything lay. But calm and rational discussion is difficult when, to make yourself heard, you must stand right up against the other person's ear and bellow at the top of your lungs. At length, they agreed on their best guess as to the way down and resolutely plodded ahead. After an eternity, repeatedly suppressing fears that they might be going in the wrong direction, they were overjoyed to see a cairn on the trail. But when they got to the cairn, they realized that they were back on the north side of the mountain, precisely 180 degrees off course!

Now they had to again face the risks and difficulties of crossing that same snowfield. Their tracks, of course, had been long since wiped out by the wind-driven snow. Furthermore, the wind had increased considerably, the snow was now deeper (covering more of the cairns), and they were much more tired. Somehow they managed to swim or sink or wade or flounder across the snowfield. Finally, out of the implacably swirling clouds and snow, they saw their packs ahead, encrusted with snow and ice.

Lesson 4—Never go anywhere without a compass. It is hard to imagine getting turned around 180 degrees on a familiar summit, but it happened in this case and can happen again. Once you lose that all-important sense of direction, the alpine world suddenly appears featureless and inscrutable—and totally hostile. Without a compass, you're dead lost.

Lesson 5—Don't count on following your footprints. The wind can blow them to oblivion in a minute or two. The hole left by an ice ax lasts somewhat longer, so look for those rather than your crampon tracks; but nothing lasts long in a serious Presidentials' gale.

Lesson 6—Never separate yourself from the equipment you require for survival. These two reckless but lucky adventurers eventually found their packs before being overcome by fatigue, darkness, or just plain inability to find the way. Without their packs—spare clothes, sleeping bags, tent, stove, food—they would have surely perished in the open. With their packs, their chances of surviving were considerably improved.

All of these exhausting perambulations not only left both father and son fatigued, but also consumed a considerable part of the daylight hours. It soon became clear that they had neither strength nor daylight left to climb the enormous summit cone of Mount Washington, 1,000 more feet of elevation, on which the wind's fury would certainly increase.

Lesson 7—Remember that early winter days have the fewest daylight hours. As Yogi Berra once said, "It's the time of the year when it gets late early." This fact needs to be kept in mind in all winter trip planning.

They were now confronted with the prospect of trying to set up a camp where they could survive a night immobilized in an awesome storm. Having come this far, they were now many miles of formidable mountain terrain from any trail that led out of the alpine zone to a nearby road. The only trail nearby was the Sphinx Trail, which led sharply down into a vast wilderness area known as the Great Gulf, through which they would have had to lug themselves and their enormous packs for miles through several feet of unbroken, unconsolidated snow—that would now become considerably deeper because of this storm. Going that route would have meant the total defeat of their plan, and perhaps two hard days of dispirited plodding through the woods back to safety.

So they felt strongly committed to sticking out the storm. Perhaps it would die down during the night or in the morning. (Mountaineers tend to be ridiculously optimistic when all of nature is screaming evil tidings at them.) They noticed that the temperature felt warmer, and mistakenly took that to be a promising sign. Dropping a bit below the crest of the ridge, they carefully selected a spot in the lee of some large rock outcroppings, where they laboriously leveled a site for the tent. As they got the tent up, they noticed that the snow had changed texture—it was more like sleet or freezing rain. The temperature had indeed climbed, but that meant trouble, not relief.

They managed to get set up inside the tent just before dark. Then the wind shifted. That night proved even more frightening than the day out there on the snowfield. The wind repeatedly swelled into great buffeting blows, at which the helpless inmates of the tent would grab its A-frame poles, trying to hold it together against the force of the tempest, wondering how long the fabric would hold up against this punishment. Fortunately the tent did last through the night, but just barely. Between the worst gusts of the storm, the father spent a full hour methodically scraping the encrusted ice and snow off his wool shirt, which had been exposed on the outside of his pack during the day. He correctly reasoned that it would be vital to survival, since down garments lose their value as they get wet, and thus the time spent cleaning the ice off the shirt was a good investment. But the price of lost sleep was a stiff one to pay.

Lesson 8—Always take the time to pack essential items properly. Failure to stash an item inside your pack can result in it becoming so soaked that it is useless for the rest of the trip—or it can be torn off the pack unnoticed and turn up missing when it is needed.

Early the next morning, the wind finally wore down the battered tent. Shortly after daylight, a brief but unmistakable ripping sound announced that the outer fly had given way. Within seconds, it was reduced to tattered shreds flopping noisily at the downwind end. Father and son knew it was unnecessary to wonder how long the main fabric of the tent might hold out.

Lesson 9—In setting up a tent, never assume that the current wind direction will hold constant. It's also reasonable to assume that no tent can stand up to the fury of a Presidentials' storm at its worst. You're better off not putting your confidence in any above-tree-line shelter if you have no easy escape route. Snow caves or igloos offer a better chance for survival, but they are time-consuming to build, can get you very wet in the process, and cost daylight hours that can probably be better spent getting to some less-exposed spot, preferably one below tree line.

Somehow father and son got the tent dismantled then desperately set off to get out of the wind. The Sphinx Trail proved extremely steep and difficult to negotiate with their gigantic packs. Between the time it took to pack up, the difficulty of the descent, and the formidably deep, soft snow down in the woods, they made very few miles that day, stopping for the night at one of the shelters that have since been removed from the Great Gulf Wilderness. By nightfall, the storm had abated. It stopped sleeting, but this only brought a new danger. All of their clothes were soaking wet and the temperature again began to drop.

Lesson 10—In winter, neither wind nor cold are as deadly as relative warmth and rain followed by cold. When a winter storm drops rain, look out for your life. Be prepared to get out of the mountains fast, especially if your clothes and equipment are wet.

Father and son spent their worst night yet, shivering in down sleeping bags that had lost most of their insulating warmth from the soaking they had received. They both wore all of their clothes, but those big fluffy down jackets that had felt so warm earlier now clung to their skin, damp and clammy.

Lesson 11—Layers of wool are more valuable than the finest down gear when wetness is a potential problem. Most experienced mountaineers place little reliance on those big down parkas because wool is warm even when wet. Newer, even more mountain-worthy fabrics are now in widespread use, but this was 1968. And it remains true that multiple layers of sweaters, shirts, and underwear—whether of wool or newer fabrics—are far more reliable than one monster parka.

The next day was spent plodding through bottomless soft snow, laboring under huge packs, oppressed by the sense of having been totally defeated by a typical period of bad weather in the Presidential Mountains. But they were a foolish pair who didn't know when to give up. After spending a morning in a laundromat, they set off at noon the very next day to climb Mount Washington, this time using the 8-mile long, summer auto road for the ascent. Where the road rises above tree line, there used to be emergency refuges at half-mile intervals, each one a 7-foot cube, with one double door for access and one double window for light. Our intrepid pair reached one of these at 5,500 feet on the afternoon of December 31. They did not leave it until January 3.

What happened was another storm, this one making the previous blizzard look like a faint breeze. For three nights and two days it was unthinkable to even move on that mountain. The summit weather observatory recorded winds of more than 100 mph for 23 hours straight, with peak gusts well over 150 mph. The temperature dropped to –26 degrees Fahrenheit on January 1 and ranged between –11 degrees and –18 degrees on January 2, warming to a mild –3 degrees on the following day. When they started their stove, the temperature inside the refuge rose above zero but never above 10 degrees; they lived inside their sleeping bags.

Their biggest problem, besides boredom, was getting snow to melt for water. Any loose snow had long since been blown into the next county. To get snow, one of the two would get dressed in full climbing regalia, including face mask, monster mitts, and crampons. Then the other would open the doors, and the first would hop out and wrestle the outer door while the second slammed the inner one shut. Ice ax in hand, the person outside would creep up the slope to where a cornice of hard-packed snow had accumulated. He would spread open a stuff sack, holding it open with one knee and one hand. Then he would strike the cornice repeatedly with his ice ax. At each blow, chunks of snow would dislodge and immediately be carried off by the wind—but some of them would land in the stuff sack. This was repeated until enough of the precious snow had accumulated to satisfy the water requirements for the day. Then the weary, frozen climber would creep back to the box, knock hard and jump inside. The next half hour would be devoted to assiduously sweeping snow off sleeping bags and everything else, since opening the doors even for a few seconds resulted in filling the box with a thin coating of spindrift. It was vital not to allow snow to stay on the sleeping bags, where it might melt and soak the down.

Boredom was combated by resorting to the reading matter brought along in anticipation of being pinned down. The son made out all right with some mystery novels, but the father had made the mistake of bringing Dostoevsky's *Notes from the Underground* and a poetical translation of *The Iliad.* Such heavy stuff had absolutely no appeal in those surroundings and went unread!

Lesson 12—Sex and violence are the only subject matters that command attention at 5,500 feet in a howling tempest. Can the culture.

They also ripped out the last fifty-two pages of a small memo pad and made an impromptu deck of cards. In the ensuing poker games, each used his precious lunch and snack items for chips. This resulted in a deadly serious game. When you are staking your last candy bar on three nines, you've got to be sure they're winners! Even a small piece of hard candy needed the support of a pair of face cards, at the least.

On January 3, with the wind easing into the general neighborhood of 50 mph, they struggled to the summit and back, then descended along the road, much subdued and humbled by their vacation in the mountains. But they were the lucky ones. They survived despite all their mistakes and inexperience. Others have been less fortunate.

Lesson 13—Never trifle with winter in the mountains. If you decide to undertake this special madness called winter climbing, prepare yourself well. Read up on it, get the correct equipment and, most important, hook up with someone who has experience in that unique world. Start slow, with day hikes at first, then get plenty of overnight experience below tree line, where you can learn to deal with the cold without the additional devastating problem of wind.

It's not just that the wind feels stronger and colder in winter—it actually is stronger. The average wind speed on Mount Washington in July is 24.7 mph; in January, it is 43.8 mph. From 1948 to 1975, the strongest wind recorded during July averaged 80.7 mph; in January, it was 124.9 mph. Everybody knows where winds like these take you on those famous windchill charts. You can profit from mistakes: the son went on to become an outstanding mountain climber with first ascents in the Canadian Rockies and Alaska, climbs of exceptional difficulty. The father went on to many more years of pleasurable winter climbing in New England. Clubs like the Appalachian Mountain Club in the White Mountains, the Green Mountain Club in Vermont, and the Adirondack Mountain Club in New York State offer programs to help novices gain experience from those who have been through it all.

BENJAMIN DAVID POTTER

Poking the Dragon

I have climbed in wonderful places all over the world, but the mountains of New Hampshire and Vermont are my home, their views and challenges take my breath away just as well as the Dolomites, the Swiss Alps, or the Sierras. I'm strictly a hobbyist mountaineer, no pro by any means, and I idolize those hardened men and women who chose to take on the challenges that I currently do not, who reap the benefits of very high altitude or remote mountaineering, and sometimes the awful consequences. Their path to adult happiness differs from my own, and though I may sometimes envy it, I like to think that they would sometimes envy mine as well. Their practice was described to me once as "poking the sleeping dragon," or tackling an endeavor containing very real dangers, with the silent hope that the worst will not happen, that the dragon will fail to wake up and strike. I may not be able to travel to Tibet or Alaska very often, but I can sometimes find those challenging conditions here in the Northeast, and then—unleashing the boy that still lives inside me—I can pretend and, for the moment, I am one of those intrepid souls.

The following is a tale of ill-advised adventure, since in my humble experience, those can sometimes be the most rewarding or the most memorable. It was March 2006 and smack in the middle of a cold New England winter. I had been checking the weather the night previous at my grandmother's house in southern New Hampshire, and the report was of a snowstorm moving in, bringing lots of wind and well below zero cold. I wanted to climb the next day and was hankering for adventure, so I decided to head up Mount Washington. The weather for the mountain observatory said that the wind should be 90 mph and up, wind chills down around −50 degrees and much worse at the top, with lots of driving snow. I figured I would give it a shot—even if I could not gain the summit, it would be a great effort trying!

I drove up in the pre-dawn darkness and arrived at Pinkham Notch around 6:15, the light still dim and the snow crisp. I packed my snowshoes, crampons, piolet, and all of the other essentials and signed into the visitors'

Ben Potter on Mount Lafayette summit.
Photo by Alex Potter

log. The access trail to the Hermit Lake Shelters was so very peaceful in the dim morning light, with slowly falling snow being blown every direction by wind. I stopped at the waterfall to admire the cool aquamarine color of the frigid waters and unzip a few vents in my outerwear. I will admit to being somewhat of a mountaineering introvert in that I enjoy isolation in the hills; therefore the weather keeping most people away was fine by me! I had decided the night before that since I was alone, I would take the commonly traveled Lion Head trail, thinking that there was a lot of new snow, and going up the headwall alone with feet of new snow and no one around was a bigger dragon than I wanted to provoke at the time.

I had my first encounter with other hikers as I headed up the steep area of Lion Head, where on crowded days traffic jams begin. The trail was now consumed with ice and I was happily working my way up the flow with my ax and crampons when I met two men who were roped up and on their way down. The gentlemen stated that they had almost gotten to Lion Head but turned back due to the cold and weather. They had completed this climb plenty of times and the wind and low visibility didn't entice them today. I pondered for a minute on the merits of their being roped up and having a partner, and continued on. It was not until I finally reached the tree line that the magnitude of the weather that day dawned on me.

The cold was phenomenal, and my layers were not sufficient, so I descended until the scrub trees were high enough, and performed the task that I think is dreaded second-most by mountaineers, which is stripping down in the driving wind and snow to remove sweaty layers, replace them with dry ones, and stack a few more on so that the cold doesn't bite quite as hard. (In case you are wondering, the number-one most dreaded activity is probably answering the call of nature, and if you have had to do so above the tree line in a snowstorm, you know what I mean!) So after the religious experience of freezing myself thoroughly and chanting like a maniac to stay warm, I put on the clothes that I'd planned to wear at the summit, in addition to my thick mitts, balaclava, goggles, and hood. This is a part of mountaineering that I find most enjoyable: the armor. I call it armor because it feels like you are invincible in your Gore-Tex fortress. The wind cannot assail you, the snow cannot touch your skin, and the biting cold is held at bay. Fully suited up, I climbed upward past Lion Head, and then promptly flew back down past Lion Head.

It turns out that the ridge just above Lion Head acts as a sort of wind funnel and, as such, is absolutely brutal on a day like this one, brutal enough to lift a 175-pound guy with a 35-pound pack off his feet and deposit him on his back scooting down the hill in a hurry. I now understood why those gentlemen had turned back. If wind this strong was enough to knock you down if you stood up straight, heck, it would lift you and knock you down even if you were stooping. Having felt hurricanes on the beaches of Cape Cod, I can tell you that this was worse, a real force to be reckoned with, and great fun! One had to basically crawl along the ice to stay right side up and make forward progress. With my crampons I was leaving scratches in the ice as the wind pushed me back that looked as if a giant cat had been dragged downhill against its will. I was knocked down twice trying to get past that ridge. Each time I told myself I would try once more, and if I could not gain the snowfields that time, it was time to turn around. Halfway between Lion Head and the snowfields I plopped down behind a cairn and considered my choices. Thinking that if *this* ridge was so bad, what must the rest of the mountain be like, the temptation to turn around and head for a warm fireplace was great. But it seemed that one more try would do it, and from that cairn I crawled on all fours, ice ax first, until the wind calmed after the ridge. The battle with the wind on the ridge that day was some of the most fun I have had in the mountains, a true challenge and a testament to the power of Mother Nature—more the rule than the exception on Mount Washington in the middle of winter.

The snowfields that followed had the wonderful quality of being in the lee of the summit cone, so the wind was less, but the snow was falling very thickly and I was well into the clouds, so visibility was only about 15 feet at any time. The problem was that the cairns are much farther than 15 feet apart but, having hiked this trail a few times, it was possible to remember the vague direction, and if I became uncomfortable I had a GPS (the secret weapon) stashed in my jacket, with a trail track from a previous trip. It is a great feeling hiking when there are no other tracks, a kind of peaceful march in the mist. When the clouds and snow surround you, and there isn't so much as a rock to provide contrast to the endless white, the feeling is surreal. It is as if you are in a white room and someone just closed the door; the horizon melts into the sky and you are swallowed whole. The only force to wake you from the trance is the eternal howling wind.

The cairns led higher into the steeper terrain, where the rocks and ice have been blown bare of snow and one needs no trail map to find the way, merely proceeding up, forever up. Many who will read this have likely climbed in the bitter cold of –30 degrees or more, and know of the hardships found therein. But for the benefit of those that have not, there are a few unique inconveniences. I enjoy these hardships because, as was mentioned before, they help create the illusion that one is on the top of the world, fighting not only for the summit but also for survival, and I revel in that semi-fiction for the moment.

One such inconvenience is getting a drink. There are many ways to beat the deep freeze, but I choose to carry bottles of water surrounded by goose-down jackets, since any CamelBak would quickly freeze, as would any uninsulated water bottle, no matter how deeply buried in your daypack. But these down bottle-jackets can often keep water liquid just about all day, although it is fun to take the bottle out and watch the water on the top freeze before your eyes in seconds. Another inconvenience is eating, not because the food is cold or buried in your pack, but because if you stop to eat, things get chilly fast, and shivering all alone in a snowstorm on the side of a mountain is not as much fun as it sounds! So some pack like a hamster might; having many small stashes of food in their pockets, which allows you to eat as you walk, keeping the energy up, and with energy and food come optimism and warmth. The last challenge I will describe is breathing. As any skier knows, if it is very cold out, you need to cover your face to prevent frostbite, and this practice becomes ever more important as the mercury continues to fall. The eternal problem is that, no matter what, your breath will freeze into ice on just about any fabric and, before long, your face cover has become solid and you feel like you are breathing through your bed pillow—no good if you are panting and breathing hard! So you must either find another way to shield your face, or adopt the practice of turning from the wind regularly to remove your face shell and sneak a few deep breaths.

The hike continued beyond the comparatively quiet snowfields, up onto the summit cone and into the rocks that characterize the last 1,000 feet of the climb. At this point a simple routine is the best practice, breathing and stepping with an unsung (or sung) rhythm, keeping your progress constant and satisfying, even though visibility still doesn't betray how far you've come or have yet to go. Your footing feels infallible under the crampons, your ax acts as a cane to stave off your exhaustion—it is a wonderful, unstoppable feeling!

Reaching the summit of Washington—for all of the challenge to get there, the adventure found in the weather conditions and, sometimes, the view—is in my opinion very anticlimactic. The ice-covered parking lots, small village of buildings, and slew of meteorological gear bring my visions of "climbing in the vastness of nature" to a premature end. However, as I gained the summit this time, I understood why the buildings are chained down, why all of the structures are reinforced, and why there was no one else outdoors. The wind was brutal. Making headway was nearly impossible when not in the lee of some structure, and even crampons could not keep you stationary on the icy ground. I spent just a minute up there, but even though there was no view, I consider it my favorite trip to the summit of Washington. I was able to take one picture before my camera lens froze, and it serves as a reminder of the thrill of that day.

The descent was steady and calm. The cushion of the snow removed the jolting knee torture of a typical descent. The snow was falling more slowly and the fog of clouds consumed me. I can recall my amazement at the fact that the wind, in just the space of an hour or so, had completely erased my tracks. The GPS was useful in the snowfields, to guarantee that I did not wander too close to the rim of the headwall, and I was glad for the twenty-first-century safety blanket. A slow and peaceful descent was a perfect reward after a difficult climb, and I soon found myself ambling back to the Pinkham Notch lodge, signing myself out of the logbook, and shedding my suit of armor.

That day I gained a new appreciation for wind and cold, and a new place to go in my head when school or work loses its appeal. Escape was the reward for some hard work and determination, along with memories of a fulfilling adventure when the sleeping dragon was not roused by my prodding, and I passed from its reach once more, a bit wiser, though exhausted! Since then, other winter traverses and summits have all seemed just a bit more tolerable, with that memory of what wrath the weather can inflict.

LANDON G. ROCKWELL

Porky Gulch and Above

During the midterm break in February of my senior year at Dartmouth College, four of us planned to visit the Mount Washington Observatory on the peak's summit. We would spend three or four days up there, helping with chores, and maybe make a tour over the Northern Peaks to Mount Madison and back. At the last moment I was delayed. My friends went as planned and I drove up to Pinkham a day later. I spent the night there, intending to ski solo up the road to the summit the next day. That morning I was in luck—a brilliant day, not too cold, no sign of wind. Perfect conditions! But it was to be my toughest trip.

I had brought my packboard because there were usually odds and ends at Pinkham waiting to be carried to the observatory crew. I asked Joe Dodge, the general manager of the Appalachian Mountain Club (AMC) hut system, what there was to go up. He took me to a storeroom and pointed to a pile of things: "Any of that stuff you want to take." I dug up a couple of cartons and eventually lashed much of the pile on the packboard.

Just as I finished, Joe came in. "How are you doing?"

"Fine."

Joe took a look at the pack, hefted it, and looked at me. "You're crazy—8 miles and over 4,000 vertical feet with that rig? Who the hell do you think you are, Paul Bunyan?"

"Oh, come on Joe—it doesn't weigh more than about 70 pounds. You're getting soft, sitting on your butt figuring out how you're going to catch a bobcat with your bare hands."

Joe had a big thing about this. It really was one of his ultimate objectives. And he almost pulled it off a couple of years later. Joe was one of those who became an authentic legend in his own time. There was practically nothing he hadn't turned his hand to. He was one of the most generally competent men in the North Country and one of the most colorful. I never knew anyone who worked for or with him for any length of time who didn't have an enormous respect and affection for him. Pinkham was known as Porky Gulch to its intimates and Joe was the Mayor of Porky Gulch.

Joe's talents did not end with the practical. He was also an artist. He could relate a simple and routine event with such verbal orchestrations that it came out in symphonic dimensions. His virtuosity in cussing was awesome. He could cuss for two minutes without repeating himself. Those who heard him for the first time came away with a changed perspective on life. He had a number of words that served as spare parts for almost anything. One of them was "rig." Most anything could be a rig—a car, a radio, an outcrop of rock, a woodpile, bookkeeping accounts, stew. If Joe wanted to tell you how to put this or that together, it could go something like this: "You take this rig and rig it up to this rig with this rig and then you'll have one hell of a *^#+ fine rig!"

I'd carried dozens of loads heavier than that, packing provisions up to the Moosilauke Summit Camp as a hutman,[1] and I had plenty of time for the trip to the summit. Appropriate humility was not then one of my stronger points. I took the old Jackson Road, a shortcut of about 2 miles that hooked into the auto road a couple of miles up. The snow was perfect, untracked, hard-packed—and the packboard rode high and easy. The air was like champagne. I felt like Pippa in Browning's poem: "God's in His heaven—/ All's right with the world!"

I was just well warmed up when I came to the junction with the auto road. The trees here were hardwood—mostly birch in some stretches—so that you could see far into the woods. Shadows from the trees, all running parallel uphill, slicing across the snow, made startling contrasts in intensities of light and shade against the muted white of the birches.

Two miles more to the Halfway House on the auto road. The snow squeaked under my skis and poles. But the air was just comfortably cold enough to keep me from sweating, probably about 5 to 10 degrees above zero. The road here made a dogleg to the right as you faced Mount Washington from Pinkham Notch or the Glen House, where the road started. At the upper end of the dogleg was the Halfway House. I got there about three hours out from Pinkham. Four miles, three hours—just about the time I had estimated, considering my load.

I had spent two nights there on previous winter trips. It was closed and shuttered out of season, but winter parties could get a key to one room where they could sleep on the floor and use an old iron cookstove. It was a dreary, run-down box of a dump, but a welcome sight in the winter wilderness. There was a large bulge of rock right next to the house. I came alongside it, close aboard like a ship about to tie up, and slowly shrugged off my pack. It would be much easier to get it back on, propped up waist-high on the rock. There were some old steps on the southeast side—in the sun and mostly blown clear of snow. I stretched out and had lunch, then it was onward and upward again. But, during the 20 minutes while I was having lunch, that pack seemed to have gained about 25 pounds.

The Halfway House is just below tree line. After a couple of turns in the road and then a big hairpin turn, I was above tree line on another dogleg bearing southeast toward Nelson Crag. The big hairpin was blown clear of snow (as it usually was), but there was a nasty base of gray seepage ice. I almost went down several times while getting off it to the much rougher, but much more secure furrows of snowdrifts over to the side. Then it began to happen. The hard work of fighting against falls on the ice, off balance, with a broken rhythm, had taken much of the wind out of my sails. The snow had a hard wind-pack, but it was not thick enough or hard enough to support my weight. As anyone with experience knows, breakable wind crust is one of the most fatiguing surfaces to travel on, particularly on skis and uphill. After a few hundred feet I was leaning on my poles, head down, feeling like a tapioca pudding and breathing like a horse that has just finished the Kentucky Derby. One mile more to go on the road, then almost two miles on the shortcut over the backbone of Nelson Crag and up the cone to the summit. Two thousand vertical feet.

I put it in low gear and joined the road again. The terrain was much less rough on the road and the wind slab had mercifully given way to light powder. Finally I reached the shortcut to the left over Nelson Crag, a massive shoulder jutting out to the east, just north of the summit cone. It is a dominating feature of the mountain architecture from several points on Route 16. The shortcut route was prominently marked by a line of 4-foot-high cairns about 200 feet apart. I had traveled that shortcut more than once, when halfway between two cairns you couldn't even begin to see either. But now it was brilliantly clear. Cased, as usual, in heavy rime, they stretched along the gently rising plateau like a long line of pillars of salt. Lot's wife in multiples.

Halfway across Nelson Crag, all my energy and strength suddenly drained out through my boots into the snow. I would make it to a cairn, lean heavily on it, head limp on my chest, and gape unfocused at the snow. Then, summoning all of my remaining resources, slowly make it to the next cairn. And the next, and the next. Nothing hurt, and I wasn't yet cold. In fact, I had something of a non-physical feeling of well-being. I felt utterly detached from myself. *That poor guy; glad I'm not in his boots, he ought to know better.* In fact, I was way out of condition. Because of academic work and extracurricular responsibilities, I had taken no mountain trips that amounted to anything since we had closed the Moosilauke Summit House in September. At my age it simply never occurred to me that there was such a thing as being out of condition. I could have dumped the pack. But that didn't even enter my mind as an available option. You just do not do that. It just wasn't in the nature of things.

Now and then I was aware of the view. It was spectacular. To my extreme right, across the Great Gulf, rose Mount Jefferson, Mount Adams, and Mount Madison, totally white against a sky of royal blue; across the valley to my left were Carter Dome and Wildcat. But I saw them only as pictures in a book. *Sometime I ought to go up there and see that view.* Fuzzy thoughts of how the view would look modulated into fuzzy hallucinations—voices, blurs of music coming from nowhere. Once there was a trumpet. For a few seconds it seemed unfuzzed. "The trumpet shall sound and the dead shall be raised . . ." *Strange place to be giving the Messiah. Usually it's before Christmas.* I don't think my subconscious was signaling anxieties of death, although doubtless it had an interest in my being raised—about 1,000 vertical feet at this point. I had an overpowering desire to sink down in that beautiful soft snow and sleep. It wasn't really snow anymore. Simply warm seductive down. Just a short nap would bring me around and I would be full of beans again. But if I started to sink I would be asleep before I hit the snow. And I knew it. That was that one sliver of awareness that was still alert and informed. I had had plenty of experience to know the lethal consequences of yielding to such compelling temptations. By now my arms and legs were vaguely cold.

I was, in fact, in a state of hypothermia—the loss of central body heat which, if unchecked, leads inevitably to death. My exhaustion had slowed my exertion to a worm's pace. That had radically reduced my normal production of body heat (which must be considerable in near zero temperatures) possibly by 50 percent. When that occurs, one's physiology automatically presses certain buttons to sustain the core body temperature. This reduces the flow of oxygenated blood to the brain and withdraws heat from the appendages. Hence my fuzziness, the hallucinations, and the progressing coldness in my arms and legs. Although I did not realize it at the time, I had crossed a threshold beyond which a path to death would have probably been easy and painless. In those days we had never heard of hypothermia. We simply called it exposure, but we recognized its symptoms and dealt with it the same as one does today.

Immediately beyond was a short, steeper rise that led up to a shelf at the foot of the cone. I stared at it. *Mount Everest. Mount Everest hasn't been climbed yet. Can it be climbed?* More voices. No music, just voices. This time they were not coming from nowhere; they were coming from somewhere. Somewhere was ahead and above. As I was worrying about Mount Everest, two figures seemed to be moving down over the skyline. That just about did it—voices, music, voices, and now the cairns were taking off. But they weren't cairns; they were people—two of my friends down from the summit. Joe Dodge had told the observatory crew that I was being a complete chowderhead and, if I didn't show by a certain time, somebody had better start down and check me out. They didn't have to ask how I was. Two pairs of hands took the pack from my back and two voices asked, "Can you make it?"

"Yes . . . I can make it."

About an hour later we were inside the observatory. Wordlessly I slumped down on a bunk—asleep before I actually hit the mattress.

LANDON G. ROCKWELL

Skiing Mount Washington

Bill Lingley, a close friend and classmate, and I experienced some rough Mount Washington weather one March day. We skied up the auto road, reaching the summit just before dark. The entire summit of Mount Washington had become a gigantic, elegant wedding cake. All of the structures on the summit—of which there are far too many—had been transformed, like Cinderella, from plain and ugly to beautiful and breathtaking. Nature's cosmic Michelangelo had been at work. The rime formations—frost feathers—were the most enormous I had ever seen. They had built up into the wind, in some places between 3 and 4 feet long. Fluted and intricately convoluted, they were bold and carved in heroic style in some places, infinitely delicate and complex in others. The textures were so fragile it seemed incredible they could have been wrought by the onslaughts of storm.

We were in for a stormy night. The barometer had dropped fast and far. When we hit the sack the wind was ripping furiously across the summit. It sounded as if an endless freight train were rumbling by and as if we were lying on the tracks beneath it. The observatory building vibrated constantly. Every once in a while it would shudder as if it were about to die or take off. We had some difficulty sleeping with all that battering noise.

Then there was the cat. In the previous spring, the crew had acquired a cat from somebody or other who didn't like cats. None of the crew particularly liked cats either, but it seemed like a good idea at the time to have a pet around. By fall they decided that wintering on the summit with the cat would be a little too thick so they drove it down the mountain to Gorham, 16 miles away. There they gave it to a friend who liked cats. About two weeks later, Sal was outside reading instruments when something ran between his legs. It was the cat. By means miraculous and mysterious to man, that cat had found its way all the way from Gorham to the summit of Mount Washington.

By morning, the wind was gusting around 100 miles an hour. The temperature was about –25 degrees Fahrenheit. It was by far the most severe combination I had ever seen. Naturally we all spent the day inside, mostly playing cards, trying to keep warm, and trying to sleep. By evening the wind had dropped to 60 or 70 mph and a warm spell had moved in. It was just about zero.

The following morning it was snowing furiously. The wind was still up there at around 40 mph, but the temperature had moderated to about 20 degrees. We had to be back in Hanover that night. The crew told us we were crazy; on the radio, Joe had said it was storming hard down at Pinkham so we'd be in this stuff all the way. And no matter how well we knew the mountain—and we both know it intimately—we could get totally confused in the whiteout and end up God knows where. Or just end up. We were fully aware of those possibilities. At one time or another we had both become badly fouled up above tree line on terrain we knew intimately. But we were young and full of confidence and, on this particular morning, also full of the spirit of adventure. We were also well equipped. We had plenty of warm clothing, windproof parkas with fur-lined hoods, goggles—the works.

So despite entreaties, dire predictions, and insults about our sanity, we left. Outside it was wild. Getting our skis on was a production because of the wind and the confusion of blowing snow. Finally we were all set and started down the road.

After a 100 yards or so I shouted to Bill: "Why don't we go down the cone to the Alpine Garden and then either down Tuckerman or Lion Head?"

"The road's much easier to follow."

"I know, but it's more exposed, and the cone would be a lot more interesting."

"Maybe." Bill really didn't have to have his arm twisted.

We turned off the road to the route that would take us down the cone to the Alpine Garden, a shelf of tundra terrain that separates the cone of Mount Washington from the various descent routes eastward to Pinkham. We made relatively short zigzag traverses, trying to make each zig the same length as the zags, and the angle of each turn more or less the same. This enabled us to maintain a crude, dead reckoning as we descended in zero visibility. Theoretically it was not a bad procedure. Actually it was very vulnerable. The terrain was rough and the roughness varied considerably. Some zigs were shorter than the zags and the angles of our turns were anything but constant in order to avoid rime-covered boulders or sudden sharp dips that studded the cone. We kept as close together as we could—three or four ski-pole lengths. Even so we lost each other frequently.

"Bill, where are you?"

No answer. The wind was too noisy.

"Bill, where are you?"

"I'm here."

I moved in the direction of his voice and—plump—there was Bill, right in the middle of my stomach. It was often like that: contact visibility only. At some points we literally couldn't tell whether we were going up or down. The air was so opaque with snow we couldn't see where the air ended and the snow-slope began. It was like skiing inside a gigantic milk bottle full of milk. Like blind men, we would probe ahead of us with our ski poles. The shorter pole was downhill.

Finally the slope eased off and we stopped to take our bearings.

"Bill, where are we?"

"We're on the Alpine Garden about 1,000 vertical feet below the summit."

"Sure, sure, but where in hell on the Alpine Garden are we? It isn't exactly the size of a tennis court."

"Well, I'd say . . . [long pause] we're in that flat-ish area between the rim of Tuckerman headwall and the ridge that leads out to Lion Head."

"Which direction is Tuckerman?"

"That way," pointing a ski pole, the end of which was just a blur.

"Maybe or maybe not, let's check it out with a compass."

"I forgot to bring my compass. I'll get yours. Which pocket of your rucksack is it in?"

"It's in Hanover."

"God, we couldn't even make tenderfoot scouts."

"Oh, come on, Willy, this is really great! We're totally on our own, alone on a mountain in a wild storm and we're going to hit our descent route right on the button."

It was great. We were having a ball. A ball very close to a line of danger. Danger from exposure, if we opted for the Tuckerman route. Danger from a nasty fall, if we opted for the Tuckerman route and missed the exit slope in the whiteout. Danger simply from getting hopelessly lost. But that's exactly why we were having a ball. Challenge. The mountain was cutting us down to size. Very small size. Microscopic. *So—you think you know me. Try me now and see how you do.* For an instant I was back in the book of Job: "Then the Lord answered Job out of the whirlwind and said . . . gird up thou thy loins like a man: for I will demand of thee . . ." A mountain can become very personal. Mount Washington was now very personal. It had suddenly become an angry geological and meteorological Goliath, slinging everything it had at us. Maybe not even angry—scornful perhaps, or just toying with us in a low-key game of Russian roulette.

Tuckerman Ravine from Lion Head.

Photo by Steve Boheim

We had to choose between the Tuckerman and the Lion Head routes. Simultaneously and silently, we both realized the insanity of the Tuckerman route. A headwall 600 vertical feet high, close to 60 degrees at its steepest point, severe avalanche danger, and an ambiguous approach—even with good visibility—to the only exit point. We checked each other's faces for frostbite and shoved off, bearing slightly to the left. Lion Head is the north sidewall of Tuckerman Ravine. It is a peninsula-like ridge sloping gently for a few hundred yards, then narrowing, plunging roughly down through scrub, then woods. You come out just below the floor of Tuckerman Ravine and ease right into the ski trail down to Pinkham. We had to hit the base of that peninsula as it played out from the substantial acreage of the Alpine Gardens. Flying totally blind, we could only feel our way along a line that would keep us on relatively high ground. That was our only compass. Under the circumstances, it wasn't a bad one.

Bill was barely visible a few yards ahead—suddenly he yelped and step-turned, off balance. Then I saw it. Rocks. Rocks plastered with a foot of rime and piled one on top of another, 4 feet high. Bill had almost clobbered himself into a cairn—one cairn in a whole line of beautiful, beautiful cairns that led straight down and off Lion Head. We had it made. We swapped looks of tremendous relief and then went into the inchworm routine. One of us would stand by a cairn until the other sniffed out the next one. Then we'd join forces and repeat the process. It was slow but secure. Toward the end of the ridge we took our skis off for the trail descent of the steep, rough head of the Lion. With the skis now on our shoulders for those last few yards above tree line, the more furious gusts of wind jolted us into instant weather vanes. Then we bounded down into the relative calm of the woods.

A man named John F. and a companion climbed Mount Washington to ski in early April, but Tuckerman Ravine proved impossible because of heavy, wet snow. The men continued to the summit in dropping temperatures, which froze the snow hard and smooth. John slipped on frozen corn snow and slid 900 feet to the Alpine Garden rocks and death. I have always remembered this because two of my close friends found the body. I have learned enormous respect for winter slopes above tree line.

ALAN VIA

A Wild Day in the Presidentials

My first trip to New Hampshire was a memorable one. The second weekend in September, five of us drove to Pinkham from Albany and decided to sample New England hiking by staying at Mizpah Spring Hut, Lakes of the Clouds Hut, and Madison Hut. Wanting to eke out every ounce of views, we began with the Webster Cliff Trail, enjoying every minute of our first hike in New Hampshire. It was a cool and beautiful September day and we were looking forward to our first stay in the hut system we'd only read about. Our second day was a carbon copy with cool, clear blue skies, with little humidity—just a perfect day for a hike over Clinton, Ike, Franklin, Monroe, and down to Lakes. A couple of us took a quick nip up Mount Washington, and the rest explored the Bigelow Lawn and over to the edge of Tuckerman Ravine.

Clouds were rolling in by evening and as darkness fell it was raining. At breakfast, the weather was ominous—foggy, icing, windy, and the temperature on the summit of Big George was an even 32 degrees Fahrenheit. We had reservations at Madison Hut, a date with Washington, Jefferson, and the various Adams summits, and a decision to make. Everyone else who was staying at Lakes of the Clouds Hut was either going to wait out the weather or head down. None of us wanted to end this trip—not a smart call, but a five-hour drive from home and a long awaited trip sometimes has a way of influencing a decision. We were all very experienced hikers in great shape and had lots of extra clothing and gear. A woman who was at Lakes by herself also had reservations at the Madison Hut and was sensibly reluctant to hike the northern Presidentials by herself, so she asked if she could join us, and we quickly learned that she had all the essentials to do so.

We stepped out into the elements. Visibility was 30 yards near the hut and diminished greatly the closer we got to the summit of Washington. Our progress over icy footing was measured by walking cairn to cairn until we got to the summit, and there the wind was gusting 70 to 80 mph with a steady 50-plus mph. We were getting blown all over and the strain of keeping the party together on the way up was tiring. Our new friend had a frame pack that really caught the gale up there and she was blown around worse than we were, plus we were heavier than she. We put her right in the middle of us for the day.

Coffee and a museum tour allowed us to regroup and we set off for Mount Clay, keeping within 3 yards of each other. The fog, roar, and icing were disorienting! The Northern Presidentials on a day like this required every bit of care and experience we had, which included climbs of the winter Adirondack High Peaks. I remembered a potentially lethal mistake I made on one of those climbs, an overnight to the trailless peaks Panther and Couchsachraga, when I experienced advanced hypothermia. I'd eaten and drunk too little, photographing the mountains all day, and I told my friends to go ahead. Alone, I began falling, sometimes headfirst, and increasingly often. My clothing was soaked from snow and greater shivering and heavy fatigue set in. *I'll sit down and rest,* I thought. Then I realized with dismay that this had to be advancing hypothermia; if I went to sleep, death could result. My knowledge of hypothermia, a strong will to survive, and excellent physical conditioning kept me descending. My friends redressed me in dry warm clothing, put me in a sleeping bag, and huddled close. I was shivering uncontrollably and was so nauseous that I could not swallow

View from Mount Monroe to Lakes of the Clouds, the Crawford Path, and Mount Washington. *Photo by Dan Stone*

beverages or food. Only later could I tolerate warm Jell-O and tea, and it was even later before I could eat anything solid.

The summit of 5,712-foot Mount Jefferson was wild and wonderful; the summit rock had an ice pennant 18 inches long and, when I bumped it, the hurricane-velocity wind launched it downwind like a golf ball. Visibility was around 20 feet and the wind was screaming, making even shouted conversation almost impossible. We headed down to Edmands Col, where the wind compression was so strong we had to alternate between crawling and duckwalking! It was essential that we stay close together and look out for each other. We sought respite for fifteen minutes in the metal emergency shelter[2] and I remember our pulling off face masks and hollering excited conversation over the roaring wind; we were exhilarated by a combination of fun, fear, and the excitement of surmounting the worst the mountain could throw at us, or so we thought. Visibility decreased even further and the gusts increased on the climb up 5,774-foot Mount Adams. As we stayed close together, the cairns were not visible from each other and we needed to pay close attention to the route, keeping the compass bearings dialed in as we slowly picked our way up the last few hundred feet to the summit. The summit of Adams had the same inches-long rime ice pennants; we sought a bit of inadequate shelter in the lee of a summit boulder to decide on our route down to the Madison Hut. We descended very carefully, taking advantage of every large boulder where we might find a little shelter.

Mentally and physically exhausted, but pretty pleased with ourselves, we walked into the hut late in the afternoon. During the night the wind died, the stars came out, and we had almost perfect cold-weather hiking conditions and fabulous visibility. I photographed the sunrise from the Mount Madison summit, and as the sun lit up the spectacular scenery missing from the previous day, I enjoyed looking back at what we'd traversed in very extreme conditions.

MATT HARRIS

Haunted

The Lakes of the Clouds Hut is the most exposed and, in my opinion, the most impressive of the Appalachian Mountain Club huts in the White Mountains. It is located at a pair of alpine lakes, just a mile down the trail from the peak of Mount Washington. The only vegetation is small alpine flowers and grasses, some of which is federally protected as endangered species. *Walk on the rocks,* they tell you. The signs at the start of the krumm-holz say, "You are now entering an alpine zone, we grow slow here." It was fairly cold inside the hut, so I found a window seat where the sun would warm me. A turkey dinner was served promptly at 6:00. Splendid views, a nice hike, a hot turkey dinner with cranberry sauce and gravy—what could be bad? Only memories.

This place has haunted me since September 1984, when I came here with ten friends for a weekend hike from Pinkham Notch, across some of the most stark, exposed terrain in the Northeast.[3] The entire 9-mile trail across the Gulf and over Mount Washington is well above timberline, marked with rock cairns spaced about 50 to 100 feet apart in case of whiteouts, which happen often. One moment could be clear, sunny skies, and the next a cold rain. This is the nature of weather in the Whites and signs warn of this at many trailheads. In 1984, I wore jeans and flannel shirts, bad attire in a cold, driving rain with plenty of exposure. I remember crowds of people caught unprepared for the weather and becoming hypothermic at Edmands Col, 3 miles into the 9-mile hike. We had reservations at Lakes of the Clouds Hut; about half the guests there that night did not, and ended up sleeping on and under tables in the common area. Many had left the summit with just sneakers, T-shirts, and shorts, so they were far worse off than my group. I read logbook entries in the hut library, the first one by a member of our group:

Sept. 1 I left the Madison Hut at 9:30 a.m. in slightly overcast and windy conditions with a temperature of 50 degrees. On the summit of Mount Adams, I knew it was going to be a severe day with winds of 30 to 50 mph. Rain, fog, and high winds battered us all day. There were eleven people in our party, some not properly prepared. For the first time in my six years of hiking I observed several effects of hypothermia—slurred speech, tiredness, sloppy bouldering. During the six-and-a-half-hour trek, I experienced both exhilaration and fear. Given the right set of circumstances and Murphy's Law, the mountains have the ability to grab you. I'm finishing this by flashlight. It's 42 degrees and the winds are still high; the hut is overfilled by about twenty-five people, all caught by very bad weather and improper clothing.

—Steve T., Long Island, New York

Sept. 2 I shall never forget September 1. Midday storms caught your typical casual hiker (read: *unprepared*) and Lakes Hut was mobbed by cold,

CLIFF NOTE Cotton clothing does not dry quickly when wet and clings to the body, drawing out heat from the core that can lead to hypothermia. Wool retains warmth even when wet. When climbing high peaks in any season, wear quick-drying synthetics and layers of clothing.

CLIFF NOTE Construction of the Lakes of the Clouds Hut was planned after William Curtis and Allan Ormsbee were killed by an ice storm and gale on June 30, 1900. Curtis died near the hut site and Ormsbee not far below Mount Washington's summit building. (See "Tragedy among the Clouds.") The hut's construction was completed in July 1915; in early September, a raging snowstorm stranded six hikers there for four days.

Nearby Madison Hut was built in 1888, while the Mizpah Spring Hut was completed in 1965. It is somewhat ironic that the existence of these shelters—and their reservation system—occasionally lures people into dangerous weather. As more than one story in this volume shows, it can be dangerous to place too much value on keeping a hut reservation.

wet people, half of whom should never have gone above timberline such as the pathetic couple huddled in blankets all afternoon and night, and this morning; three guys from New Jersey wearing sneakers, T-shirts and jeans, hypothermic, desperate for cigarettes, and most infuriating, totally ungrateful for the patience and help the crew delivered; the gang of teens who barged into the kitchen and rudely asked for dry clothes, food and a way out; the ignoramus who extinguished his cigarette in my soup! The arrogant guy who helped himself to our precious milk. Sound angry? Well, as cook for the day, I have a right to be upset with the rudeness and lack of respect and/or lack of intelligence displayed by many persons that day. Of course, the "good" crowd helped or took their own garbage out or was pleasant to be around. Maybe the abruptness of the weather led to the general commotion and to my bitterness. For future readers, I hope the saying "take things for granted"—like a hut above tree line, Forest Service rangers, a tolerant hut crew—acquires some new meaning.

P.S. It feels good to get the bitterness out. Try it, you'll like it. What a great day to be on the crew, after yesterday's mayhem.

—Scott Anderson Lutz, Croo 1984

Sept. 1 We are here at Hard Rock Cafe. But we wonder why we are? If you call hail, rain and high winds fun, well, you're ***damn right! Life is boring unless one pushes himself to new or higher limits. But what qualifies a new experience as being a higher limit? It's all in the head! Therefore, climb on!

ELLEN MCDOWELL RUGGLES

The Great Gulf

Two of us talked about leading a moderate-paced but challenging July hike into the Great Gulf to the summit of Mount Washington. We would start early enough to reach the summit by early afternoon, then descend the better-known and relatively easy Tuckerman Ravine Trail. Soon we had a group of ten interested hikers, some of whom we knew from previous hikes. One of us had spoken by phone to those we didn't know or hadn't hiked with recently, to get an idea of their hiking ability. There can be safety in numbers, but also risks when abilities and expectations vary. How much can be learned through a phone call? Some say that phone conversations are better because they bring out more honest answers, whereas e-mail messages aren't as effective, because potentially unqualified "hopefuls" can think about what's being asked of them, and practice their responses. I've learned that both methods have benefits and drawbacks, and finding the best ways to discuss a good fit comes with experience and different communication methods. My friend and I are easygoing. We described our trip as 12 miles and a 5,000-foot ascent, keeping at the pace of the slowest among us.

We'd left cars where we planned to finish, at the Pinkham Notch Visitor Center, then carpooled together to the Great Gulf Trail parking lot, 5 miles north on Route 16. Before starting we reviewed common expectations for group hikes. We were expected to stay together. If someone got ahead of the group, as can happen, he or she was expected to wait at trail intersections or landmarks, or where the trail might be confusing to follow. As groups spread apart, those in front become impatient, while those in back become discouraged at being unable to keep up, which can develop discontent.

The high peaks were hidden in overcast skies as we started out in the wide valley, but the forecast was for clear skies and a nice summer afternoon, with temperatures in the sixties and winds averaging 20 to 30 mph. Summer mornings are often chilly, but the going that day quickly felt hot and sticky. At the first break I removed the zip-off legs on my pants, converting them to shorts. I wore a light T-shirt of breathable material. Others similarly "layered down," except for a burly young man who wanted to keep his thick wool sweater on. He insisted that he was fine that way. *Who were we to say how others might feel most comfortable,* I thought, but we kept checking in with him in case he was mistaken. The Great Gulf Trail follows a narrow abandoned roadway and portions still show crumbling pavement, but dirt, leaves, and roots cover up most of the remains. At the first intersection the trail turns left and crosses the Peabody River on a thin, bouncing suspension bridge that extends gracefully across the rocky streambed. The next portion of trail consists of logging roads, some heading off here and coming in there, remnants of days when the White Mountain forests were overharvested. The route is clear but other possibilities wend their way through the open woods. A spur path joins from the nearby Dolly Copp Campground; cross-country ski trails come and go, with signs placed high for winter visibility; informal pathways split off to link with little-known swimming or picnic spots along the river. The traveling was gentle and so was conversation in the group.

After the Osgood Trail heads off for Mount Madison, the Great Gulf descends into a dark narrow hollow, then ascends to the bluff, where we expected views toward our destination. That was not to be—the sky remained mostly overcast, the air heavy with humidity. Small blue patches showed potential for clearing skies, I thought, as I recalled the maritime question my grandmother taught me: "Is there enough blue sky to sew a Dutchman's breeches?" In *When a Loose Cannon Flogs a Dead Horse There's the Devil to Pay: Seafaring Words in Everyday Speech,* Olivia A. Isil defines it this way: "To a sailor, a patch of blue sky signifies the breaking up of a storm at sea." But why a Dutchman's britches? "The Dutch were famous for their thriftiness," the book explains. Ever the optimist, I expected a positive change in the weather.

The trail continued with good footing, as the trees in the forest became more dense and evergreen. We passed another landmark, a stream crossing that could be confusing because the trail on the other side was not obvious. Next, the Madison Gulf Trail turned off to the right. For hikers heading out, this trail coincided with ours for a short while, and then turned left to meet the Mount Washington Auto Road, which some consider a possible escape route in bad weather (it's good to note the alternatives, I've learned). Following that was Clam Rock. How do landmarks get their names? This one became obvious—a cabin-size boulder broken apart to reveal an open-jaw shape. Next, the Chandler Brook Trail split off to the left with a trail sign that clearly marked where we were. This would be another good option for an aborted plan; it led to the auto road and potential rides down.

We took a break for water and snacks at the stream where the Wamsutta Trail came in, then climbed steeply up loose gravel to a clearing. There we saw nothing—nothing but gray sky above, beside, and below us. I separated myself from the group and listened to the weather radio I'd brought; the report called for a 30 percent chance of showers at higher elevations. Hmmm. The optimist in me again thought, "Well, that's still positive." The weather cup wasn't even half-full of bad news. Upward we went. The next marker was for the Six Husbands Trail, which heads steeply for a difficult climb of Mount Jefferson, known also for caves, ladders, tricky footing, overhanging ledges and possible areas of old snow on the upper fields. It's not an easy trail and not recommended for descending, but the adventure of it appeals to the more experienced. Then we passed by the start of the rugged and demanding Sphinx Trail, which culminates at the col between Mount Jefferson and Mount Clay.

Still optimistic, we encouraged the group along, reinforcing the idea of staying together, as some of us had slowed down and others advanced. Suddenly, from around a bend in the trail, a young man hiking solo headed toward us, the second person we'd seen all day. He seemed overdressed in Gore-Tex jacket and pants, and was wearing a hat and gloves. Most of us were still in shorts and T-shirts! He looked like he'd been through the wringer. Stopping briefly, he said that the weather "up there" was horrible, the worst that he had ever seen, and that he'd abandoned his plans in order to get below treeline. All he wanted to do now, he said, was set up his tent at the first available spot, heat some water, and climb into his sleeping bag to get warm.

While his words certainly seemed worthy of our attention, it also appeared that his circumstances were different than ours. He was hiking solo; we were in a group. He was from Canada, hiking in unfamiliar territory, and while we hadn't been on this trail before, we "knew" the area. Although some began to feel unspoken doubt about what was ahead, we continued up. This was confirmed as a good choice when we met two men hiking down, who told us, "It isn't that bad . . . just a bit foggy and windy." Who were we to believe? We went on, wanting to believe the best of what we'd heard. The trail now was wet and slippery, with moist roots and soggy, moss-covered rocks. Picturesque waterfalls drew our attention from the increased difficulty of the trail. Soon we were mostly boulder-hopping, stepping cautiously from one slippery remnant of the glacial era to the next. Occasionally large slabs of exposed rock meant that any misstep or slip would drop us into the water. This went on "forever."

At 2:30 we arrived at Spaulding Lake, barely visible in the fog. We were behind schedule. Trail junctions and landmarks were mostly behind us and the summit was a little over a mile farther. We ate again and prepared for the higher elevation, where trees were short, then scrubby, then nonexistent, as gnarled and weathered krummholz holds an impenetrably rugged stance. Cookies and trail mix were shared amidst genial conversations; the group used rocks for chairs and tables. Everyone seemed ready for the half-mile ahead, climbing 1,600 feet up the steep ravine to the headwall and then to the summit of "The Rock Pile," as Mount Washington is referred to. The trail, we knew, would not be easy, the footing not at all like the comfortable trail we'd started on, and also quite different from the large boulders and slabs of ledges we'd just clambered and slipped over.

We were entering the alpine zone of the White Mountains. "Fragments of stone, many of which are loose" make up this section, explained the AMC's *White Mountain Guide,* but the views of the valley floor beneath and the northern Presidential summits above can be spectacular. Except that we didn't have any views today, and that was disappointing. Rock cairns are infrequent in steep, treeless terrain like this, because they are often swept away by avalanches, which can be common in winter. Nothing stays the same for long. At a break, I noticed "Sue" pulling jeans on over her shorts. Cotton clothing is a big no-no in this hiking environment. Some call cotton comfortable, others refer to it as "death cloth" because it absorbs damp-ness, pulls warmth away from the wearer, and becomes heavy. Why was she doing that? She was experienced and knew better about appropriate gear! I didn't want to embarrass her, but offered an extra pair of rain pants I'd brought along and quietly insisted she change out of the jeans.

As we made our way up through scrubby trees, loose rocks, sand, and boulders, the visibility seemed to decrease into a wet fog. Soon the group spread out between those who were able to climb quickly and those who could not; I was in the middle, unable to catch up but not wanting to stay behind. The difference in paces was especially notable on the steep climb to the headwall. I felt like a recording: "Please stay together." Some followed my pleas, others did not choose to, and some could not. The friend I'd planned the trip with was at the end, encouraging the slower ones. When I approached "Brenda," sitting next to a sheltered ledge, I asked how she was feeling. "Fine," she responded, "just getting out of the wind for a minute and waiting for the others to catch up." Good for her, I thought, as bits of sleet hit our faces. Where were those who were ahead? I checked my thermometer: 52 degrees Fahrenheit. Icy pellets must be an anomaly that occurs around headwalls, I thought, where wind and weather compete.

"Allen," who'd vanished into the gray above us, suddenly reappeared, emphatically exclaiming "It's dangerous up there! We must turn around and go back out the way we came in." Could it really be so bad that we should retreat? If we turned around, it would be a good 7 miles back, over very tough going. The summit was now less than a mile away and soon we'd top out and cross the tracks of the cog railway. At the summit, we could take shelter and buy soup or hot chocolate. I couldn't imagine that retreating would be the better choice. I knew that headwalls often create exaggerated conditions with temporary turbulence. *Forest and Crag,* by Laura and Guy Waterman, confirms this, saying, "There are no easy ways out of the Great Gulf." These authors declare that "the incomparable 'rough and difficult' trails of the Great Gulf are a fitting memorial" to Warren W. Hart, the man who created this trail in the early 1900s, breaking away from an earlier form of designing trails for comfortable going. I looked at my co-leader and saw by his expression that he and I agreed we must go on, and so, although normally of a democratic temperament, I asserted that heading down was not an option.

The climber's bible, *Mountaineering: The Freedom of the Hills,* compiled by "The Climbing Committee of The Mountaineers," writes that a "climbing party is more than the sum of its members . . . the group is nothing apart from its members." At the crest I spoke to the group about safety in fog, as we could see only a few feet around us. I requested that everyone keep their eyes on who was ahead of them and maintain an awareness of who was behind them. In these harsh conditions we were each other's lifelines, so I reminded everyone that we had agreed to hike this day as a group and as a group we must remain. Separating out, as we sometimes had done below, would be dangerous here. Another problem was that we all looked different than when we were down lower, wearing shorts and T-shirts and still getting acquainted. Allen had been known by his navy T-shirt, but that was now covered by a red shell, with a black hat covering his graying hair. Betty had on baggy black shell pants and a yellow rain jacket with a hood. Others were dressed in a variety of black garb, sold by outfitters who were cautious not to make clothes in colors that wouldn't sell. Were we the same group? Who was in control? It was hard to tell. I felt like a recording again: "Please stay together." The difference in peoples' paces became especially notable on the steep climb to the headwall. The wind—whirling off in different directions—prevented our calls of confirmation to each other from even being heard, much less understood.

A great deal had changed, but not the weather. With the wind in our faces, we clambered across the cog railway's tracks, then turned left at an intersection with the Crawford Path, and finally achieved the actual summit. But it wasn't as simple as that. The trail here required a lot of concentration. Giant rounded boulders and great broken slabs were uneven under foot. Some were loose and tippy. Many were lichen-covered and slippery as ice when wet. Winds blew as strong as 57 mph, not unusual for this summit. The weather had worsened rather than improved—fog and mist and showers, with temperatures in the low 40s. Eventually we arrived at shelter in the Visitor's Center. To my dismay it was now five o'clock, well beyond our schedule, but at least we had made it.

Except for Mary—where was she? Had she gone into the bathroom? The gift shop? The museum? Was she taking pictures outside? We must find her soon, because we had a change in plans to discuss. What we didn't know was that Mary had become separated from the group some time before.

We waited. When and where had we last seen her? The others shook their heads. No one could say.

Later, Mary described her experience. She had been climbing, stepping carefully, and when she glanced up, she realized that no one was ahead of her. She turned around and looked back. No one was there either. Everyone had simply vanished. Frightened, but retaining enough composure to stay somewhat calm, she climbed up over the jagged boulders on her own, calling out occasionally for assurance. She continued up, even though it didn't seem to her to be a trail. She never took an easier route around, which is how some lone hikers go astray, sometimes finding themselves still lost when darkness falls. Finally, through the gray fog, she spotted what she thought must be one of the summit buildings. She wandered the perimeter until she found a door that would open.

Mary was greeted with hugs, cheers, worried expressions, and a few reprimands—brought on by our own fear of what might have happened. That we had lost someone, for even 20 minutes or half an hour, stunned me.

Most of us seemed to have had enough for one day. Wisdom dictated that our wet and tired group, sober from realizing that we hadn't taken good enough care of each other, should not hike down the Tuckerman Trail for four more miles, as originally planned. For those who keep lists of hiking accomplishments, it can be difficult to give up completing a full hike, so there were a few objections to this decision. But group leaders sometimes have to make decisions that are not wholly popular. I signed us up to take the tourist van down the auto road and offered to pay for anyone who didn't have funds for the ride. The choice wasn't unusual. The Park Service estimates that nearly 50 percent of people who hike up take a ride off the mountain.

Lessons: The mountains can fool us. We must be willing to modify our plans. As Joe Owens, a guide on Mount Hood, taught me in a simple word: "Reset." What you needed on your last hike will probably be different from what will work best on your next. A Mount Whitney guide I know has learned that people's ideas of their abilities can be flawed, that they often haven't honed the skills to climb on the routes they desire. The head guide for an International Mountain Guides climb on Mount Rainier told of watching a climber he suspected might not be prepared to summit. Because he didn't want to tell her that she shouldn't continue, he waited. He held off long enough for her to make that decision herself, then was supportive of it, with ideas for alternative activities while she stayed behind in camp with a friendly guide. She might have felt disappointed, but not discounted.

What should I have done differently in co-leading this hike? How does one recognize voices of fear or trepidation? When are we reaching beyond our self-proclaimed boundaries to stretch ourselves, to find new horizons? When is a change of plan the sensible route? How do we know we are not engaged in stubbornly forcing a desired outcome? It worked out this time, but I made the decision to learn to listen more closely, to hear the voices of wisdom and reality. It had been a pretty good hike. Or the worst ever.

CAROL STONE WHITE

Tragedy among the Clouds

Among the Clouds was the "only newspaper printed on the summit of any mountain in the world," according to its masthead. In addition to announcing "Printed Twice Daily on the Summit of Mount Washington: 6300 feet," the July 7, 1900, special edition reported: "Frightful Storm on Mount Washington—Raging Wind and Driving Sleet." Here is an excerpt:

After a quiet and pleasant day and an unusually calm evening on Friday, June 29, the summit of Mount Washington was visited by the most ferocious ice storm, lasting until Monday noon, ever known at this season of the year. The guests and residents of the Summit House retired in the calm, comfortable evening with anticipations of a pleasant morrow, and found in the morning an arctic storm with a howling, shrieking wind at about 75 mph and every rock coated with ice from one to four inches in thickness. At the end of the three-by-four-inch turntable lever, there projected on Sunday morning a solid block of ice in the teeth of the wind a foot and a half in length.

As the storm progressed, the lumps of ice grew according to the position of exposure until cakes weighing at least 200 pounds were formed all around the Summit House. So rapid had been the formation of the ice, and so fierce the velocity of the wind, that even small particles, driven like from a gun, broke dozens of panes of glass. The storm lasted sixty hours and during that time, more than forty panes were broken. The curious and fantastic shapes that the ice took were a study. Between the northeasterly corner of this office and the northwesterly corner of the Summit House, where sometimes seems concentrated all the breezy energies of New England, appeared one of the most beautiful sights presented anywhere. The wind seemed to have blown in a series of 100–200 small circles, for in an area of one rod square projected regular rows of ice bulbs three inches in length and the same in thickness, standing at an angle of 45 degrees and pointing northwest.

On June 30—the day described in this excerpt—the Appalachian Mountain Club (AMC) was holding their summer meeting on Mount Washington. They had selected this site for their field meeting twice before, in 1886 and 1894. It was to be a multi-day affair, featuring several days of hiking, so nearly 100 people were coming up to the Summit House by rail. Beautiful frost formations were noted on the ascent. Telegraph wires were coated with ice, with the wires becoming as thick as ropes and, near the summit, "great crystal festoons a foot or more in diameter" decorated the landscape. The club members arrived in an ice storm and blizzard of epic proportions: "The wind estimated to be 60–70 mph caused the staunch old house to rock like a vessel in a storm."

Almost everyone made it inside, including the Nichols party, who had ascended the Davis Path and camped on Mount Isolation on June 29. The temperature had fallen 23 degrees overnight and, luckily, the party rose very early, leaving for the summit by 5:30 a.m. By 11:00 a.m., with the brutal blizzard rapidly increasing in intensity, they had made it to the open spur, where they had to crawl and seek shelter during the worst gusts. Ice formation occurred rapidly on that afternoon of June 30. The party's guides descended on the Crawford Path, where two expected attendees, William Curtis and Allan Ormsbee, were ascending to the meeting.

Frank H. Burt, publisher of *Among the Clouds,* wrote feelingly about Curtis, aged sixty-three, and Allan Ormsbee, aged twenty-eight, in his article, "Victims of Storm." In 1868, Curtis had been one of the founders of the New York City Athletic Club; he was known as the father of athletics in America and looked upon as a "final authority on all athletic questions." In 1878 he founded the Fresh Air Fund. In 1898, he visited the White Mountains and "tramped and climbed extensively. He was perfectly fearless and would climb alone and in all kinds of weather, so confident was he in his strength and skill. . . . He was so thoroughly inured to cold that even in midwinter he never wore an overcoat." A regular feature of his hikes was the announcement that the hike would go, regardless of the weather. Ormsbee was likewise a trained athlete, Fresh Air supporter, and a member of the Crescent Athletic Club of Brooklyn.

My husband David and I are Adirondack Mountain Club guidebook authors for the Catskill Forest Preserve, where Curtis and Ormsbee cut a beautiful trail up its highest peak, 4,180-foot Slide Mountain. A stone monument on their trail, at 2,500 feet, notes simply "Curtis and Ormsbee Trail to Slide, 1900." Whenever I pass the monument, I'm reminded of

View from Mount Monroe to the Southern Presidentials. Mount Eisenhower, where William Curtis and Allan Ormsbee signed in, is the round summit in center. *Photo by Ben Potter*

important matters that were well described by the chairman of the AMC's Excursion Committee at the June 30 meeting. He made "explanatory and cautionary" remarks about "the dangers that mountains as high as these present to those unaccustomed to their peculiarities and sudden weather changes." Rules were established to govern the conduct of parties going out under club auspices.

Curtis and Ormsbee were climbing up the Crawford Path during this meeting. In my opinion, a series of poor choices—from the beginning of that day—resulted in the untimely deaths of these two extraordinarily able, well-liked, and altruistic men. The cause, I believe, was that they felt they were invincible. They had been hiking for a week before the meeting and, on June 30, they inexplicably chose to hike Mount Willard before starting up the 8.2-mile Crawford Path to the summit of Mount Washington, which actually totals 8.6 miles if also summiting Mount Pierce (Clinton) and Mount Pleasant (later Mount Eisenhower), as they planned to do. From

Mount Willard they certainly would have seen Mount Washington, socked in with heavy clouds. The nearby Crawford House was in regular contact with the Mount Washington summit by telephone and, although weather forecasting wasn't as scientific then, valuable information was available there to hikers en route to Mount Washington. But the men did not stop to review current conditions on Washington's summit before crossing the road to the Crawford Path.

The Crawford Path skirts the summits of 4,310-foot Mount Pierce, 4,761-foot Mount Eisenhower, 5,004-foot Mount Franklin, and 5,384-foot Mount Monroe, allowing hikers to avoid dangerous weather. Curtis and Ormsbee took extra time hiking to the summit of Mount Pierce and again more time taking the loop trail over the summit of Mount Eisenhower. The terrain from the Eisenhower-Franklin Col to the Mount Washington summit is totally exposed to the weather. There are few places that are so spectacular and relatively easy to traverse—as long as the weather is favorable. If Mother Nature offers her worst, there are few places more dangerous.

On July 5, a hiker found this entry in an AMC cylinder on the summit of Mount Eisenhower: "June 30, 1900. Wm B. Curtis, A.M.C. Allan Ormsbee. Rain-clouds and wind 60 miles. Cold." Two woodsmen, employed by the Crawford House, had been cutting growth on the Crawford Path that day. James C. Harvey reported that they saw Curtis and Ormsbee ascending Mount Eisenhower just after 2:00 p.m., that they hailed them and tried to warn them, but failed to stop them. After descending from Mount Eisenhower, Curtis and Ormsbee met Walter Parker and Charles Allen, the two guides who had accompanied the Nichols party up the Davis Path; these guides very strongly advised Curtis and Ormsbee not to go up Mount Washington. They told them about the dangerous conditions, how they'd been severely challenged by wind strong enough to compel crawling and brief runs to sheltering boulders on Bigelow Lawn, which took two hours to cross from the open spur to the base of the cone. On the cone, the Nichols party had constantly fought the fury of sleet driven by gusts of up to 100 mph, requiring stops every hundred steps to recover slightly, behind any rock that offered respite; the boulders were encrusted with ice.

Meanwhile, the fears of those at the Summit House about Curtis and Ormsbee had been allayed somewhat, knowing that the two guides would meet them and describe the extreme conditions above. Surely Curtis and Ormsbee would turn back, or they would descend on the Fabyan Path,[4] cut in June of 1886 and refurbished in 1896, at the northern end of Mount Eisenhower. They did neither. By the time they reached the area of Lakes of the Clouds, they were in desperate trouble. The two made an improvised shelter in the scrub, under the lee of the larger of the Mount Monroe summits (no hut had yet been built).

When it became possible to leave the Summit House, after the storm abated on Monday, Louis Cutter hiked down the Crawford Path by himself and found Curtis, "thinly clad," near Lakes of the Clouds. One camera and an empty milk bottle were found near the edge of Oakes Gulf, presumably to mark their shelter spot. Curtis's camera and some bread were found later. Cutter continued to the north side of Mount Eisenhower and met some hikers who had not seen anyone else. After much speculation, the best guess was that Ormsbee had left their tiny shelter at about 4:30 p.m. and reached the base of the summit cone before ice had yet formed at that elevation. Youthful and strong, Ormsbee would have thought he could make the summit for help, in spite of the cold rain driven by gale-force winds. He didn't foresee the incredibly icy conditions that existed near the summit. Once he was substantially up on the cone, there was nothing to do but try to make it.

Ormsbee's body was found within a 5-minute walk of the Signal Station, in the great boulders off the path, by his good friend, Professor Herschel C. Parker. Parker knew what Ormsbee would have tried to do—go straight for the top. The place where he fell was in an exact line between the Lake of the Clouds and the top of the mountain. That route had taken him off the wandering Crawford Path, and into the jagged icy rocks. His lacerated hands and injured limbs showed that he might have found it impossible to keep upright in the intense wind, on boulders like blocks of ice, and that he was forced to crawl near the summit. With the onset of hypothermia, he may have lost use of his extremities.

Among the Clouds reported that a Mr. T. O. Fuller said that he had made barometrical measurements and found that Ormsbee was 130 vertical feet from the platform of the hotel. Fuller found Ormsbee's glasses in a 2-foot hole in the rocks; they were double concave glasses, so powerful as to indicate that Ormsbee had been extremely nearsighted. Could loss of his glasses have caused even further difficulty? Frank Burt wrote: "He wages a heroic yet hopeless fight with the tempest, suffering fall after fall on the icy rocks, until at last, with only a few rods more to shelter, bruised and bleeding and crippled,[5] he too falls to rise no more. A struggle such as no other person ever passed through on Mount Washington ends in defeat and death."

A very interesting comment was made in "Lessons of the Tragedy," another column in *Among the Clouds.* "Men less strong and hardy would probably have given up the attempt [to reach the summit] and sought safety below, so it may be truly said that their extraordinary strength was in this case their source of danger." Other "lessons" included the following: avoid stormy days, don't hike alone, and don't undertake more than your strength will permit. But there will always be people who are equally strong, experienced, and knowledgeable who do not believe that Mother Nature can overpower them. They truly believe they are invincible. I know some people who feel that way, but this cautionary tale proves that *no one* is invincible.

One insidious effect of hypothermia is an increasing inability to think clearly. Well over 100 people have died on Mount Washington and the immediate environment of the Presidential Range (not counting vehicle deaths): 30 from hypothermia, 12 from avalanche, 19 from natural causes such as heart attacks, and 42 from falls. Drowning accounts for 6 deaths and falling ice 5 more. "People can overestimate their ability and/or underestimate the force of the elements," Peter Crane writes. "I find something admirable in testing one's self against challenges, but with that must come a sense of balance, in striving to soberly assess risks and benefits, and to recognize, as early English alpinists would stress, the difference between difficulty and danger."

The article on lessons learned from the Curtis-Ormsbee tragedy observed that, although one may be fearless of consequences to oneself, one must consider dangers to others who might attempt a rescue. Fred Ilgen had left Curtis and Ormsbee to climb Twin Mountain; he then took the train to the Summit House in an already severe storm. When he reported that Curtis and Ormsbee were climbing up the Crawford Path, there was general alarm. Two guides with the AMC event—Thaddeus Lowe was one of them—tried to descend from the Summit House with lanterns, but the wind immediately extinguished the lights. Due to the ferocious wind and ice, these seasoned mountaineers had been forced back just yards away from the door. To proceed over the icy rocks in darkness and that fearful gale would have been to go to almost certain death, with scarcely a chance of finding the missing persons. If Fred Ilgen had hiked with Curtis and Ormsbee that day, one wonders how the outcome would have been different.

The New York Fresh Air Fund created memorials for both men. A rudimentary shelter was soon erected, and the construction of the Lakes of the Clouds Hut was completed in July 1915. Just two months later, six hikers were stranded in the new hut for four days by a raging snowstorm! What is mountain safety? Know the route and its condition; know the weather and the condition of your team; be fully equipped—even for the surprises; and be prepared to use plan B—an early descent.

It was said that the June 30 ice storm and gale were the fiercest ever known on Mount Washington in "mid-summer," but it can be wintry in the mountains on any date. This past July, someone inquired about the "easiest" way to climb Mount Washington. One respondent said, "Whatever you do, make sure you are prepared for winter-like conditions any time of year, no matter how nice the weather is at the bottom." On June 30, 2011, exactly 111 years after the Curtis-Ormsbee calamity, a cold front stalled out for two days on Mount Washington, causing a thick blanket of fog throughout the day, with rumbles of thunder and a persistent risk of showers. The wind speed was 58 mph with a low temperature of 38 degrees Fahrenheit. If the temperature had dropped another few degrees, all the potential for the disastrous weather of June 30, 1900, including the extreme icing, would have been there. Three major storm tracks converge over Mount Washington, which is why this forbidding peak is famous for its erratic, turbulent weather in every month of the year. The bottom line: severe winter-like storms can occur at any season.

In 1894, when the second AMC field meeting was held on Mount Washington, a party of fifty members hiking in Tuckerman Ravine had just passed through the snow arch when 100 feet of it fell. Several people were struck by falling ice but luckily no one was injured; eight years earlier, on July 24, a fifteen-year-old boy had been killed when the snow arch fell just as he stepped under it.

My husband and I agreed that we would climb Mount Washington in winter when the temperature was higher than the wind speed, but it is good to remember that 3 to 5 degrees Fahrenheit are lost for every 1,000 feet of elevation gained, and Mount Washington is a 4,300-foot ascent from Pinkham Notch. On December 28, 2003, the sky was the deepest, beautiful blue, but the brilliant sun, low in the sky, offered little warmth. At the base of the mountain, the temperature was about 30 degrees, with the wind at perhaps 25 mph. The narrow steep section of the Lion Head Trail, below tree line, was like Grand Central Station, with hikers ascending above us and behind us in an enthusiastic line. Nineteen days later—on our thirty-ninth anniversary—the summit temperature was −43.6 degrees, with sustained winds of 87.5 mph. We didn't celebrate it on Mount Washington.

MICHAEL N. KELSEY

Green in the Whites

Some colors just don't go together, like green in the White Mountains. On that frigid winter weekend in late December 2001, when the cloud-white snow measured waist-deep and the temperatures sunk below zero, Branden and I were as green as it gets. At the beginning of our intended full traverse over the 34.5-mile Pemigewasset Wilderness mountain loop, the price tags still dangled from our newly purchased snowshoes and our dress was nine-tenths cotton. This multi-day trek is a challenge in any season, particularly winter, when heading into the woods unprepared is the leading cause of hiker fatality.

We were new to New Hampshire, new to peakbagging, and new to snowshoeing. Blame it on youth. Blame it on excitement. Blame it on bad advice, but these two optimistic adventure-seekers, with wills and tenacities of steel, were dead-set to take our hiking trips to the next level. We were both accomplished three-season hikers, with some winter camping experience under our belts, but neither of us was prepared for the challenges that lay ahead in this introduction to New Hampshire winter. Among the lessons learned—and there were many—was that during winter in the White Mountains, the only greens that are tolerated are of the coniferous type. And even those evergreen and fir trees know enough to lay dormant all winter long, waywardly sagging, ice-covered and bent over beneath layers and layers of frozen white rinds. We would have been wise to learn from their example. Instead we ventured deep into the New Hampshire wilderness—under-prepared, over-ambitious, and more than a little naïve. Our intrusion into the white winter became a bout with nature, in which mere survival represented a marked victory.

The idea to snowshoe some New Hampshire peaks first surfaced the day after Christmas. Branden and I splurged all our Christmas gift money on oversized Tubbs snowshoes (in later years, I would come to dismiss these as "clown shoes"). During that purchase, the store clerk probably suspected the severity of our under-preparedness. He directed us to an auto mechanic who was pursuing the White Mountain 4,000-footer list.

When we walked into the garage bay, the mechanic was busy under the hood of a car. "We're headed to New Hampshire to snowshoe a mountain tomorrow," I said. "Know of any good ones?"

"I just returned from hiking the Pemi," he told us, using the affectionate name hikers have given the region—an attempt, perhaps, to soften its strenuous and severe topography. "Follow me. I'll show you photos from my Labor Day weekend trip."

Topo maps served as wallpaper in his office. He traced the outline of the Pemi traverse on the map, showing how it began and ended at the Lincoln Woods trailhead, with some 30 miles and 18,000 feet of elevation gain, most above treeline, in between. The trail meanders over some of the premier New Hampshire peaks, including the remote Mount Bond and its sister mountain, the craggy Bondcliff. "If you're seeking adventure and wilderness, it doesn't get any better than the Pemi!"

We thanked him and embarked on the six-hour drive from New York to New Hampshire. In our pockets was the map he'd loaned us; had he known our level of inexperience, he might not have been so generous. We were too green to know that trail conditions and weather are much different in December than in September, or that, at high elevations, the travel rate is more like 1 mph than the 2.5 mph lowland rate we were accustomed to.

At 45,000 acres, the Pemigewasset Wilderness is New Hampshire's largest and wildest outdoor playground. A series of connected trails run in a horseshoe-shaped crescent over three mountain ranges that together take the hiker over ten mountains, eight of them on the White Mountain 4,000-footer list, with side trails leading to four more.[6] Although difficult and challenging, the payoff is huge—on the open ridge the views are stunning—and, on the second day, that was our experience atop 4,698-foot Mount Bond. Near and far were rows of snow-covered mountains of varying height and contour, each radiating differing shades of blue and gray against the white foreground of snow. Wispy clouds rising between the peaks added mystery and grandeur. The gray cumulus puffs overhead seemed to cap each range like a crown.

"This is amazing," wide-eyed Branden beamed when the clouds parted, granting us a brief mountain view.

The awe had begun around 9:00 a.m. when, not far from our wooded

Bondcliff summit, with West Bond in background.
Photo by David White

tent spot, the trail had opened to a tall rock wall, proclaiming that we had reached the boundary of 4,265-foot Bondcliff. Here on a snow-capped ledge we fumbled with handholds and footholds to climb, at times on our belly, up the signature Bondcliff shelf, where we both would achieve our first New Hampshire boasting rights. A sign declared that we had now entered the alpine zone, where plant life was more fragile. We were overwhelmed to think that, for the next 20 miles, our journey would be on an open ridge winding over mountain after mountain. The trail, now devoid of trees and hemmed in by clouds, angled upwards toward Mount Bond. Scattered everywhere were snow-dusted boulders and jagged, pointed rocks, giving the mountain a feeling of isolation and coarseness that suggested a wild geological past. Branden darted up the rough route, the exhilaration making him forget about the heavy backpack on his shoulders. I followed equally in awe.

We were not averse to hardship. In fact, overcoming obstacles has always been one of the appealing challenges about outdoor adventure. But this trip, owing to our inexperience, would have more than its share. Some of our mistakes betrayed years of otherwise sound training. Take, for instance, my decision to hike in cotton trousers because I had outgrown the vintage wool pants that—eons ago, as a first-year scout—my now deceased scoutmaster, Frank McFarlin, had taught me to wear. He'd sit us down at troop meetings, week after week, ingraining the do's and don'ts of winter camping.

"If your feet are cold, put a hat on, as much of your body heat escapes through the head."

"Dress in layers and always change your clothes at night because, during the day, sweat builds up that will freeze and make you cold."

"Never wear cotton. Cotton kills. Instead wear synthetics or self-wicking materials like silk, polypropylene, wool, or burlap."

I knew better than to trek in winter dressed in cotton and yet, with limited funds, I chose snowshoes over new winter pants. Other mistakes were due to plain stupidity, such as the flawed logic which convinced me that using cheap yellow rain pants to cover my cotton Dockers would keep me dry. We were not even 2 miles into the hike before they began cracking in the single-digit temperatures. This meant that my pants were susceptible to wetness whenever we sat on the snow—and the weight of our 40-pound packs enticed us to take frequent breaks. If the sight of my cotton pants underneath the deteriorating yellow rain pants wasn't indication enough of our inexperience, the poor decision-making that followed certainly must have been.

That was most likely the impression we gave to a robust couple from Canada, who we encountered soon after ascending a trail lined with high-altitude pines. She was bundled in layers, adorned with a burlap poncho. He sported a beard that Saint Nicholas would have been proud of. Immediately they expressed wonderment that we carried our gear in backpacks, on our shoulders, rather than towing it in sleds, as they did. Sleds might have eased our burden, saving us time in the limited daylight. As it was, we were completely unaware that the sun would soon set or what that would mean to the temperature. The Canadian couple had pitched their camp in a clearing, slightly off the trail, and they pointed to a spot suitable for our tent. This should have been enough of a prompt, but instead we told them we were headed over both Bondcliff and Bond to the Guyot Campsite, still 4 miles and significant elevation gain away. The worried glance they shared did not escape me as the fellow blurted through his beard, "Well, we'd better not keep you then, as you still have a long ways ahead of you."

No sooner did we leave them than we received our first views, through leafless trees, of the valley below. The sky paled to lavender and soon we spotted the full moon rising in the cloudless sky. (It would take several more trips before we learned that cloudless nights meant frigid nights, because clouds serve to insulate.) Out came my 35-mm camera to photograph the evening sky. I was proud of the special fingerless gloves I'd brought for this trip, as I could snap away without exposing my entire hand to the cold. What I failed to realize was the susceptibility of my fingertips to the chill, something I didn't notice until I could no longer feel the shutter. I would have been better served if my scoutmaster's ancient counsel had reverberated sooner: "Be extra careful to cover up your extremities—ears, nose, cheeks, fingers and toes—lest frostbite set in."

I inserted my numb, white fingertips into my gloves, making fist pumps to try and stimulate blood flow. Although this technique provided some relief, it would be two full weeks before I recovered complete sensation in my fingers, a condition somewhat intensified by nerve damage incurred in an automobile accident a decade earlier. After sundown, the temperature plummeted. Icicles formed on my month-old beard and soon our faces were feeling the blistering chill. The decision to abandon our far-off destination and pitch camp in haste was a shared one. It was derived in part by panic brought on by the harshness of the cold; it was unlike any either of us had ever felt. Frantic to take cover, we haphazardly plopped down our tent directly on the trail, violating even the most basic rule of trail etiquette. While we had had the sense to bring foam pads to insulate us from the ground, neither of us knew enough to bring along a four-season tent. The bulk of our body heat therefore escaped through the tent's vented walls and loose-fitting fly.

We cooked inside on account of the cold, melting snow as a substitute for our frozen Gatorade. Again, we failed to adhere to Mr. McFarlin's able advice: "Use a thick sock to insulate your water bottles and turn them upside down to slow down the freezing process." In our haste to prepare dinner, we failed to realize that the rising steam would saturate the tent's walls before freezing, adding unnecessary weight when we rolled it up the next morning.[7] We pulled the drawstrings on our mummy sleeping bags so tight that only our noses peeked out, and fell asleep dreaming about the views above treeline from the summits of Bondcliff, Bond, and the other eight mountaintops that awaited us.

The dreaded reality check—that "in over our heads" moment—came on the summit of Mount Bond. We had followed fresh snowshoe prints, presumably from the Canadian couple, who must have passed us as we slept in the early hours of morning. I can only imagine their head-shaking at our tent placement, and at our poor time management, as we again failed to maximize our use of the daylight hours by starting before sun-up. On top of Bond were several medium-sized rocks, perfect for sitting, resting our loads, and eating lunch. Snow-covered alpine shrubs encircled the bald peak like a tonsure, while thick clouds hovered overhead. Desolate and barren, it was the closest to winter tundra I had ever experienced. At noon, some glorious moments occurred when the clouds parted for a few minutes to show us that extraordinary Pemigewasset panorama of winter bliss. The imagery was uplifting, almost euphoric, the type of sensory overload and winter grandeur which would motivate us both to return to the Whites a month later, to experience it anew.

After marveling at the views, we prepared to get the blood flowing again and decided to review our situation. Yesterday's hike had been slow going; the rugged terrain today, up and over Bondcliff and on to Bond, had taken us 4 hours; we were still 0.7 miles from the Guyot Campsite, yesterday's destination, with 20 miles and six peaks still left to go on the traverse. Now on Bond—halfway through our second day—with only Gatorade slush to hydrate us, a frozen tent to shelter us, and damp cotton clothes to warm us (the torn rain pants were of no further use), it was apparent that, if we continued, our Pemi traverse would not end well, if we could complete it at all. We lacked enough food and provisions for this extended trip. Our experiences so far suggested that we might become victims of hypothermia, severe frostbite, dehydration, or worse—a typical example of how lack of preparation, combined with over-ambition, caused yet another hiker death.

"We're wasting time discussing this," Branden said, shouldering his pack and starting on the trail toward the Guyot Campsite. "We need to go."

It was like a bomb dropped when I verbalized what hitherto had been unthinkable: "In which direction?" Here at noon, atop the most remote peak of New Hampshire's 4,000-footers, on the second day of our intended three-day traverse of the Pemi, we made the decision to turn back. Hobbling back down the rocky, snow-covered cobblestones was hard on our feet, but harder still on our pride. We retraced our steps to Bondcliff, still mesmerized by our surroundings, despite our setback. Our senses still exploded with the alpine conditions, high above the tree line where rock, snow, ice, and mist were all that the eye could see. Soon we were at Bondcliff's famous 10-foot ledge, which hours earlier we had struggled to climb. It served as a natural barrier separating the start of the alpine zone from the wooded ridgeline leading downward. Earlier we had tackled this section brimming with excitement, now we were only saying farewell.

We passed the spot where our tent had been pitched, and a wooded overlook which the night before had offered glimpses of an inspiring full moon, rising against a purple, cloudless sky. With many miles to go, we passed by without pause. Moving through the forest, with thoughts and emotions running deep, we walked out under a different sort of cloud. Our bodies ached and morale was low as Branden and I made the late-night death march back to our car. On our tongues was the taste of defeat. This was a trip cut short by an acceptance of the facts: we were in over our heads, behind schedule, and under-prepared; we had been beaten by the White Mountains and the perils of winter.

Although we knew our decision to turn back was the right one, now was not the time to bask in our good judgment. Instead we took turns being angry as our feet reversed the previous day's steps on the monotonous 4.7-mile Lincoln Woods Trail. At times one of us would hurl a backpack as far in front of us as he could. When we reached the pack, we would throw it again—if we could muster the energy. More commonly we just gave it a solid kick, causing it to slide forward on the icy road. It took us 7 hours to reach our car from the summit of Bond, then two more before we found a room in North Conway. By then we were too exhausted to recognize the feat we had just accomplished—or the fate we had smartly avoided.

We'd turned bad judgment into good judgment, while summiting what is considered to be among New Hampshire's toughest peaks, at the cusp of winter, when the sun shines for barely 8 hours and temperatures rarely rise above freezing. There's a seasoning process required before green wood dries and becomes usable. We too had been "seasoned" by the White Mountain winter. Green no more, we left for home with a new appreciation for—and a renewed commitment to—backcountry preparation.

"You climbed the Bonds in winter?" Hearing these words exclaimed in a bar, six years later, was our after-the-fact consolation. The surprise redeemed our experiences during those cold December days of 2001. The speakers were newly introduced White Mountain peakbaggers, people who knew the mountains as well as the severity and ruggedness of Northeast winters. Their astonishment increased when I told them the Bonds had been my first New Hampshire peaks. My retelling of our winter trek gave me instant acceptance into a seasoned group. Months later, I would join them for a three-day post-Christmas marathon up seven New Hampshire peaks, including many of those along the Pemi Loop that had been forsaken on my trek with Branden. Now an experienced mountaineer, that inaugural alpine trip up Bondcliff and Bond ranks as my most memorable, not because of what went wrong, but because Branden and I had had the good sense to know when we were beat and when to turn back. Ironically, that acknowledgement of defeat became our real accomplishment.

When I think of the Bonds today, I don't think of failure, I think of the complete exhilaration and total saturation of the senses, the thrill of conquest, and the feeling that life does not get better than mountaineering in winter. Today when I relive my experiences on the winter Bonds, I feel that white-green color combination recurring again, except this time it's not the green of inexperience or the white of frostbitten fingers. Instead, while wishing to be atop Bond when the clouds part, I become green with White Mountain envy.

JOHNATHAN A. ESPER

Extremes at the Top of Maine

A permit, a sizeable fee, and a group of at least four people are prerequisites to spending a night in Baxter State Park in winter. My dad and I needed to climb Baxter and Hamlin Peaks, so we recruited Phil Hazen to join the group. I had met Phil the year before in the Adirondacks, and he had proven to be a suitable hiking partner. Phil found three other friends to join our team, and we applied for and received permission to attempt the summits during a four-day period in February 2000. We all converged on a small town just south of the park, then proceeded to our starting point: a heavily used logging road called the Golden Road. We spent the first day hiking 15 miles on the park road (open to traffic in the summer) that leads to Roaring Brook Campsite. Even though my dad and I were snowshoeing and carrying full packs, we managed to keep up with the others, who were skiing and pulling sleds.

That night we slept in a cabin. I awoke as a park ranger was urging us to pack quickly and hike the three miles up to Chimney Pond. It was snowing heavily, and over a foot had already accumulated. By the time we arrived at Chimney Pond, in late morning, everyone was tired except my dad and me, and no one else wanted to attempt any mountain, especially in that weather. That afternoon I explored the South Basin under the Knife Edge, while my dad packed the trail up Hamlin Peak for the group's future climb. Though capable of summiting, he was forced to turn around above tree line, because park rules mandate a minimum of four for any summit attempt. The next day's weather proved very windy; it would be poor for climbing, but my dad persuaded the whole group to attempt Hamlin, as Baxter Peak would be even more exposed.

Above tree line the wind was stronger, though not yet knocking us over. We were in whiteout conditions, barely able to see in front of us. Leading the way, I thought we were in the clouds but, when I saw blue sky above, I realized it was yesterday's snow blowing off the ridge. About a third of the way up the exposed ridge, it cleared slightly and I was able to see the ridge rising up ahead. It was an awe-inspiring but fearful sight: white clouds of snow blowing over and off the ridge's crest. In my heart I wanted to turn around from fear, but my dad caught up with me and encouraged the whole group to continue. My fears proved well-founded; the wind got worse, reaching 70 mph. One of my snowshoes kept falling off at the worst locations. I was forced to take my hands out of my gloves and kneel on them so they wouldn't take flight as I fixed it. The snowshoe itself also would have blown away—if not for its claw gripping the wind-packed ice and snow. I stayed in the lead to the summit, and thankfully did not have to wait long for the others. I noticed a large swollen area about the size of a Kennedy half-dollar on the exposed cheek of one of the climbers, who was quite helpless at this point. My dad took his hand out of his glove to thaw the other's cheek to prevent frostbite. We'd been above tree line and in the wind for almost 2 hours.

Surprisingly, the others wanted to try to follow the broad plateau over to Baxter Peak. I knew the idea lacked sense, considering the risk of becoming disoriented in the deteriorating weather conditions, so I told everyone to retreat before we succumbed to the elements. On the way back down I was again in front. The wind grew even stronger, forcing me to crawl. At times I could not even crawl, but just hung on to the ground or a rock. There was virtually zero visibility, although I could perceive that I was still on the crest of the ridge. I began to wonder if we would ever get back down to the tree line. I found shelter from the wind behind a large boulder, where I rested and waited for the others to catch up, but after 10 minutes they still had not appeared out of the whiteness. As the winds increased to over 80 mph, I grew more concerned. But, to my great relief, they eventually appeared, and the rest of the way down proved uneventful, though very tiring, as we continually fought against the relentless wind to remain standing.

On the following day, all six of us attempted Baxter Peak. We hiked up the Cathedral Trail past tree line until we were even with the First Cathedral, the first of three large rocky outcroppings. By that time the fair sky had become clouded, flurries were beginning to fall, and the wind had begun to pick up. I could see ribbons of snow blowing between the rocks ahead and didn't wish to repeat our experiences of the day before, and neither did the group. We turned around and, though I felt that was the best decision, my dad and I knew that the next day would represent our last opportunity to summit.

I awoke before dawn, anxious to see what the weather was like. I stepped out into the frigid air and gazed with wonder at Katahdin bathed in moonlight. It was the first time I had seen Katahdin in its entirety, unobstructed by clouds or blowing snow; the full moon only accentuated the spectacular view. I felt overwhelming excitement, confidence, and gratitude to God for giving us this clear morning. However, no one else shared my enthusiasm for another summit attempt. They pointed to the clouds of snow being blown off the summit, which I had conveniently ignored. By mid-morning, my dad and I managed to convince two others to attempt the summit with us, fulfilling the minimum requirement of four persons in a group. We retraced our steps up a steep snowfield and gained the ridge. Though the sky was perfectly blue, the wind was about 40 mph. I was obliged to keep my face completely covered, because the wind chill factor was −40 degrees! The Cathedral Trail proved to be a breathtaking route, and, praise God, I successfully reached the highest point in Maine. The two other climbers followed my dad's and my footprints and soon joined us. After risking frostbitten fingers for a few quick pictures, we hurriedly descended. Though tired and thirsty, we decided against taking the time to get anything out of our packs, as one's fingers became numb after only 15 seconds of exposure.

When I reached the top of the 45-degree snow-slope, just above tree line, I took out my ice ax, sat down, and slid, using the ax as a brake. I reached the bottom in less than a minute. The others, afraid of starting an avalanche, decided to follow along the top of the snowfield and take a longer route back to the tree line. Their footsteps severed the top of the snowfield, and I watched as snow suddenly came rushing toward me, pushing over and burying small trees in its path.[8] Fifteen feet in front of me, the snow mass piled up and—fortunately—stopped. Needless to say, the other climbers were unnerved. One recalled that he looked at the snow below him and noticed it was moving!

Our primary mission accomplished, my dad and I headed down to Roaring Brook Campsite. Although the rest of the group would leave in the morning, we felt we might not have another chance that winter to climb the third 4,000-foot peak in Baxter State Park, North Brother. We therefore planned to hike 23 miles on the road around Katahdin to the North Brother trailhead, bivouacking when necessary. By 3:00 a.m. we had covered 13 miles on the road (a snowmobile trail in this season), and stashed our unnecessary gear in the woods by the 2-mile spur trail leading to our car. We continued north on the park road, walking another 6 miles to the summer trailhead of North Brother, stopping only once to rest.

Though I was exhausted and had virtually no food left, we climbed to the summit of North Brother, reaching it by dusk. It seemed to take forever to get back to the trailhead in the dark and, when we finally did, I was too exhausted and hungry to continue. We put our pads and sleeping bags directly on the snow in the middle of the trail. My dad was so tired that he fell asleep standing up, hands tucked in his pockets for warmth. I told him to take off his boots and get in his sleeping bag. Having hiked 33 miles that long day, I quickly fell asleep with the most satisfied and cozy feeling, as snowflakes began to fall softly on my face and cover my bag.

Addendum

Because Phil notified park rangers of our plans, they searched for us on snowmobiles, found us sleeping at the North Brother trailhead, and made us ride out with them. Park headquarters sent us a letter saying we had been banned from entering the park for one year, as we had violated winter park rules by splitting up the group. Would I do the same thing again? Probably yes. However, my dad sometimes laments that he didn't teach me to respect authority, and has second thoughts about what we did.

PART II

Rescues in the Mountains

Many of the following tales convey the extraordinary courage, caring, and competence of search and rescue teams, both professional and volunteer, throughout the Northeast. Other accounts show that knowing wilderness first aid and the symptoms of hypothermia and frostbite can help us aid our fellow hikers and perhaps save limbs and lives. But let's begin with how a search and rescue expert deals with his own physical and mental challenges.

DOUG MAYER

A Leg Up
Challenges of a Self-Rescue

Two are better than one . . . for if they fall, the one will lift up
his fellow; but woe to him that is alone when he falleth, for he hath
not another to help him up. —*Ecclesiastes 4:9–10*

If you enjoy hiking and mountain climbing enough, you try to do a lot of it. And, should you manage to find enough time to get up into the mountains for more than one or two trips a season, you begin to throw new twists into the process. You may start climbing in the winter. You may begin to feel comfortable going out on your own. After a few seasons of winter climbing and hiking, you get used to the excitement and unpredictability of the season's weather. You come to have a pretty good sense of what to bring along, and of what your capabilities are. This was where I found myself in December 1989.

No one ever expects to be the victim of an accident. We read *Accidents in North American Mountaineering* each year and assess the mistakes of our peers. Though on some level we know that it could just as easily have happened to us, in hindsight the errors all seem obvious. Still most of us manage to push ourselves through the routines: toss in the first-aid pack, the sleeping bag, the matches, the compass; leave a route description; check a weather forecast.

December 1, 1989, was a very cold day in New Hampshire. At the observatory on the summit of Mount Washington, Peter Crane reported on the WBNC morning weather show that the current conditions were –15 degrees Fahrenheit with a 72 mph northwest wind. The summit forecast predicted a warming to –10 degrees, with winds averaging 50 to 70 mph with higher gusts.

I had been wanting to get out for a good winter hike for a few days; maybe a summit or two, with a swing by the Randolph Mountain Club's new Gray Knob cabin, on the side of Mount Adams. The night before, I had filled my pack with all the usuals: sweater, shell, pile pants and jacket, Dachsteins, overmitts, balaclava, crampons, bivy sack, two-way radio and spare batteries, headlamp, map, compass, food. The radio was a leftover from my summers spent working in the White Mountains, when I often hiked alone for miles at a time. Several times the radio had proved useful, and I did not begrudge the extra weight. I also tossed in a large pack of toilet paper, for Paul, the caretaker at Gray Knob. We had joked a week or so earlier about his running short. Finally, I left behind a description of my intended route. I was planning to hike up the Valley Way, then loop over Madison and Adams and down to Gray Knob.

I arrived at Appalachia around 9:30 a.m. and headed right out, dressed in polypro, pile pants, and double plastic boots. About eleven or so I was getting near tree line. The trail was slippery, with not quite enough snow to cover the ice. In many respects, however, it was a perfect winter hike: a cold, clear, and windy December day, with no one else on any of the trails. No signs of anyone having been through, either. Near the Watson Path, I stopped for some hot chocolate. It was evident that, above tree line, the hiking was going to be a classic winter experience with lots of ice, lots of high winds, and bitter cold. On most days, I would have been looking forward to such an adventure, stopping just below tree line to get "suited up" and ready for entry into the arctic scene above. Today, though, I just didn't seem into it. I have rarely, if ever, found myself with such a feeling. So I packed up and turned around. *Don't force it,* I thought, *you're up here to enjoy yourself.*

Fifty feet later, I tripped on a rock. I heard a snap and a soft crack as I fell. Before I landed, I knew what had happened. The thought that went through my mind was very simple and objective: *So that's what it's like to break your leg.*

I kidded with myself, trying to calm down. *Maybe it's just a bad bruise.* I tried, slowly, to get up. But something was different. My right leg collapsed under only part of my weight and I fell again. I felt the broken bones grating against each other. *Damn.* The next few thoughts seemed beyond my control, presenting themselves automatically. I sensed that they had to be brought out into the open and answered if I wanted to work past their presence. This was a worst-case scenario. *If I didn't get someone on the radio, I could be here until early morning before help comes. If it's a bad break, there might be internal bleeding, damaged nerves, or other problems. I could be in serious trouble. I could go into shock and then . . .*

Nonsense! I pushed that last thought away. The notion was so unreasonable that I spoke out loud: "You've got years of outdoor experience. You're an EMT, you're just a few miles from help, you can handle a night out. Just stay cool, Mayer, and everything'll be fine."

In these situations, staying level-headed is all that matters; the rest will fall into place. If you lose your cool, then you will have beaten yourself. So don't freak out—just deal with it.

I took off my gloves and got out the radio. The Randolph Mountain Club frequency. "KAD4855, this is unit 93, to Gray Knob or Randolph, anyone around?" No answer. Again. No answer. Again. Silence. *Come on, answer!* I switched to the AMC repeater, but couldn't key it up—the mountains were blocking the path to the summit of Washington. *Damn.* I switched to scan—no one on any frequencies. *God damn. Bad luck, Mayer.*

At that point, my mind switched gears, effortlessly. Without any prompting, it simply went into a new, no-nonsense level of operation. *No one is on the radio. Forget the radio. Put the radio away, your hands are freezing already. Just forget it. No one hears you. Move on to the next step, this one is not working.*

The choice was pretty clear. I could stay and wait, trying to stay warm, or I could try to work my way down the trail. My old first-aid training reminded me of things I really did not want to know. If I moved my unsplinted leg, I risked cutting into any one of several decent-sized arteries. I could lose circulation in my leg for several hours, and face a much more serious injury. I could also injure a nerve and realize permanent damage to my leg.

The other choice was to wait: get on all my clothes, break out the bivy sack and play mind games to pass the time. But it was *cold.* There also was not enough snow for a good snow cave—and I hadn't brought my stove. *Mayer, you idiot. You always bring your stove in the winter.* Hypothermia presented itself as a prospect. *No way can I sit around for 12 hours. Self-rescue is the way to go. Now is your chance to take complete responsibility for yourself. Solo hiking in winter—this is what you have to be ready to deal with. So, deal.*

I pulled myself over to a few branches that had fallen across the trail. I grabbed one and smashed it against a tree, breaking it to a 4-foot length. Same process with another branch. I pulled the straps off my crampons and tried to improvise a splint. *Too damn cold.* My fingers just didn't work at all—totally useless, completely clumsy. Couldn't tie a simple knot.

Your fingers are worthless like this. Forget the splint. Rewarm your hands. The splint idea will not work. Forget it. Move on to the next step. Your hands are freezing. Keep your warmth. Bundle up now, before you lose heat. The next step is to bundle up.

I put away the crampons, and put on all my warm clothes: sweater, pile jacket, storm jacket, balaclava, mittens, overmittens. *Avoid going into shock. If I go into shock I'm in real trouble.* I took my pulse. *One hundred, seems strong at my wrist, steady.* Not bad. I took ten deep, slow breaths, and drank half a quart of hot chocolate.

I grabbed my two sticks. Time to move. *Can I stand with these sticks? Can I walk?*

I stood up. My right leg was nearly useless, but I could balance off of it. I could move. *Nice trick, Mayer. You must look pathetic. But you can move yourself!*

I began to move, ever so slowly, ever so gingerly. Each step was carefully selected. *What's underneath that snow? Is that a rock? Don't get snagged on that stick! Slow, slow, put your weight down slowly. Okay . . . good, good. Now, what's next? Okay . . .* Any jolt to my foot sent a wicked surge of sharp pain up my leg. A good incentive to treat it gently. *See that tree? Here we are, great, you did it! Good job, Mayer. Good job! See that gully? Our next goal, that gully. Take it slow.*

My mind cruised along at full speed: strong, focused on the moment, no other thoughts. It was dragging an injured body out of the woods. It was on a mission, for me. *Don't think about how far you have to go. Pick easy goals, take your time, remember all those stories.* I had been reading a lot of mountaineering stories recently. I would never have thought that those tales would be put to this kind of use. *Remember* Moments of Doubt? *Brad Washburn and Bob Bates in Alaska? How about* The Breach—*Rob Taylor coming off Kilimanjaro after that fall.* Touching the Void—*Joe Simpson's three days' crawl through the Andes with a shattered leg! Your situation is zero compared to those guys. This is nothing at all. Those guys could do it—you can do this little walk.*

But every now and then my mind did wander. I began to get my hopes up—perhaps someone really would come along this trail. *It's a Friday afternoon, the Valley Way's well traveled.* I began to imagine the scenario: "Hi, uh, I don't mean to bother you, but I just broke my leg . . . can you give me a hand here? Boy, it's great to see you!" Every time, though, my mind put the focus squarely back onto me. *No one will come. No one is coming up this trail today, no one at all. That's all there is to it. So get back into it and keep moving. No one will come up the Valley Way today.*

Talking out loud seemed to add some much-needed levity to the situation. "Not one of your better days, huh Mayer?" "Okay, this is the last leg of your trip." "Sure would be a shame to slip and break the other one too." "Don't worry, you've got a leg up on the situation." "If I were asked, I would have to say that today really is one of my less enjoyable days."

I made pretty good progress. On the steeper sections, I would slide on my back, right leg high in the air. It would have been an odd sight, but no one was watching. "Oh, hi! Hello! Nice day, isn't it? Why this way? Well hiking just gets so damned boring sometimes . . ."

It was 4:45 when I got out to the trailhead, just dark—a 5-hour trip over 2.5 miles or so. I waited at Route 2 for a car, a truck. Nothing. *This is the worst day of my life. Don't I get any luck today? None, huh? Okay, to hell with it.*

I unlocked my car door, pushed my pack onto the passenger's seat and slid the driver's seat all the way back. I got the car started, with a short jab on the accelerator. A fresh, warm burst of pain flared up my leg. *Oh, yeah, times like this you sure wish you'd taken that automatic they had on the lot, huh Doug?* "Well, personally, I like the automatic because it's just so much easier to drive with a broken leg." I got the car into first gear, set the cruise control at 20 mph, put on the flashers and headed along the breakdown lane to Barb and Don Wilson's, 2 miles away. *Four thousand rpm, kind of revving the engine a bit high today, Doug.* Second gear just wasn't worth the effort.

Pulling into the driveway, I honked for several seconds and waited. *Hah! No one's coming . . . of course! Remember, you're just out of luck today. The final blow. Where now, Mayer?*

Don Wilson appeared at the door! I had been wondering for the last hour or so how he or Barb would handle this upcoming conversation: "Umm, hi Don. Doug Mayer. I, umm, broke my leg on the Valley Way and, uh, need a hand." *He's going to think you're joking. He's going to think you're nuts.*

Perfect. Fabulous! Less than a minute later he was outside with an old pair of crutches, giving me a hand inside. Totally calm, very helpful. I couldn't have asked for more. *You're okay, Don. You're the best. Now I can turn this mess over to other people. I can relax.*

A phone call, then an ambulance ride to Berlin from Gorham Ambulance ("Say hi to Mike Pelchat for me. Tell him I walked out 'cause I knew otherwise he'd be treating me and carrying me out and you can naturally imagine how scared I was of that prospect!" A good laugh with the EMTS.)

Others have had much more spectacular accidents. For me, December 1 was just a long and tiring day of intense emotion and pain. I may have been on the edge of a life-threatening situation, but I always managed to keep it at bay. I ended the day in surgery, with a handful of screws and a metal plate in my leg, to repair three broken bones and a few disconnected ankle ligaments. Four days later I was out of the hospital. Seven weeks later I was off crutches. In March I was done with physical therapy. This June I plan to join four friends on a trip up Denali's Muldrow Glacier.

Despite the accident, I can't imagine doing anything much differently in the future. I will remember the stove, and I'll watch the trail a little more closely. When the opportunity presents itself, I will still hike alone when I have a day free and can't track down a partner. For the simple pleasure of cruising the woods, stripped down to the basics: a mountain, a person, and the sound of boots meeting the trail. Solo hiking may not be for everyone. One needs to feel at home in the woods, on the mountains, and on the trails—in all weather conditions and various states of fatigue. This takes time. Most importantly, one must be committed to the principle of self-rescue, for, as I realized, there can be times when there is no other choice. But, for many, the risks of hiking alone will still outweigh the pleasures. After all, it is always possible that an accident will occur where self-rescue simply is not practical.

If I did come away with anything from last December (in addition to the crutches and an endless flow of medical bills), I came to understand what I had always heard but never really listened to: that such accidents are a challenge not just to the body, but also to the mind. I consider myself fortunate, for I experienced only a brief minute of fear, of those fleeting, unanswerable thoughts: *Will I get out? How bad is it? What will happen to me? Can I stay warm?* After that, my mind took over the situation, like a bystander coming to the rescue. Those fears, those questions I could not have answered, were pushed aside. They were subverted to the task of getting me to the trailhead. In *Woodsmoke,* the late New England outdoorsman Ross McKenny wrote: "Within the shadows of the forest I have also learned the meaning of fear—fear that is within all of us and which can turn into terror and cause embarrassment of disaster; fear that can be governed and overcome in self-reliance. . . . Have you ever given deep thought to this hidden fear within you? What would you do in an emergency? Think it over, it's time well spent."

Plenty of climbers have good stories to tell, and most are far wilder than anything I will ever approach in my lifetime. I suspect almost anyone else would have reacted in much the same way—at least, anyone who would consider hiking alone through the White Mountains in winter. Hike and climb enough, and in the end it's not unlikely that the odds will catch up with you, whether in the Brooks Range, the Himalaya, the White Mountains, or the Blue Hills. At least the odds should be working in my favor for the next few years.

TODD BOGARDUS

Sub-Zero Weather Incapacitates

In mid-February 2003, a man started out from the Nancy Pond Trail on Route 302, planning to complete a 15-mile hiking/snowshoeing/cross-country ski trip through the Pemigewasset Wilderness. He lost his way on the trail around Norcross Pond. He did find his way back to the Carrigain Notch Trail, but eventually ran out of steam and couldn't go farther. Slumped on his pack against a tree, he sat with his dog through the night and all the following day, exposed for more than 24 hours to bitterly cold temperatures and high winds.

On February 13, New Hampshire Fish and Game search and rescue teams headed out in search of the overdue hiker. One of the teams, Samuel Sprague and Brian Abrams, set out from the Nancy Pond Trailhead but, as darkness fell, they still had not found the missing man. Sprague and Abrams pushed on through the darkness and cold. Communications were hampered because their radio batteries were getting low, and transmissions were limited because a fire had damaged the communications building atop Mount Washington. At 9:30 p.m., the search team lost all radio communication after Sprague fell into an area of deep snow. The team continued to battle their way through the snow, at times chest deep, at the same time coping with temperatures reaching 30 degrees below zero—not including wind chill. The extreme temperatures also affected the operation of their radio and GPS equipment, but the two did not turn back. Sprague and Abrams valiantly kept up their search through the night, and eventually they came upon the exhausted hiker. Suffering from hypothermia and severe frostbite to his feet, the man could not walk. The search team needed help to transport him, but the radio was still out. Sprague and Abrams did what they could to keep him alive through the night. They built a fire and gave him warm drinks, food, and extra clothing.

At 8:00 the following morning, a crackly radio transmission went through. The team would need an airlift from their location, 8 miles into

The hand of Old Man Winter.
Photo by Dan Stone

the backcountry. Later that morning, a National Guard helicopter swooped in to fly the hiker to Laconia Airport, where he was put into an ambulance and taken to Lakes Region General Hospital. Before leaving on his 15-mile wilderness trek, the man had wisely left an itinerary of his planned route with his innkeepers. Had he not done so, he would most likely not have survived the ordeal. The helicopter then returned for the search team and the dog, culminating a successful rescue by New Hampshire Fish and Game.

"Sprague and Abrams braved deep snow, extreme cold and high winds, overcoming their own exhaustion to persist in a very difficult search in the backcountry—an effort that saved a man's life," said Major Jeffrey Gray. "These officers are real heroes. Without their extraordinary efforts, Mr. L.

Frostbite is the freezing of body tissue and usually affects the extremities and exposed areas. Mid-February 2003 was a period of intense cold, when an extensive solo outing would not have been appropriate. In the situation described in this story, self-rescue became impossible. Check the weather forecast before heading out! While you are active—and your heart rate is up—you might not feel cold, but when your activity stops, the sudden drop in core temperature can plunge you into hypothermia, especially in extremely cold weather. Know your limits. And always tell someone your route and expected return time. It could save your life.

would not be alive today." Sprague and Abrams received Lifesaving Medals from the New Hampshire Fish and Game Department in recognition of the remarkable endurance and professionalism they demonstrated during the rescue. Although this saga had a successful outcome, Gray cautioned that the man's experience is a grim reminder that hikers, snowshoers, and skiers need to be extremely well prepared when venturing into the backcountry.

MARIAN ZIMMERMAN

Fall from Saddleback Cliff

Bob Zayhowski and I decided to hike three peaks in the Great Range of the Adirondack High Peaks—4,960-foot Mount Haystack, 4,827-foot Basin Mountain, and 4,515-foot Saddleback Mountain. We were unable to get up to the Garden parking area due to ice, so we parked in town and climbed the extra 1.6 miles to the trailhead. At Johns Brook Lodge, 3.5 miles in, we met other hikers who described icy conditions on the peaks. We bare-booted it past Bushnell Falls and Slant Rock until the pitch became so steep that we needed crampons and snowshoes. We summited Haystack with minor difficulty in icy spots, then dropped below tree line beyond Little Haystack to eat lunch. We continued on to Basin where conditions were good, as was our progress. As we climbed near the summit of Basin, the wind increased, requiring additional layers of clothing. Coming down Basin, some very steep spots required care but we negotiated them without undue difficulty. We arrived at the steep cliff of Saddleback at 3:20 p.m., just as two other hikers were descending. This is a particularly difficult spot, and we spent over an hour trying to find our way around the thin skin of ice and snow. We decided to try to work our way east along the edge of the rock. Eventually we came to a place 20 feet below the summit that was impassable; we doubled back and picked up the regular trail on the rocks.

We were so close! Once up to the summit it would be an easy 8.3 miles back to Keene Valley. Bob and I had been having an ongoing dialogue about whether the peak was doable under these conditions. After a short way on the icy trail, Bob prevailed upon me to give up the quest. But, as I was turning around, I lost my footing. I will never know exactly what happened, but I somehow slipped, then fell about 60 feet.

Much of what happened after that remains in a fog. What I did know, after Bob helped me up, was that I was not going to be walking out. Bob remembered our conversation with Maciej Domanski and Arkadiusz (Arek) Pasikowski, the hikers we'd met at the cliff's base; they were camping that night in the Saddleback Basin col. He took me a quarter-mile to Maciej

To the summit!

Photo by Ben Potter

and Arek, then left me in their care. (Returning in another season, I was amazed that I was able to cover that distance.) Bob retraced our steps to the accident site and gathered the scattered contents of my pack's map compartment; he also encountered another hiker camping in the col, who accompanied him back over Basin to get help. The wind had picked up, obliterating our tracks, and they had difficulty following the trail. It was only because we had just been there that Bob could remember the trail off Basin and find the way. They arrived at Johns Brook Lodge between 2:00 and 3:00 a.m. An Adirondack Mountain Club (ADK) volunteer radioed for help at daybreak.

It seems that the pilot thought we were at Slant Rock and it took some sorting out to locate us. Then, after the helicopter first came to the col between Saddleback and Basin (where we were) it left before anyone came to us on the ground. All we could do was to wait and wonder why it had left and when it would return. Maciej and Arek were very supportive and reassuring.

What I do remember is the pain of them putting me into Maciej's sleeping bag. We were fortunate that it was relatively warm, 10 to 20 degrees Fahrenheit. I could not have asked for two kinder, more thoughtful helpers. Maciej and Arek stayed up the entire night heating tea to keep me hydrated and warm. One funny tidbit: as they sat up through the night with me, they talked . . . in Polish. In my fog, I thought that French had really gotten away from me, because I couldn't understand a thing they were saying!

When the helicopter returned I was airlifted to an emergency room. The paramedic explained my options and suggested that a sling would probably be less painful, given my injuries. I agreed—only to learn, once off the ground, that the sling did not support my upper body. That is also when I discovered that I had no use of my right arm. As I dangled from the cable I realized that, of necessity, I had to dig deep, to find the strength to hold on with only one arm. The crew had to pull me 200 feet up. Once in the helicopter, I tried to relax and enjoy the magnificent day and the beauty of the mountains. My ability to focus lasted perhaps 30 seconds. I remember nothing else until hours later.

My injuries were extensive, requiring multiple hospitalizations and surgeries and months of disability leave from work. The weeks following my rescue were enveloped by a fog that kept my energies focused on the tasks at hand: healing and getting home. This proved to be a time of seeing the Adirondack winter hiking community and my other friends at

CLIFF NOTE The hike described in this story is a 21.6-mile round-trip from the village of Keene Valley, with a total ascent of 4,500 feet. From Saddleback's summit, Keene Valley is 8.3 miles downhill; retracing the route over Basin requires 11.2 miles, including some re-climbing and a further ascent up a trail needed to connect with the Phelps Trail. The late hour, their fatigue, and their location—only 20 feet from success—all played a part in Marian and Bob's reluctance to turn back. They could have attempted to approach Haystack via the State Range Trail, descended Saddleback using ropes, and returned via the easier route. Or having done the extra road walk—and knowing the difficulty that Saddleback often presents—they could have hiked only Haystack and Basin. A minimum of four hikers is recommended for a winter trip because, in the event of an accident, one person can stay with the injured party while two safely make the long trek out for help. Marian's life was saved by the fortuitous presence of two others camping in this remote spot in February.

their very best. Hiking is about adventure and experiencing beauty in the mountains, but it is much more than that for me and, I suspect, for many others. Hikers that I barely knew helped me in many ways—some invited me to dinner to break the boredom of convalescence; some drove me places because I couldn't drive myself. Someone was always there to lend a hand.

When my boss saw me for the first time after the accident, months later, she asked if I had been afraid of dying. This caught me by surprise. In all honesty, the possibility had not entered my mind. Yes, I knew I was in a precarious situation and was dependent upon others, but neither the thought of dying nor the fear of it occurred to me. I still remember with great delight the marvel I felt as, hovering in the helicopter, I viewed the mountains in their morning splendor, sparkling like diamonds from light reflecting on the snow.

I returned to the scene twice while getting back in shape for completing the forty-six High Peaks in winter—and to make my peace with the mountain. On Labor Day I explored all of the area around Basin—our attempted route, the standard route (where I fell), the probable tent site, the actual place where I slipped, and Saddleback's summit, looking down on the scene. In December I went up the Orebed Trail to Saddleback to avoid climbing the cliff, and was grateful that I had not been trying to ascend the sheets of ice there that day. After the New Year I received a call from Maciej. I had written to thank him for saving my life and to keep him updated on my recovery. We planned a reunion hike to celebrate the chance encounter that made such an important difference in my life. Maciej, Arek, and I met again in February 2000 to bushwhack into the Dix Range.

A year later, my friend Bob Zayhowski was tragically killed by a drunk driver while bicycling.

My Fall, the Prequel

Two years to the month before this calamitous misadventure, Craig LeRoy and I hiked from Tahawus to Flowed Lands on a well-traveled trail and crossed the edge of Lake Colden to the junction, a 15.5 mile round-trip. It was a beautiful day. A foot of new, untracked snow made the going slow as we hiked up the steep 1,950-foot ascent from the lake. We were unable to locate the trail where it passed through some immense boulders and, after much searching, I was ready to turn back, but Craig persisted and eventually found the route. Above tree line, the windswept rocks were icy.

About a quarter-mile from the summit, we encountered a short, steep, icy stretch where crampons would have been helpful, but the late hour and brisk cold winds urged us to keep moving. After quickly enjoying the summit's beauty, satisfied to have made it, we headed back, but descending that steep icy stretch proved more difficult than the ascent. I slipped and tore the muscles, tendons, and ligaments in my left ankle. It was 4:00 p.m. and we were a good 7 miles from the car. I said to myself, *Okay! You have a choice. You can find a way to walk out of here or you can go home tomorrow—in a box!* I slid down the mountain on my butt, changed into dry clothes, then limped out to Tahawus. It was a long, slow trip. My ankle took the rest of the winter season, and then some, to heal.

ARLENE HEER STEFANKO

Injury Miles from Nowhere

My sister Doreen and I were looking forward to this hike on St. Patrick's Day. It would bring our count of winter peaks to twenty-two, and we were going to hike with our friends Tom and Jane Haskins. The alarm at the Keene Valley Hostel went off at 4:30 a.m. At the last minute I grabbed a garbage bag to line my pack, and so did Doreen; the bags would keep our extra clothes dry if the light rain continued. We left Jane's car at the Bouquet River trailhead parking lot, then I drove us back to the Dix/Round Pond trailhead. I pondered taking a lighter pack, since it was going to be a long day, but decided to go with my usual winter gear even if it was a few more pounds. We were on the trail by 6:30; it was overcast, with temperatures in the twenties. The hike to Dix was beautiful—and very steep. It was fun to look down through our legs at the climber below, but also sobering, knowing that we needed to be surefooted to avoid tripping and knocking the person below off the trail. We were exhilarated on the summit, with clearing skies and views of the range.

Abundant spruce traps kept our pace slower on the way to Hough, but we had many laughs at each other, struggling to get free. Tom skirted "Pough" on our way to South Dix, and sidehilling in snowshoes on the steep mountainside was a challenge. The trail to East Dix was a section we hadn't been on, having previously ascended East Dix via the Great Slide to achieve our forty-sixth High Peak. Tom recommended descending at the South Dix/East Dix col rather than down the Great Slide—a relief to Doreen and me; with the snow so icy we were concerned that the Great Slide was too steep to descend safely.

Earlier rain had created a hard, icy crust that you broke through every few steps, jamming your leg just below the knee. Doreen had endured two such jams with painful expressions; my knees were sore as well but I was mentally trying to ignore the pain and focus on getting back. We were all happy to have four more winter peaks under our belts. We stopped at the base of the East Dix Slide and could almost see the summit; it was 5:00 p.m. We came upon a small stream flowing with the start of spring snowmelt. Tom was the first to cross on a log, then Jane. Doreen stepped on the log with her snowshoe and slipped, ending up on her back in the stream.

The pained look on her face, coupled with her immobility, spurred me to action. I grabbed her hand and encouraged her to pull herself out. She hesitated, saying she had injured her leg; I pulled her out of the water. My first thought was: *She's injured—and wet.* After assessing for obvious fractures or external injuries and finding none, I wrapped her knee with an ace bandage. Doreen was wearing a Gore-Tex jacket and pants; these proved to be lifesavers, keeping her from getting soaked. But her knee injury meant that she could only take small, painfully slow steps; it was clear that we would need help to get out. Tom decided to run ahead, suggesting that we continue as far as we could. Jane thought to retrieve some items from his pack, including his PrimaLoft jacket and emergency bivy. With great resistance from Doreen, we divided up her pack contents and I took her pack. We entered into a bit of a screaming match, since she insisted on carrying her own pack. Even though I am the little sister, however, I won! Jane was quite entertained by the exchange.

Doreen said it was easier to hike with snowshoes; they made her more surefooted, and any slips on the snow brought excruciating pain. We devised a three-legged walk to inch ourselves along: I supported her injured leg by offering my snowshoe for her to step on—thus ensuring that it did not slip as she used her other leg to place her next step. Jane led, following Tom's tracks, until we came to a larger stream. We lost his tracks there and it was getting too dark to proceed safely. We started putting on more clothes right away. Jane put on Tom's PrimaLoft jacket, I gave Doreen my PrimaLoft jacket, and Doreen gave me her lighter-weight fleece jacket. It had stayed dry during her fall because of the garbage bag inside her pack. I also helped her put on my spare dry socks. My own boot heaters had long ago run out of juice, but I could move about to stay warm—Doreen was nearly immobile.

We had no watch and lost all concept of time. We needed fire and shelter; the skies had cleared and the temperature was falling into the single digits. Our first attempt at a fire was unsuccessful. Using a small folding saw, we took turns sawing small branches for a shelter. When it was big enough for our torsos, we instructed Doreen to lie down in the emergency blanket while we added more branches. When we adjusted the branches, dried needles would fall on Doreen's bare face, providing us with some comic relief. Jane and I then climbed in with Doreen but our feet were still very cold. Jane had the idea to put our feet inside our packs for added insulation, but my feet were so painfully cold that I determined to again attempt a fire, and was again unsuccessful.

We knew we had to stay positive, to do everything we could to keep moving, and to keep Doreen warm. We tried isometrics, singing songs, playing word games—anything we could think of to generate heat. I was praying silently. We kept staring down the stream, thinking we saw headlamps coming. When we looked up at the stars through the trees, then down at the stream, it created a hallucination of lights in the forest. Since this was St. Patrick's Day, we joked that leprechauns were playing with our psyches, or that Tom was playing games with us. More than once one of us said, "Look! Here comes someone!" We would blow the whistles and turn on our headlamps. In reality, Tom was at the Keene Valley firehouse assisting with our rescue. Doreen was kept stationary, only moving her arms to generate heat. She and I tried getting in the bivy sack together, but it didn't seem as warm as moving about, even slightly. Our next attempt at fire was conducted with greater urgency, as we had all gone beyond just cold. Jane and I took turns sawing wood, while Doreen hobbled about collecting dead branches. We had a baby fire going when Doreen called out, "I see headlamps coming and I see more than one!" Jane and I didn't take her seriously until she said again, "There they are, coming right toward us!" We counted five headlamps coming at us and we were *very* relieved—it was 2:30 a.m.

Tom had reached a phone by 8:00 p.m. and called for a rescue. The team identified themselves as forest rangers Joe and Chris, and search and rescue volunteers Ron, Lauren, and Charlie. Lauren was a physician assistant at Lake Placid hospital and attended to Doreen's injury. She then put her into dry, warm clothes. Someone handed me a down coat; I was immediately grateful—and felt instantly warm (except for my feet!). We were fed, given hot tea, and treated to a roaring fire. As the other women drifted off to sleep, I listened as the team planned Doreen's rescue. They discussed the finer points of making her a harness from nylon straps. I interjected that Doreen thought she would be hiking out in the morning with their help. They said she would be convinced otherwise in the morning. I noticed the first light of morning at 4:30 a.m. and was relieved that this night was ending.

When Doreen woke, the rescuers explained that a chopper was coming for her at eight o'clock. They told her exactly what she was to do and how it would feel to be lifted into the helicopter. The rest of us divided up Doreen's stuff, because she couldn't take anything with her. We also couldn't leave anything on the ground to be blown about by the helicopter. A call came that the chopper was delayed, so we again sat by the fire. When we could hear it coming up the valley, the rescuers put boughs on the fire to signal our location. Doreen was harnessed up and ready. I gave her a hug and, with tears in my eyes, ran behind the rock that would shield us from the turbulence created by the chopper. We were instructed to stay behind the rock and not to look—or we would risk getting embers blown into our eyes. But I just couldn't resist a picture. Weeks later I surprised Doreen with an 8-by-10 photo of her on the cable, being lifted into the helicopter.

With Doreen safely on her way to Lake Placid hospital, we began our 5-mile hike to the Bouquet trailhead. The path was beautiful, even with the 24-hour lack of sleep. As the last mile near the Bouquet River was very icy, we put our crampons on. Charlie was the only one without crampons and nearly ended up in the river after slipping on an icy section. He prevented a near disaster by quickly grabbing a branch. Many Department of Environmental Conservation vehicles were at the trailhead with other search and rescue personnel. After a stop at the Keene Valley firehouse, we headed to Lake Placid to pick up Doreen, then went back to the hostel to pick up our belongings. Everyone was anxious to hear about our adventure and rescue.

After a much-needed shower and change of clothes, we started our 4-hour drive home. It was 4:00 p.m. and I wasn't sure how I was going to stay awake after the long hike, with no sleep for nearly 32 hours. But after a good meal I felt alert, refreshed, and blessed with reserves I didn't know were in me. We thoroughly discussed how differently we would pack after this misadventure.

Within weeks, Doreen would have surgery for a torn ACL and meniscus.[9] After her recovery, she was even stronger than before. We went on to complete the Winter 46 in January 2006, doing all the climbs as day hikes. I feel grateful to have climbed these High Peaks with my sister; she's my best friend.

Addendum: Doreen's Story

After Jane and Tom crossed a small tributary on a log, I stepped onto a partially submerged log; it kicked out, trapping my right snowshoed foot while the rest of me fell backward into the brook. I could hear and feel the pop in my knee on my way into the very cold water. Shocked, I just lay there as my sister, Arlene, asked if I was okay. I couldn't get up—the pain had initially paralyzed me. Arlene called to Jane and Tom, who came back

Doreen being lifted to a helicopter in the Dix Range.

Photo by Arlene Heer Stefanko

and helped her get me out of the brook. I had Gore-Tex pants and coat on, but the layers under them were soaked. We were all prepared quite well with an emergency blanket, extra socks, spare fleece, and matches.

After a few tentative steps, with my leg popping out from under me, we knew that I would need a great deal of support. Tom left his extra jacket and said he was going out to get some help. Dusk was imminent and we were not on any trail. It was a bushwhack out for Tom and a long night in the mountains for Jane, Arlene, and me. I told them I would like to try going as far as we could, following Tom's snowshoe tracks before total darkness. We did a very painful but slow shuffle with Arlene holding my right snowshoe stable while I took a step ahead; we ended up doing about a quarter-mile.

I was in good spirits with Arlene and Jane joking with me to keep my embarrassment at bay. I had already changed into dry clothes but, with the temperature dropping steadily, it was very cold. The girls tried to start a fire, but with no dead wood, it quickly went out. They then built me a shelter out of boughs that I crawled into for awhile. Time stood still. We had no doubt Tom would get out to round up help. Arlene and Jane kept moving in place to stay warm. They knew that with my limited mobility, I would need more of the extra clothes, so they managed with less. We sang songs and joked around to pass time.

At 2:30 a.m. we saw headlamps and heard distant voices. The rescue crew had found us based on Tom's directions. We were so happy to see these wonderful, skilled, experienced rescuers. They had a large fire going in no time, and each of them worked on a specific job. So synchronized and impressive! I was helped into more dry clothes and my injury was checked out. We were given hot tea and sandwiches. I was a little hypothermic, so was advised to climb into a down sleeping bag for a few hours sleep.

Unbeknownst to me, there was a helicopter scheduled to pluck me from the woods at eight o'clock. They roped a harness on me and gave me instructions on how to avoid trees while being lifted up through the forest canopy to the hovering helicopter. Before I knew it I was on my way to Lake Placid Hospital. The pilot flew me over the peaks we had summited the day before; it was beautiful and kept my mind from the painful knee. At the hospital it was determined that I had ruptured my ACL and ripped my meniscus. A month later, in Syracuse, a donor ACL was placed and the meniscus was repaired. I went on to finish my Winter 46 in 2006!

I think we did a lot of things right during this event. We could have been more aggressive with a fire, but we never panicked. We were smart to stay put when we lost Tom's tracks. Arlene and Jane were instrumental in building the shelter and working to keep warm. Due to Tom's experience in the mountains, skills in bushwhacking, and great climbing condition, he got out of the woods safely to activate a rescue. The rescue team was able to locate us quite easily based on Tom's account of where we were. We came away realizing we needed everything we had in our packs. I will be forever grateful to everyone involved. It's humbling to know you have caused such a ruckus, but no one ever made me feel bad.

Addendum: Tom's Story

Our plan was to take the side trip over to Macomb Mountain, with a return to South Dix, before heading to our final peak of the day, East Dix. However, we were running a bit behind our time estimates and agreed that it was best to skip the side trip, thereby assuring we'd be off the mountains and down into the Boquet South Fork valley before sunset. We were concerned that once we were into the valley, the route—a bushwhack—would be difficult to follow, and we wanted to cover as much of it as possible in daylight. As a backup plan, I did carry a GPS with a handful of programmed waypoints to help us navigate that portion of the hike in case we were overtaken by darkness. The ridge walk to East Dix was pleasant and uneventful, then as we descended East Dix toward the valley, the atmosphere was cheerful and upbeat with the difficulties of the day behind us.

Still ahead were 5 to 6 miles of bushwhacking, but the terrain would be gentle and we were all veterans of end-of-day forced marches, common to climbs in the Adirondack High Peaks. Off the steep slopes of the mountain ridge, we crossed a few small tributaries and worked our way towards the headwaters of the South Fork. I was a few minutes ahead of the pack, so waited; when nobody showed up after 5 minutes, I headed back to discover that Doreen had somehow fallen into the water while crossing a tributary and, due to a knee injury, had required assistance to even get out of the water. Jane and Arlene were getting Doreen out of her wet clothing and into dry spare clothing that we all carried in our winter packs.

We quickly came to agreement that I would hike out for help, while Jane and Arlene would stay behind to make Doreen comfortable and prepare a bivouac. I left most of my emergency gear and headed down the valley. I was familiar with the terrain and moved quickly to put as much distance behind me as possible before nightfall. In typical mountain-stream fashion, the streambed wandered back and forth between its steep banks, requiring me to make several stream crossings. I was still wearing snowshoes and decided that it would be best to stick with snowshoes even for stream crossings; changing several times between snowshoes and crampons (or bare boots) would have cost precious time with little, if any, benefit. After following the South Fork for a few miles, the route crosses over a low pass into the valley of the North Fork and here I was overtaken by darkness. So, GPS in hand, I abandoned my efforts to stay on the regular route and began connecting the dots from waypoint to waypoint. I knew that the open woods wouldn't hinder my efforts, else the remainder of the hike out might not have gone so smoothly. Not long after dark, the GPS batteries went dead; I had spares and before long was back on the move. At our vehicle, I banged balls of ice off my snowshoe bindings with my trekking pole and poured my remaining drinking water over them to thaw the last bits of ice.

I drove to Keene Valley, stopped at the hostel, and placed a phone call to DEC dispatch to initiate a rescue effort. I was instructed to meet the rescue coordinator, Officer Charlie Platt, at the Keene Valley firehouse. There I was debriefed by the rescue team. I described the location of the accident (although I hadn't thought to take a waypoint at the accident site), and also informed the team that those still in the woods would not have moved from that point any farther than was needed to establish a good bivouac. I was also asked about the nature of the injury and the condition of not only the victim but the other group members as well. Knowing that the accident involved a soaking in the stream, and with overnight temperatures hovering around zero degrees Fahrenheit, the team decided that the rescue should commence immediately rather than waiting for daylight. I was kept in the loop during the rescue. The team reached the ladies at around 2:00

a.m., and decided a helicopter lift was called for. In the morning Officer Platt updated me on the timing of the rescue, and I was able to hike in and meet Jane and Arlene as they hiked out with the rescue team.

Looking back, I truly believe that our decisions throughout the day, based on knowledge of the route selected, having an itinerary as a guideline, and regular evaluation of the weather and the condition of each member of the group, kept us on track for a safe and enjoyable hike. The decision to skip the side trip to Macomb is a good example. All members of the group were experienced winter hikers who would have raised the red flag if there had been any hint of concern, and no member of the group would have pushed the others to take on more than they were comfortable with.

Nonetheless, the accident happened. Preparation and good decisions are no guarantee against accidents, but they do stack the odds in favor of a good outcome if an accident does occur. Fortunately our experience and excellent physical conditioning put us in a good position to deal with the situation. The emergency gear we each carried was sufficient to meet the challenge. Our action plan resulted in a successful rescue with no injuries beyond those incurred during the accident. Importantly, we were blessed to have a highly experienced and devoted SAR team at our disposal. Had going for help not been an option, I'm confident we would have been able to assist Doreen back to civilization safely, most likely with a full second-day effort, but knowing professional help was nearby made our decision easy.

Addendum: Rescuer Ron Konowitz's Report

After skiing Mount Marcy that day, I was having dinner with Lauren when the pager went off. At the Keene Valley fire hall, the reporting party and two rangers and numerous firemen were there. Our plan was to hike in, assess, and keep everyone comfortable overnight to fly the patient out in the morning. We left our rescue vehicle at the trailhead, with two firemen staying all night to assure radio communications; this route to East Dix has proven to be spotty for radio transmissions. We started from the North Branch of the Bouquet River in the dark by headlamp. The first river crossing was fast-moving open water, so we bushwhacked by full moon to cross the south fork; again the water was open and rocks were covered with ice—it was zero degrees. The only way to cross safely was to step on submerged rocks that didn't have the coating of wet ice.

The injured party had tried to start a fire unsuccessfully with wet wood.

They were very cold, not planning on spending a night in the woods! My wife, a physician's assistant, assessed the injured hiker while we got a ripping bonfire going—the Ranger Way. We gave warm clothing to everyone, gathered wood to keep the fire going all night, and stayed up telling jokes. At first light we scoped out a place where we could do a helicopter hoist operation and it flew in with a state police pilot and ranger hoist operator; we safely lifted Doreen up and she was most appreciative of our efforts. We were back at noon and met other firemen and rangers who were on standby until we were safely out of the woods. As always, my brothers and sisters in the fire service and the rangers put their lives on hold to help someone in need—that's how we roll!

KIMBERLY J. LAPORTE

A Mount Marcy Helicopter Rescue

August 8, 2009, started out perfectly: a great, sunny, warm day. I was at the Adirondack Mountain Club's campground on my annual hiking trip with the Tramp and Trail Club of Utica. For the previous four years, it had rained on this trip weekend, so I was looking forward to my hike more than ever. I was also in the best shape of my life since high school, so I decided that it was time to conquer 5,344-foot Mount Marcy, the highest peak in New York State and my fifth High Peak. I consider myself a pretty experienced hiker and I was with many other experienced people that day, including my stepfather; but I was not prepared at all for what happened.

I've hiked many mountains over the past ten years. Clouds or high winds often prevail on summits, but that day was so warm that I had a tank and shorts on; there was no rain in the forecast. I was with my now-fiancé, Dan, and Marcy was his first mountain climb. The hike up was great, as always—good people, good surroundings, and good conversation. We reached the top in about 4 hours, had a leisurely lunch, and took many pictures—I could see everything for miles. It was almost too good to be true, and it was. After about an hour, we all started to pack up and descend; it was getting late and chilly air was starting rolling in.

I shouldered my pack and walked about 100 yards. Then it happened. I turned to talk with someone next to me, learning the hard way that I can't walk and talk at the same time. My right foot rolled over a ledge of a rock, and *snap!* It sounded like someone had snapped a piece of celery. I fell immediately, pain shooting through my foot and ankle. No one else even realized that I had fallen, except Dan. I looked at him and said, "I think I just broke my ankle!" I could see the panic in his face immediately. He called the group over to assist. Some of the hikers in our group were retired doctors but, as it turned out, all of the doctors had hiked a different mountain on this day.

We took my shoe off and you could already see a bulge coming out from under my ankle bone. I immediately panicked and started to cry.

Everyone was telling me to get up and try to put pressure on it; I tried and it was a failure. I was stuck on top of the world. We immediately went into survival mode, searching my bag and discovering that I'd left my phone, identification, and first-aid kit at the campsite. I had some water and food but, besides the leg extensions for my pants, only the clothes on my back. The thing that kept going through my mind was *I am going to be stuck up here for days and die.* We told the rest of the group that there was nothing they could do. They descended the 7.4 miles back to the trailhead, while my fiancé and stepfather stayed with me. I could not help but think the worst. *How was I going to get down?*

Some people that we didn't know stopped to show concern; I later learned that they were Carol and David White. They insisted that we take their warm clothes, stressing that it would get cold on this open summit by the time help arrived; they also gave us a flashlight. Carol fortunately had the New York State Department of Environmental Conservation's 24-hour hotline for emergencies, 518–891–0235; two men arrived with cell phones and DEC was contacted. These strangers waited with us until DEC could call us back. The rangers said they would either send up a rescue crew with a stretcher to carry me down—yeah, right, that would take days—or a *helicopter!* Guess who watches too many movies and is scared of flying? The rangers said they were having a busy day, so I was on a waiting list. After almost 4 hours, it became cold and windy and the sun was low in the sky. I thanked God for the complete strangers who gave us clothes, a cell phone, and a flashlight, because we needed them.

Dan and my stepdad Roger provided many laughs up there as we tried to make the best of it. Finally a helicopter could be heard in the distance. It circled the top of Marcy three times, but did not land. This bad situation was getting even worse. I started to cry again, screaming, "It's going to crash into the side of the mountain—I'm going to die!" The helicopter finally stopped circling. It hovered over the summit, and down came a ranger on a wire—it was a scene from *G.I. Joe.* To this day, we still refer to the ranger as G.I. Joe. He came over, stabilized my foot, put a brace on it, then stood me up and wrapped a harness around my waist.

"What's this for?" I asked.

"This is going to connect you to that wire," he replied. "You are going to go up into the helicopter the same way I came down." Shock set in. I was trembling so hard that he thought I was having a seizure. He calmed me down, of course—well, kind of! The ranger and Dan lifted me up, act-

CLIFF NOTE The key to this accident is in the sentence, "I turned to talk with someone next to me, learning the hard way that I can't walk and talk at the same time." Like drivers, hikers must learn to talk without turning their attention from the route ahead. "When you are moving, watch your footfall," says marathon hiker Timothy Muskat, whose epic adventure appears later in this book (see "Curses, Excursus"). "Most hiking accidents—and I'm talking slips, falls, tumbles that lead to broken bones below the waist—happen because the victim, if only for a split second, takes his/her eyes off the path. When you are moving, then, *watch your step;* be aware not only of the trail before you, but the 'foot' trail you are making. Note: I'm not saying one should literally look at one's feet while in motion—that might lead to disaster or at least a sizable bump on the head. But by all means, be roundly aware of what you're walking on, and what lies (most immediately) ahead of you. If you want to stop and stare at something—whether near (lichen on a stone, a junco hopping about in the scrub) or far (breathtaking views), by all means *stop* all forward progress. Don't simply slow down—cease; be motionless. Breathe, get your balance and bearings, then look about you all you want." Part of Tim's "Rules of Engagement for Climbing the Whites in Winter," this is excellent advice in any season in the mountains.

ing as my crutches until the wire reached me and was connected to my waist. The ranger told me to hold onto the wire, put a helmet on me, and said not to look up. I was in the helicopter in under a minute—it was a breeze. Then the ranger came up and we took off. The helicopter did not have enough fuel to make it to the hospital with any additional people, so Dan and Roger had to climb down Marcy in the dark. That flashlight the Whites lent Dan sure was needed!

I felt horrible because I had ruined the day. I did, however, get to fly over the High Peaks and it was beautiful. At the hospital I had X-rays, but the images were unclear because of the swelling, so they wrapped me up, gave me crutches, and drove me back to camp—all within 2 hours. I made it back to camp even before Roger and Dan descended the 7.4 miles from Marcy's summit! I ate dinner and started to drink some wine, when the Whites stopped by to learn what had happened. They reported that they'd heard the helicopter flying to Mount Marcy when they were below Indian Falls, and again at the Phelps Mountain junction, when it flew toward Lake Placid. The men made it back to camp at 9:00 p.m.

We still enjoyed ourselves that night and the next day. I went home and saw a doctor that Monday. I had a detached ligament and was on crutches for eight weeks. To this day, I wear a special brace on this foot, and will forever, whenever I run or hike. My foot still swells when I exercise or wear a pair of heels for too long. I will take it, though, over what might have happened. I was not prepared—no extra clothes, no phone, no identification—because I assumed that I would be O.K. Thank God for the strangers who literally gave me the clothes and tools off their back.

MELINDA BROMAN

A Fall from Grace

At 1:00 p.m. on a late December day, my friend Lynne and I stepped out on an outcrop on Crane Mountain. It was mild for this time of year, mostly cloudy, but the clouds parted and a brilliant sun shone through as we selected an open, rocky place and sat down to enjoy the view. We pulled out snacks and congratulated ourselves on the relatively easy climbing in 1- to 2-foot deep snow. We had had to break through an icy crust below, but above 2,900 feet, the snow was soft and deeper and easier on snowshoes. Both of us had snowshoes with Tucker bindings.

Fifteen minutes later, we ascended the 25-foot ladder to the summit. The ladder was encrusted with snow, but footholds were easily accomplished. At the top, however, I regarded the place onto which I must step with dismay. It required a maneuver to the left, onto a ledge with small footholds and no handhold.[10] There was little ice or snow cover. I decided not to think about it, but to move ahead quickly. Seconds later, I lost my footing and gasped as my body hurtled straight down the icy precipice. At the bottom, I turned over and skidded down another steep incline, head first. Finally I stopped. Though badly shaken, I was intact. My companion was bending over me. I asked for my ski poles. My first thought was one of disappointment—I would not be able to walk out on the summit. But my disappointment became more acute when I realized that I could not walk at all. A sharp pain gripped my right foot. Lynne helped me up. I was dismayed to find that I could not stand at all on that foot.

At three o'clock, having handed me all the clothing she could spare, Lynne ran down the mountain, 1.8 miles to the trailhead, to get help. The first rescuer arrived at 5:30, shortly after dark; more men arrived after that, and I became the subject of a massive evacuation effort. A fire engine, ambulance, helicopter, physician, forest rangers, firemen, and search and rescue personnel of various origins came to my aid from all quarters of the Adirondack region.

I was laid in front of a roaring fire, near where I had fallen, and kept warm by blankets and outer garments. My foot was examined by a wilderness doctor, who inserted a heparin lock in my wrist to prepare for emergency administration of fluids and pain medication. Men stood about the fire communicating with men at the bottom about my ultimate removal from the mountain. I was overwhelmed by the sheer size of the rescue effort. At the height of it, I was told, there were twenty-two men on the mountain, all ministering to my needs. Was I, with my useless ankle, worth the magnitude of this response? *Push me over the side of the mountain,* I thought despondently. But the men did not seem to mind; in fact, they seemed to enjoy themselves. They checked my status and told stories and jokes to pass the time. I was given glucose and propped up on a tree to urinate.

"Have you ever had so many men paying attention to you?" they asked. I replied, "Only the contractors who renovated my house." They laughed and reported to the ranger below that I was in good spirits. I put my sweater back on and insisted on turning it right side out. "You are a perfectionist, aren't you?" a man said. I was embarrassed; he was right.

Forest rangers arrived with a Stokes litter. I was lifted onto it and covered with an orange sleeping bag. Its hood was laced up and my arms were strapped to my body, a human mummy carried down the steep mountain trail. "I'm claustrophobic!" I protested, but surrendered control calmly. Men in front and men in back shouted information and instructions, using headlamps to illuminate the path. On steep places, they belayed the stretcher with ropes from trees. We arrived at a trail junction where more men stood around another roaring fire. They were debating whether to prepare an overnight camp at Crane Mountain Pond, a half-mile on the cutoff to the west, so that my evacuation could be more safely completed in daylight the next morning. Radio communications transpired and it was decided to complete the evacuation that night. Men lifted me again and continued the belay down the mountain.

"Aren't you sorry you won't be spending the night with us?" they joked. I lay looking up, feeling calm, watching the black sky dotted with stars and the huge pines frosted with snow glide by. *So beautiful here at night,* I thought.

We reached the trailhead at midnight. With so many lights and people and Lynne bending over me, I wanted to cry. We walk up mountains to feel in charge of our lives, of our physical selves, at least. Yet here I was, as helpless as an infant, as humbled by the limitations of my body and mind as one could be. It would be a long trip back from there, to a place of forgiveness for my fall from grace, from a perfect body, from an unblemished record of forays in the wilderness. To err is human and to forgive is divine, and I am still seeking some divine forgiveness for my humanity. I had lots of time for these thoughts because I could not walk on my injured foot for six weeks.

Of course, I could not thank my rescuers enough for their good humor and forbearance through it all. "You work so well together," I said, trying to compliment them. "Like ants," came the reply. "One of us is nothing much but a whole colony is amazing to watch." Then there were the rescuers I never met, the folks in the house at the bottom of Crane Mountain who opened their door when a stranger came knocking and crying for help. That family emptied out their refrigerator and cupboards for the rescuers and allowed their garage to be used as a command station by the forest rangers. The little boy in the house waited up until I came off the mountain. They wanted to know what it was like for me up there. So, here's my report.

Although I could cite the practical aspects that might have played a part in my accident (and I will), I stress the psychological factors. The Adirondack Mountain Club's book *Winterwise* notes that accidents usually happen because of a combination of factors. This was certainly true in my case. I am ashamed to admit that I was hiking with a less-experienced companion who was, against her wildest expectations, pressed into service as my rescuer. Fortunately, her success in this endeavor has not dampened her enthusiasm for winter hiking and she is looking forward to going back again (but not on the same trail!).

Having a less-experienced person along should be a cause for even greater caution. It constitutes another detail, or set of ongoing details, to think about while traveling. Additionally, we were not well-equipped,

CLIFF NOTE Melinda's hiking partner should not have "run down the mountain" to get help. She was less experienced, after all. What if, in panic, she had also fallen? This account demonstrates the advisability of hiking in parties of four, particularly in winter, so that someone can stay with the injured person while two safely descend for help. Accidents happen to even the most experienced and well-prepared hikers.

having neither boot crampons nor an ice ax to negotiate the terrain on the summit (I had not considered the necessity of these items beforehand). These factors, in the context of the allure of the summit, set the stage for a terrible error of judgment. Although most of us who read these pages know about such hazards, I cannot stress enough the need to monitor one's psychological and practical situation at every point. If I had admitted that several factors weighed against me, instead of taking an unacceptable risk, I might have stepped down the ladder and safely walked down the mountain.

ROY R. SCHWEIKER

Midnight Rescue

It was Sunday evening of Memorial Day weekend, 1985. Four young men had backpacked over the Baldfaces in eastern New Hampshire and set up camp partway down, near Eagle Cascade. The hike leader went to the top of the falls to take a sunset photograph and slipped, tumbling down the falls and landing unconscious in the pool below. His friends rushed down and hauled him out of the water, onto a flat rock. They tucked him into a sleeping bag and built a fire next to him. The conventional wisdom is to leave one person with the victim and send two for help. There was just one problem: the leader was the only one who knew the best way to the car from there—and he wasn't telling!

Going back the way they'd come—over the Baldfaces—seemed much too long and difficult,[11] but the others didn't know where the trail they were on went, how long it was, or whether it could be followed at night, especially in the drizzle that had just started. In New Hampshire, the shortest way to a road is often along a stream, going downhill, so they bushwhacked down along the brook from the cascade. After about a mile, an old logging road with trail blazes crossed the brook and they followed it right out to their cars—how convenient! They jumped in one car and headed down the road, turning in the first driveway where they saw a light. Fortunately, they had come to the right place. The first buildings south of the trailhead are the Appalachian Mountain Club's Cold River Camp, which provides summer vacations for families. The camp wasn't open for the season yet, but that weekend, it was hosting a volunteer work party from the Chatham Trails Association, which maintains many of the trails used by camp guests. One man was still reading in the lodge; he roused the trip leader after the unexpected visitors arrived. Other workers who were light sleepers wandered in when they heard the commotion.

The community of Chatham was too small to have its own rescue squad, so they shared services with nearby Fryeburg, Maine. The trip leader called Fryeburg's emergency number and a volunteer member who lived nearby arrived shortly to assess the situation. An injured hiker in the woods would require two dozen large men to carry him out. When one of the trail workers asked where they would find so many people at midnight, he was told it would be much easier then—they'd all be at home asleep!

Some concern arose when nobody in the rescue squad's advance party knew where the cascade was. They insisted that one of the hikers guide them back to the site. But of course the hikers didn't know how to get back—except by the bushwhack they'd come down—and, having back-packed all day then rushed down for help, they were exhausted and looking forward only to occupying some vacant beds at the camp. Meanwhile my mother had woken me, asking if I wanted to help with a rescue, so I offered to show the rescuers the trail to the falls. I didn't bother telling them that I had never been to the actual falls myself, because I at least knew which trail junction to turn at. As it turned out, the leader of the advance party also knew where the turnoff was, and even remembered what kind of tree the sign was on, so they would have been fine without me.

Most of the younger members of the trail crew had gone home after supper on Sunday because they had to work on Monday, and those of retirement age didn't feel they'd be much help carrying a litter at night in the rain. So I was the only one of them to go out that night, although others were generous in loaning me flashlights and batteries. It was 11:00 p.m. when I set off with the advance party of four that I was to guide; more rescuers would arrive later with a litter. The first part of the trail was then an old woods road, so we headed in with a four-wheel-drive pickup. But the visibility was poor and the truck bounced a lot. When I got out to direct the driver, I found that I could walk faster than the truck so we soon parked it. The route to the falls was mostly on old roads that hadn't grown in too much, so we found it easily, even at night, and were glad to see that it would be good for carrying the litter down.

When we reached the turnoff to the falls, we got a radio message that perhaps the victim was somewhere else! Knowing that there were no other waterfalls in the area, I went by myself to check it out. Sure enough, at the foot of the falls was a guy on a rock in a sleeping bag, with a guy next to him stoking a fire and mumbling encouraging words. I told them help was on the way and dashed back, staying at the junction to direct the next group while the advance party headed over to stabilize the patient. Eventually the main group arrived with the litter and we all went to the falls. In the dark I never got a good count of how many people there were, or whether more trickled in later, but all of the people in the woods that night were men. I'm of average height and above-average weight, but only the lead EMT seemed smaller than I am, and the advance party leader looked to be twice my size. Women are the mainstay of many small-town volunteer rescue squads, because they are more likely to be in town during the day (the ambulance driver who waited at the road was a woman), but the dispatcher apparently took the request for big guys seriously.

The rescuers gingerly transferred the victim to a backboard on the litter and set off downhill. His companion chose to walk down too; I would have been tempted to crawl into my sleeping bag right there. I put out the fire, retrieved a medical case the rescuers had left behind, and took a couple of turns carrying the litter. It had a shoulder strap on each corner and two handles on each side, so the weight of a small man split eight ways was quite reasonable, even if one of the handlers slipped and let go for a minute. There were few stops to rest or change handlers—when you got tired, you raised your hand and someone else stepped in while the litter was still in motion. Partway out we were met by half a dozen AMC seasonal staff from Pinkham Notch who couldn't pass up such an adventure, easily distinguished from the volunteers because they had raincoats and headlamps instead of sweatshirts and hand lanterns. We also met the local conservation officer, who had been notified late and, as he lived at the far end of the district, had taken a long time to arrive. He saw that everything was under control and walked out in the rain with us, but a major newspaper reported that he had organized the rescue.

I wondered if the stream crossing would be a problem in the dark with a litter, but it wasn't. Several ATVs were there; between their headlights and people shining their flashlights, it was like an electricians' convention. It wasn't long before we reached the first of several trucks, but the rescue leader was having none of that. He decided that it would be less bumpy for the patient to be carried by hand and, with the wider road and the end in sight, all the carriers perked up. They had been walking at nearly 4 mph; every time they'd slow down, maybe to 3.5 mph, the leader would yell, *If you're tired, let somebody else take over!* Following them was a parade of bouncing trucks, ATVs, and pedestrians struggling to keep up.

The road at last! Because the patient was still unconscious, the decision was made to transport him by ambulance directly to Portland instead of to the local hospital, which would probably want to send him on anyway. (We learned later that the victim did recover.) Coffee and sandwiches were ready for the rescuers at the camp, but most just headed home to sleep. It was after daylight when I went to bed, but I got up after a couple of hours to eat breakfast with the trail crew. It was still raining lightly, so the trail work for the day had been cancelled and I went back to sleep—thinking that several volunteers from last night must now be at work at their regular jobs.

One of the young hikers had gone to the hospital to be with the victim and one was still asleep, but the third guy wanted to go up to the campsite and collect some items, including the keys to their second car! My mother offered to show him the trail up, and the trail-work leader encouraged two other trail workers to go along. They used the four pack frames that were up there to bring down most of the hikers' gear, except for a few soaking wet items that were hung up to dry and retrieved the following weekend. Occasionally, on trips to Chatham, I'll meet someone from the rescue squad who will thank me for my help that night. But they deserve the thanks—I went out once and they do it all the time. If I ever have an accident in the mountains, I hope it's somewhere near Fryeburg.

EDITH TUCKER

Two Lives Saved by Search and Rescue Teams

The lives of two middle-aged hikers who became disoriented while descending 5,774-foot Mount Adams in whiteout conditions above tree line were saved on January 10, 2007, by the combined efforts of two volunteers from the Randolph Mountain Club (RMC) and Androscoggin Valley Search and Rescue (AVSAR), and four New Hampshire Fish and Game Department conservation officers. The search and rescue team located a 55-year-old woman and a 50-year-old man at 12:52 a.m., huddled together in a sleeping bag that was rated as adequate to 20 degrees Fahrenheit. "It was –14 degrees with winds in the low 70s mph," said Fish and Game Lieutenant Doug Gralenski. The two hikers were found below and to the east of Thunderstorm Junction, where the Gulfside, Lowe's Path, and the Great Gully Trail intersect at nearly 5,500 feet in elevation.

"It was a life-threatening situation," Lieutenant Gralenski explained. "They probably would have survived the night, but we'll never know whether or not they would have survived the descent down the Great Gully into King Ravine to the valley below, because they would likely have had to deal with both frostbite and hypothermia." He said that although there was nothing wrong with the two hikers' winter gear, they "were over their heads" as far as experience in tough winter conditions goes.

The pair had spent Tuesday night at Gray Knob cabin. On Wednesday morning they hiked 1.7 miles up Mount Adams and had reached the 5,774-foot summit at about 1:00 p.m. However, as they started down, the trail became shrouded in blowing snow, Lieutenant Gralenski said. At 3:30 p.m., the two hikers reached a stone cairn on the trail and they could not see how to safely proceed; the man called 911 on his cell phone. In piecing together the sequence of events, Lieutenant Gralenski said the pair thought they were on the Lowe's Path, but they were actually about a quarter of a mile northeast of Thunderstorm Junction at the top of the Great Gully. He told them to stay where they were.

Lieutenant Gralenski said that, given the very severe conditions, he

View from Mount Adams.
Photo by David White

decided to call out members of the department's search and rescue team: Brian Abrams, Greg Jellison, Brad Morse—also a paramedic—and Sam Sprague. As he called around for additional help, he learned that Al Sochard of Randolph was already dressed in winter gear and readying himself to hike up the Lowe's Path to check on Gray Knob in the absence of the regular winter caretaker. Longtime AVSAR volunteer Mike Pelchat of Gorham also volunteered his services. In what Lieutenant Gralenski described as a "pivotal" decision, he gave the hikers' cell-phone number to Sochard, which ultimately helped him to locate the pair. "I talked with the man three times, and it was a great comfort to him to know we were on our way," Sochard said.

When the rescuers found the two hikers in their sleeping bag tucked in among some boulders, yet still relatively exposed, they first fed them hot liquid Jell-O and some food. Then they outfitted them with dry outer jackets and hats, placed heat warmers in their boots, and got them back up on their feet to walk with them to Gray Knob, arriving at nearly 3:00 a.m. The two hikers and their six-man rescue crew slept at Gray Knob until morning and then started at 8:15 a.m. to hike down to Lowe's Gas Station. Sochard reached the gas station at about 9:45 a.m. and the rest at about 11:30.

Late on the previous afternoon, Lieutenant Gralenski said he and Lieutenant Todd Bogardus had set up a command post at the home of Bill and Barbara Arnold. Arnold, a longtime member of both RMC and AVSAR, maintains radio contact between Gray Knob and his house every evening in the winter, and each rescuer carried a radio tuned to the RMC's frequency. After all the members of the hiking party had reached the safety of Gray Knob, the two lieutenants headed home and Arnold also turned in.

"The role played by RMC and AVSAR volunteers who are very familiar with the local trails in what we think of as 'our' part of the forest, working with the professional team, provides us all the ability to help save lives," explained Sochard. "Mike [Pelchat] and I have a familiarity with these trails that made it possible for us to figure out where these two 'lost' hikers were."

Mike Pelchat added to this account: "Not too long after I arrived at the Knob, the Fish and Game rescue team arrived and the six of us were ready to leave Gray Knob to start our search by 11:00 p.m. I asked Fish and Game officer Brian Abrams if he would like Al and me to go ahead and they could follow us at their own pace. Given the weather conditions, which on the summit of Mount Washington were 70 mph winds gusting to 100 mph, the temperature –18 degrees Fahrenheit and visibility zero, Brian insisted that we all stay together. Al is a very fast hiker and was highly motivated to get to these hikers quickly, so I could see he didn't like that answer. But Al, like a good team player, understood that this was safer for our whole team. If anything untoward happened to one of us up there we would need everyone's help. So we stayed together and headed up into the storm.

"The strong northwest wind was thankfully to our backs as we ascended the ridge. As we got closer to the summit of Adams Four, Al was actively searching nooks and crannies on each side of the trail where someone could possibly hole up. It was all the rest of us could do to keep following the ice-encrusted line of cairns while Al was circling us with his unbounded energy and determination. Wherever the snow was soft the trail was drifted over, quickly hiding any recent tracks. However, recently made crampon marks did remain in the old icy snow. We could barely see from one cairn to the next, but having those crampon marks visible helped keep us on track. At Adams Four we all started actively searching, fanning out a little as we continued our ascent to Thunderstorm Junction. I blew my whistle every now and then, but the ball in the whistle eventually froze. I made a mental note to buy a whistle without a ball for wintertime. I was also trying a small red glow stick on the back of my backpack for the first time.

I was told it was a great help to my teammates who could identify me much more easily, especially at times when they stayed at a cairn while I searched for next.

"We passed Spur Trail and there were a couple of old up-bound crampon marks. At Thunderstorm Junction I was really hoping to find our missing hikers hunkered down in the lee of that big cairn, but they weren't there. The trail signs were all encased in thick ice and useless. There was no way one was going to get out a map in those winds either. This is where having a mental map of the lay of the land and the five trails that branch off from Thunderstorm was an invaluable asset.

"By searching a couple of cairns at a time in each direction we eventually found a set of crampon marks going down the Great Gully. No one in their right mind would be descending the mountain via that treacherous route in these conditions, so we deduced we had found the trail of our lost hikers! Al was really charged up and quickly followed their trail yelling all along. It was all Brian Abrams and I could do to keep up with Al. The other three Fish and Game officers were left in the dust, but these Great Gully cairns were big and we knew they would have no trouble following us down. In a few minutes we heard shouts answering Al's calls. I dug out my radio and transmitted that "we have audio." Lieutenant Gralenski acknowledged and I could hear the relief in his voice.

"In a few more minutes, at the last cairn before the lip of the King Ravine headwall, we met the objects of our search—very cold but conscious, alert, and excited that we had found them. The next challenge that faced us was to get them warmed up, put boots back on, and add more clothing for the hike out—no easy trick in sub-zero temperatures at night in gale force winds! This is where my tent fly worked as a quick shelter. One of the Fish and Game officers had his crampons off so I called for him to get under the tent fly with us. Al and the others stood out in the storm, helped to pin the tent fly down, and passed us clothing when requested. Underneath the tent fly the storm was transformed to instant calm and in a few minutes it was warm enough to remove our gloves, assess our patients, get some warm Jell-O into them, and bundle them up in fresh socks and outerwear. Even though they looked like they had good shell gear on and many insulating layers, the high winds and blowing snow had entered their clothing, melted, and froze their jackets, mittens, and hats into stiff icy blobs. Gralenski said, 'They were in killer conditions.' We swapped their frozen clothing and in twenty minutes were ready to go."

TODD BOGARDUS

Life-Threatening Conditions Cause Fatality

On a Sunday morning in the third week of March, two hikers planned to do a day hike in the White Mountains, then return home that evening. They selected 5,260-foot Mount Lafayette, the sixth-highest peak in the Whites. After they were reported overdue, I coordinated a search and rescue effort involving staff and volunteers from New Hampshire Fish and Game, the Mountain Rescue Service, the Upper Valley Wilderness Response Team, the Androscoggin Valley Search and Rescue Team, and the New Hampshire Army National Guard.

The surviving hiker said that when they reached the Franconia Ridge Trail on Sunday afternoon, they could not see the cairns or follow the trail because of whiteout conditions. They built a snow cave, where they spent Sunday night. On Monday, they tried again to descend but were unable to make progress because of high winds and low visibility, so they hunkered down in a rocky outcropping close to the summit of Mount Lafayette.

New Hampshire Army National Guard personnel flew a Blackhawk helicopter over the Franconia Ridge area on Monday, after the hikers' car

CLIFF NOTE Always check the local weather forecast before setting out on a hike and never venture above tree line when bad weather is predicted. It is not a risk worth taking. The AMC *White Mountain Guide* cautions: "from Lafayette to Little Haystack, the ridge is almost constantly exposed to the full force of storms and is dangerous in bad weather or high winds."

Mount Lafayette.
Photo by Dan Stone

was found at the Falling Waters Trail parking area in Franconia Notch, but guard personnel saw no signs of them. Search and rescue crews tried but were unable to climb the mountain on foot because of severe weather conditions. The search was suspended around midnight Monday.

On Tuesday morning the search began again and crews were shuttled by helicopter to the Franconia Ridge Trail and into the Pemigewasset Wilderness. The hikers were located by helicopter personnel in mid-morning near the Lafayette summit when they saw a man in a bright jacket signaling to get attention amidst the stark ice and rock landscape of this very large mountain. The man was evacuated by helicopter from Mount Lafayette at around 10:00 a.m. and rescue personnel said he was able to walk to a waiting ambulance. He was treated for hypothermia at a local hospital, but the other hiker passed away from advanced stages of hypothermia. Those who knew them said that they were experienced hikers, with winter hiking and camping experience, and that they have hiked Mount Lafayette several times in the past.

SUSAN CAMPRIELLO

One Man Dead, One Rescued on Blackhead Mountain

Two men lost on Blackhead Mountain during a snowstorm since leaving on a hiking trip Friday evening were found by rescuers. R. was located Sunday night alive and under a blanket[12] near the mountain's summit, according to New York State Department of Environmental Conservation spokeswoman Maureen Wren. His hiking companion was found dead Monday afternoon, just a short distance away. Greene County Sheriff Greg Seeley said the cause of death appears to be hypothermia. An autopsy will be conducted today, he said. "An experienced hiker lost his life due to extreme difficulty with the weather up there," Seeley said. According to Wren and Seeley, rescuers were able to locate the two hikers through cell phone activity and "pings" over the course of the weekend. Seeley said the men, who authorities said are both around fifty years of age, arrived at a lean-to on Blackhead Mountain Friday evening where they spent the night.

Wren said the men set off at 7:30 a.m. Saturday for a daylong hike in the Windham-Blackhead Range Wilderness Area. Wren said the pair, who were following the trail that leads to Black Dome Mountain and Thomas Cole Mountain, became disoriented and got lost in the storm. One called 911 at 9:30 p.m. on Saturday, telling emergency responders: "We're in trouble." Wren said the men described the area to emergency responders but the information was not specific enough for state forest rangers to pinpoint their position. Forest rangers responded to the emergency but were slowed by heavy snowfall plaguing the higher elevations all weekend. Seeley said search crews reported that wind, rain, and snow on the mountain reduced visibility to less than 15 feet. State police helicopters could not be dispatched due to "low and impenetrable cloud cover," she said.

Several inches of snow fell on the mountain Saturday night and temperatures lingered in the low thirties, according to the National Weather Service. According to authorities, snow was already deep enough that it covered some trail markers positioned between 6 and 8 feet above the ground. According to meteorologist Kevin Lipton, wind speeds reached

CLIFF NOTE This is a tragic case of failing to postpone a planned trip and of not being fully prepared for bad weather. As guidebook authors for this region, my husband and I are out in these mountains most weekends. We watch the weather assiduously; a serious nor'easter, with high winds and stormy weather, was predicted for that weekend. This was not a routine storm, and not the time to backpack three nearly 4,000-foot peaks. If the pair had been absolutely determined to hike that day, they should have carried full gear and enough clothing to survive at least one night out. Instead, these hikers became hypothermic, losing so much mobility in their hands that they were unable to strap on their snowshoes. One also lost mobility in his legs and was unable to walk; the other attempted to descend without snowshoes. Timothy Muskat, whose "Curses, Excursus" appears in this book, writes: "The top is nothing like the bottom. Don't be a trailhead speculator: that is, don't assume that

20 to 40 mph with even stronger gusts. The hikers spent Saturday night in a snow shelter they had built and one of them went to find help Sunday morning.

"Something went tragically wrong due to the amount of snow," Seeley said.

Wren said that a combined search effort by forest rangers, the Hensonville Fire Department, and the Greene County Sheriff's Department continued Sunday morning. Ten rangers swept hiking trails in the area, she said, and R. was located at about 8:55 p.m. Other than the blanket, other hiking gear had been left in the lean-to. Forest rangers set up a winter shelter around the hiker and stayed with him through the night. He was able to walk off the mountain midday Monday and refused medical attention, she said. The other hiker's body was brought down on a snowmobile and carried out by forest rangers and volunteers Monday afternoon, authorities said. Seeley said the hikers were found on the east face of Blackhead because there seems to be a well-broken trail before you that the same well-broken trail is waiting farther up ahead. Don't assume that the sunny 30-degree day you're starting in is going to lead you into an above-tree-line balm. Pack everything you *might* need for any sort of treadway—from slickest ice to deepest snow—even as you may only require your boot soles. Moreover, never simply follow a track that's not of your own making—it could lead, trust me, anywhere. When I see a broken trail before me, I don't exult; I don't, that is, say to myself, *Cool, a cakewalk to the summit.* No, I think almost the opposite: I'm going to assume the party went 2 miles in and turned around, and that the last 2 miles of trail are caked with deep-deep snow. It's a mindset, and I recommend you make it your own. And, please, stuff everything you'll need in your backpack for an emergency. Three nights, say, in a dug snow cave at −10 degrees."

Mountain at about 3,700 feet. The mountain has a summit elevation of 3,940 feet and is the fourth highest mountain in the Catskill Mountains.

Wren and Seeley said more than a dozen forest rangers were involved with the search along with members of the Hensonville Fire Department, State Police, Windham Police, Greene County Emergency Dispatch, a DEC Investigator, and the Greene County Sheriff's Department. Rescuers remained in contact with the state police Aviation Unit over the course of the search, as well, she said. Seeley said local authorities were assisted by trained search and rescue crews from as far away as the Adirondacks and New Jersey and commended the efforts of all who participated in the effort. Wren said DEC had been called to carry out six similar search operations this winter. She said hikers of all levels of experience could become disoriented during snowstorms. Seeley said his department is also called to find lost hikers somewhat frequently but usually hikers are found by search crews relatively quickly.

JOHN SWANSON

Break on Panther Mountain

December 26 started out like many other early winter days, the temperature below 20 degrees Fahrenheit, but not bitterly cold. My friend, Nan Giblin, was leading a group of seven hikers up Panther Mountain. After a brief introduction and gear check, we headed up the trail at a steady pace. There wasn't enough snow to require snowshoes; in places bare ground showed through. The trail was a little slippery, but we easily skirted patches of ice. Two and a half hours later we reached the summit of Panther, where we stopped to snack and enjoy the view. When we started down, I fell into my role as the sweep. About 400 feet below the summit, I heard someone yell. I couldn't see what had happened, but could tell something was wrong. The upbeat jovial conversation had changed to one of concern.

I had just completed my wilderness first-aid recertification course, given by Jonathan Silver, chairman of the Wilderness First Aid Committee of the Appalachian Mountain Club. I felt a need to rush to the scene to help, but I had to restrain my urge to run—the first rule of rescue went through my mind: *Don't make yourself the second victim.* When I got to the group, one of the hikers, Russ, was sitting on the ground. He had slipped and fallen while stepping down a short rocky section of the trail. Nan thought Russ's arm might be broken and asked me to look. We were in a situation most leaders hope they never have to experience. A participant was injured, miles from the road, in winter conditions. I knew we had to act in a controlled manner to prevent things going from bad to worse. The good news: we had a strong group with adequate gear, it was not bitterly cold and we were on a modest incline which posed no additional risk to the group, the patient, or me.

In times of crises at home, we can pick up the phone and dial 911. In the field it's different. While it's possible to call for help with a cell phone, the response time is likely to be several hours. We needed to provide Russ with immediate first aid. Handling a wilderness emergency efficiently requires teamwork and leadership. Many tasks need to be done simultaneously.

Resources must be assigned to provide first aid and support the first-aid effort, as well as to plan and execute the evacuation. The group must be informed, nourished, and protected from the elements. While Nan managed the accident scene and directed the group, I focused on the patient.

I started with the basics—A, B, C, D, and E: Airway, Breathing, Circulation, Disability, and Environment. I confirmed that the first three were normal, then considered the possibility of spinal injury. We were fortunate, however, that this was not a serious accident. Russ had simply slipped and fallen, injuring only his arm. As for Environment, we had to keep Russ insulated from the cold. Cold ground sucks life-sustaining warmth from the patient at a rapid rate. In 10 minutes he could begin the deadly slide into hypothermia and, more importantly, shock. I asked him if he could move himself onto his pack if we helped. He thought it was possible, and John, another hiker, and I helped Russ off the ground. Now, we needed to ensure that he stayed warm. He was already wearing all his layers, so Nan wrapped him in her expedition-weight parka.

Priorities addressed, I reached into my pack and pulled out my first-aid kit, which is about half as big as a 1-liter water bottle. It looked awfully small and inadequate, but I knew we could put together what we needed. The name of the game in the field is "improvisation." Next, we had to work on the diagnosis and treatment of Russ's injuries. I keep an accident form in my first-aid kit to use as a guide and ensure that I get all the details recorded. I questioned Russ and found him to be alert and oriented. I did not uncover any important medical conditions. I looked for other injuries that might have been masked by the pain in his arm, but I found none.

I never doubted that the arm was broken. Russ was in serious pain, and the arm was crooked. It needed to be splinted for support and immobilization during the evacuation back to the cars. I had no SAM splint, a common commercial splint, so I started with a small foam pad. This being too small, I tried my crampon bag, which had a rigid plastic liner. That worked better, but more padding was needed, so I decided to use the foam and a small towel that someone offered. I made a sling from a triangular bandage, inserted Russ's injured arm and tied it to his body with straps so the arm would be immobilized. Then adjustments were made to alleviate undue discomfort.

We helped Russ to his feet. I asked him to take a little jump to test the splint. He jumped and confirmed that the splint felt secure. On the walk out, I supported Russ with his uninjured arm draped round my shoulders.

Keeping our balance was difficult, so I shed my pack and the contents were divided among the group. I put on crampons for better traction and we started again. Along the way we talked, telling stories and jokes to pass the time and keep up our spirits on the 3-mile hike out. At 1:30 p.m. we reached the road. Once in the hospital, the doctor confirmed that Russ's arm was severely broken. We had been lucky in being able to perform a self-rescue. Had our efforts uncovered more serious injuries that prevented self-rescue, we would have called or sent someone out to get help from the Department of Environmental Conservation.

JOHN C. GODING

A Case of the Umbles

Our eclectic group met on occasion to share adventures, chief among them hiking. Carl was a strong hiker, to put it mildly, someone who, for fun, might hike 50 contiguous trail miles—covering Liberty, Lincoln, Lafayette, Garfield, South Twin, Crawford Path to Mount Washington, out via the auto road, and up to Pinkham Notch—in 17 hours. He had been turned back twice from a winter ascent of Whiteface, but was convinced that the third time would be the charm. Mike and I answered the call to join in such a worthy quest. We'd done our share of hiking in the Whites and in Baxter State Park, and had dabbled in the Adirondacks. But neither of us had much winter hiking experience or had ever used snowshoes.

Undeterred, we prepared our gear at the Downes Brook trailhead on a near-perfect winter day—crystal clear sky and no wind, but very cold. Carl instructed us on securing and using snowshoes. The technology of the time was a woven wooden shoe with leather straps, looking like something one might see Fred Flintstone and Barney Rubble wearing on a wintry day in Bedrock. Knowing the route well, Carl took the lead, breaking trail through deep snow, with Mike and me following, flailing about with our snowshoes flopping in different directions and our arms thrashing, trying to keep our balance while crossing ten streams. Carl was blissfully unaware of the spectacle behind him and the sinking odds of success—save for the howling and cursing. But for this group of intrepid hikers, howling and cursing weren't unusual. After a good while, Mike and I negotiated an uneasy truce with the snowshoes. The spastic flailing had subsided, for the most part, but the snowshoes clearly retained minds of their own and neither Mike nor I knew when we might again be clutching the air and floundering. Still, we were settling in and gaining some confidence that we might pull this off. Carl was unaware how lucky we had been to have made it so far, well over halfway to the summit. But our luck was about to change.

Now the terrain rose sharply while, to the right of us, the mountain fell away to a stream with large sections hidden under deep snow. Carl reminded us of an earlier lesson, to swing our lead shoe into the bank of snow for purchase, and up we went. This new wrinkle proved to be a great challenge—for each step up and forward, Mike and I would slide sideways and downhill a bit, toward the stream. We were working considerably harder, wasting energy, and making painfully slow progress. Behind me I heard a *thud,* followed by cursing. I turned to see Mike splayed out in the snow. He struggled to get back on his feet and back onto the trail. Until that point, I hadn't really noticed that Mike was wearing jeans and a heavy cotton shirt—nothing waterproof. Then again, neither of us had expected to be engaged in a battle of wits and wills with an old pair of snowshoes. We continued on another dozen steps or so, and *thud.* More cursing, this time involving varied animals, parts of the anatomy, and certain actions that would curl the eyebrows of a U.S. Marine. A few more steps—*thud.*

"Mike," I said, "you really should brush yourself off before that soaks through." He answered with a glare that said, *Shut the hell up and keep walking.* When I turned at what would be the final thud, Mike had fallen and slid, facedown, almost into the river. By the time he'd struggled back up to the trail, he was spent, wet, and covered in snow that caked his clothes and eyeglasses. Carl had heard the commotion and descended to check on the situation. We brushed wet snow off Mike. At first, we had thought it was just a fall—but it quickly became clear that it was more than that.

"I can't feel my feet."

Carl and I looked at each other. We noticed that Mike was shivering markedly. Combining that sign with his degrading coordination, we real-

CLIFF NOTE Experienced hikers say "cotton kills" because only wool and synthetics retain their insulating value when wet. Cotton absorbs moisture and does not wick sweat to outer layers; it takes longer to dry and clings coldly to the body. In windy or cold weather, cotton is not only uncomfortable, but dangerous. Wool does not dry quickly either, but retains warmth when wet.

ized that Mike was becoming hypothermic and that this had the potential to become life-threatening. We had ascended over 5 miles of trail already, so this was serious.

"What do we do about his feet? We have a long walk out."

We helped Mike change into dry clothes, wrapped him in a space blanket, then had him eat a sandwich. He sat on a backpack while we took off his boots and wet socks. Carl and I took turns kneeling in front of Mike, with his feet under our armpits and on our chests, while the rest of him stayed well wrapped in the shiny space blanket. What a spectacle, should other hikers have come upon us! Was it a space alien, or some otherworldly human ceremony? While warming Mike's feet, Carl reached into his pack and pulled out a beer. What else can you do, high on a mountain, while you're thawing out somebody's feet under your armpits? "Desperate times require desperate measures," he later quipped, "and ensuring my adequate hydration and electrolyte replacement seemed appropriate!"

After a few more turns of armpit therapy, Mike put on dry socks and was willing to press ahead, but Carl and I decided that we'd dodged a bullet and had enough adventure for the day. Down we went, without further incident. It might not have been so, had the group not been prepared with extra clothing, the experience to recognize and treat hypothermia, and the good judgment to turn around. Mike's experience also highlights the real dangers of cotton in a winter situation. Winter climbing can be a lot of fun, but recognize the dangers and plan accordingly.

SUSAN P. KIRK

Katahdin Ice Climber Meets Lady Luck

Frostbite danger in winter is very real, especially if camping or spending time outside for extended periods, or if your feet get and stay wet. Before I talk about a frostbite emergency while I was camped at Chimney Pond, I'll mention my work experience with frostbitten extremities. As a registered nurse in a large inner-city hospital, I have seen many cases of frostbitten fingers, noses, and feet. It's just a fact that some homeless people, for whatever reason, will not go to a shelter on the coldest nights. If they fall asleep under the influence of alcohol or drugs or both, they can develop frostbitten extremities. The course of recovery can be long, sometimes ending in amputation of the affected part. The Connecticut chapter of the Appalachian Mountain Club offers a two-day SOLO course in backcountry rescue,[13] but the course doesn't cover frostbite. Frostbite can be a real emergency, especially if it occurs on your feet.

On a trip into Chimney Pond in the early 2000s, our group was again climbing peaks. By that time I had already completed the winter Northeast 4,000-footer list of 115 peaks, as well as the winter Hundred Highest in New England. I was up there for fun, not to complete a list, and I continue to go to Baxter State Park in winter because I love it! Even considering the high winds and driving snow, I can't get enough of that area in winter. How I envy the ranger who lives up there all season! Of course it's a tough job—you are on your own, and most likely the initial responder for any emergencies and rescues. Winter's danger, so far away from civilization, is real and can offset winter's beauty. On this trip we had lots of snow and wind—but not many opportunities to go above tree line. We were able to climb Hamlin Peak but, due to the poor visibility that rolled in after we reached the summit, none of us were willing to risk the long traverse across the tableland to Baxter Peak in such conditions.

Our group wasn't alone at Chimney Pond; a small group of ice climbers were camping about a half mile away from the cabin. Snowshoeing to the outhouse, I met one of the climbers and we got to talking. I invited them to come over to our cabin for a cup of tea, to dry out their gear and warm up. None of us were going anywhere on this windy day with blowing snow—what I call ground-blizzard-like conditions. The visibility was so poor that we discussed tying one of our climbing ropes from the cabin to the outhouse, so we wouldn't get lost on the way back!

The ice climbers came over to our cabin in the afternoon. Two of them were in their late twenties, but the third was a kid who looked really young. It turned out he was seventeen. I noticed right away when he came in that his gait was off—he was limping slightly. I made tea and offered the seventeen-year-old a seat near the stove as he looked cold. The two older climbers decided to take us up on the offer to dry out their gear and went back to their tent to retrieve some stuff to dry. In winter, down sleeping bags can be great; they are warm and light, but have one downfall—they can get damp from body evaporation and lose their insulating quality. Some winter hikers I know use plastic liner bags to protect the down from getting moist on multiple nights in the field. I can't stand the clammy feeling that results when you use liners, so avoid them. We had clotheslines all over the cabin, but our group was all right with this.

I started chatting with the young man after the other climbers left, and invited him to take off his boots. "Might as well warm up your boots, too," I said. He was holding one of his feet like it was bothering him. He was a stoic and I could tell he was not about to complain about anything. I asked him point-blank, "Are you having problems with your feet?" His answer was a sheepish "Yes." I asked him if he would mind if I took a look, explaining that I was a nurse and trying not to be too intrusive in my questions. He then took his boots and socks off. I was horrified. His feet looked dusky, grayish in color! I checked his pedal pulses (the pulses on top of your feet)—they were very weak. Then I asked him to look away, held his great toe, and asked which toe I was touching. He wasn't sure! That is a test for sensation in your feet; when checked, all his toes had the same diminished sensation. I was very alarmed. This seemed serious, most certainly a case of frostbite, with severe loss of sensation to both sets of toes! It also occurred to me that, since he had now started to warm his feet, he shouldn't walk on them, to avoid damage from pressure on his warming tissues. I explained to the young man that his toes might be frostbitten and he should stay in the cabin with us tonight. He was okay with that, glad actually.

I quickly approached our leader and explained what I thought, also mentioning that the boy would most likely need to be evacuated. A family practice physician in our group also checked the boy. He reached the same conclusion that I had—the boy had frostbitten feet! We notified the ranger right away. It was decided he would spend the night with us and be evacuated in the morning by the rangers. It was getting dark and late and really cold—I am sure that's why they didn't take him out immediately. Also, he didn't seem to have much discomfort. I had read that, when an extremity starts to thaw, it can be painful. I offered him some Motrin, since I couldn't imagine that he wouldn't have some kind of discomfort eventually.

When the two other climbers returned, we briefed them on their companion's situation. They were shocked, totally unaware that he had even had a problem. Young men sometimes don't want to admit weakness. Maybe he was embarrassed to mention anything to the older guys; maybe he didn't want to cause complications; maybe it was a macho thing. But, the next morning, the seventeen-year-old was carried out by rangers, on a large sled that attaches to the back of the snowmobile. His two friends went out with other rangers who arrived to assist with the rescue. The young man was transported to the trailhead, then to the hospital.

Life lesson here: if you get your feet wet, then stop, dry them out, and change socks. If your feet feel cold, tell someone. The group can stop and make gear adjustments; adding a hat or extra layers helps, as does running up and down, jumping, and moving your toes around in your boots as if you are playing the piano with them. Worst-case scenario, you put your feet on someone's stomach to warm them up. Anything's better than frostbite! I believe that even one episode of frostbite can cause some loss of microcirculation and sensation, predisposing you to future frostbite more easily. I never did hear what happened to that young man. I hope he is okay!

Another Episode Influenced by Lady Luck

A strong party of eight climbers camped at the Marston picnic shelter area, planning to hike South Brother and Mount Coe and descend via the Coe slide. I was the group leader and made it clear that being safe was our most important goal, besides bagging peaks. We divided the communal emergency gear among the group—a first-aid kit, sleeping bag, bivy, stove, and ground pads—but we all carried our own stuff for winter: extra layers, down jackets, space blankets, ice axes, food, goggles, several layers of gloves and liners, wind pants and jackets. Although the snow was deep and we were mostly on snowshoes, we all had full crampons—not insteps or Microspikes. During our first night, a ranger visited on his snowmobile, to check on permits and paperwork. Inquiring about the group leader, the ranger asked "Where is he?" My friends pointed out the "she" leader. After setting up our winter tents and cooking supper—the shelter was handy for that—we all went to bed.

In the morning, we anticipated a delightful and not very difficult day. The South Brother/Coe junction sign was almost buried in many feet of snow! But South Brother was glorious in the sun and, after the Mount Coe summit, it was a straightforward snowshoe to the top of the Coe slide.

Even though the snow was over 6 feet deep, however, a slide can be icy, due to wind blowing away the snow. I've had some experience with slides in the Adirondacks; on an ascent of Dix, all the snow had been blown off the slide and it was easier to crampon up it than break trail in deep snow. Would the Coe slide be the same? I planned to insist that we all use full crampons on the great descent down this slide, even though most of us had aggressive teeth on our snowshoes. One of our group had gotten a little ahead and, as I was yelling "Hey, wait up," he stepped out onto the slide on his snowshoes, without pulling out his ice ax. He took a few steps—then suddenly was skiing down the Coe slide! He stayed upright for a while, then tumbled and fell. He was sliding fast and heading right toward a pile of rocks.

"No one on the slide," I yelled, "without crampons and ice ax in your hands!"

Self-arrest skills should be practiced yearly. One can slip and fall on slopes due to ice or by simply stumbling. Without practice, you might fall too fast and become unable to stop. On a night climb on Mount Rainier, I was slightly off the route and stepped on a thin crack in the snow, which suddenly opened into a hidden 100-foot crevasse! (Crevasses often get covered with new snowfall.) Thankfully I had my ice ax, with the strap looped around my wrist. I felt the biggest adrenaline surge of my life as I swung that ax with all I had toward the outer lip of the crevasse, then dragged myself out. Most likely I wouldn't have survived the fall. Always walk on steep slopes with ice ax ready; if you fall, slam the pick of the ice ax into the snow and kick your knees in too, forming a sort of triangle. If wearing crampons, it is especially imperative to keep your feet up and use your knees, because the points of the crampons can catch the snow or ice, causing a severe ankle injury or making your fall worse.

I was already thinking of the rescue at the rocky base of the Coe slide.

The way our companion fell, he couldn't possibly escape injury—likely serious. If he couldn't walk, we had plenty of extra gear to keep him warm; if he had a neck injury, however, we couldn't improvise a litter because that would be too dangerous. The fastest hikers would have to go out and intercept the ranger, who came by only once a day. All this was flashing through my mind as we prepared ourselves for the slide. Our fallen climber had hit some kind of hump in the snow, become airborne, then stopped. I could see blood on the snow! When something like this happens, everyone wants to rush to the victim. I had taken the SOLO course in backcountry rescue the year before, and kept stressing that we didn't want any more victims. There was another registered nurse in the group; he and I made our way cautiously down.

As we descended, the climber got up and gestured. I yelled to him to sit down, in case he had a severe injury or was in shock. After all, he was bleeding. We two nurses—both trained in intensive care—checked him out. He had a nosebleed and the frames of his plastic glasses had broken, but the lenses were intact. There were no broken bones and no sprains, just the bloody nose that we stopped with gauze and snow. Although shaken, our fallen climber hiked out to the Marston Dam campsite. He refused a rescue and most likely didn't need it; he was walking fine, though sore. His vital signs were normal, neuro signs normal, pupils equal and well reactive to light. He denied hitting his head but, since he had a nosebleed, he clearly hit his face; he claimed that his glasses had hit his nose when he fell. Since he had been previously tenting with me and the other nurse, we took turns during the night to check his level of consciousness, pupils, and pulse.

The next morning we split up his gear and hiked out. He refused a check at the Millinocket hospital. Accidents happen even to the best-prepared people. The climber who fell said he didn't think he needed crampons because there was so much snow. But slides are deceiving—snow, over ice! He was a very strong and experienced winter hiker who nevertheless made an error in judgment, and was lucky. Our group left with an extreme respect for the mountains and for the dangers of winter climbing.

PART III

A Treacherous Place in the Peaks

Before learning about these accidents on the Wildcat A

slide, I was already convinced that it was dangerous in

winter—a steep, slippery slope with a drop-off below.

KEITH P. SULLIVAN

The Day "Hal's Slide" Got Its Name

As we started up the Nineteen-Mile Brook Trail on January 11, 1998, it looked to be a good day to tackle the Wildcat Ridge. The skies were slightly overcast; the wind was calm and the temperature was considerably warmer than an average January day in the White Mountains. However, one factor weighed heavily on me as we shuffled up the broken-out trail on snowshoes: What would be the conditions on the Wildcat A Slide? The previous six days had seen a series of ice storms that collectively represented the worst ice disaster the Northeast had ever experienced.[14] A huge swath of Upstate New York and Canada had been hit hardest, and although the damage in central and northern New Hampshire varied greatly, based primarily on elevation, certain locations had been hit extremely hard. It was almost a certainty, that along the route, we would be faced with an icy hiking surface and downed trees and limbs.

My hiking companions that day were a small group of New Hampshire Chapter regulars who'd all been on previous Appalachian Mountain Club winter 4,000-footer hikes I had scheduled. This was not a listed chapter hike, but rather a bootleg trip, with me as the de facto leader. Allen had been winter hiking for many years, but because he lived in western Massachusetts and had a young family, he no longer got out as frequently as before. He was chipping away at his winter 4,000-footer list and was well on his way to completing it. Dorothy was a hiking dynamo who lived in the White Mountain region. Although she had been mountain hiking in winter for only a couple of seasons, she had gained considerable experience and a high level of fitness in a short time, by hiking frequently on both weekends and weekdays. Patricia was an avid and determined winter hiker and close friend who had accompanied me on most of my listed hikes. Our final companion was Hal. He had retired from his job as a computer programmer several years earlier while only in his mid-forties, to live as simply as possible in the White Mountains of New Hampshire. A considerate and gentle man, Hal is among the finest hiking partners I have ever had, and always a pleasure and inspiration to be around.

When we arrived at the intersection with the Wildcat Ridge Trail, we stopped to tell jokes, grab a snack, and take a short break. The surface of the trail had been consolidated by previous foot traffic, then hardened by the frozen rainwater of the previous week. I was certain we would not be using snowshoes from here on. I told everyone to put on their crampons and said that they could leave their snowshoes at the intersection at their own discretion. I left mine, a decision I would regret much later that same day. We started up the moderately steep trail as it traversed the north side of Wildcat Ridge, toward the long steep avalanche slope known at the time only as the Wildcat A Slide.

As we approached the slide, everyone was feeling confident and the mood was positive. But, as I climbed, I told myself that we would not take any big chances on the slide. If it was too treacherous, I would make the call to turn around. Regardless of how unpopular the decision would be, I knew my companions would turn around with me—they were all seasoned hikers, and well-schooled in the AMC hiking principles. They respected my role as leader and would comply with my instructions with a minimum of complaining.

When the group arrived at the slide I was toward the back, with Allen, Patricia, and Hal in front and Dorothy behind. All three hikers in the front immediately expressed the opinion that crossing the 70-foot-wide slide would not be a big problem and they wanted to do so. They all looked back, awaiting my decision. Quickly, and with very little observation or analysis, I said, "Let's go, then." Allen crossed first, followed by Patricia, then Hal. I let Dorothy step ahead of me, and then proceeded a couple steps onto the icy surface myself. The surface was not quite uniform hard water ice, but it wasn't that far from it. The packed-down, snow-covered trail had been saturated with several inches of freezing rain over the previous week. It was actually a near-perfect surface for crampons, with the tips of our crampons driving a good half an inch into the surface. Most of us were wearing eight- or ten-point, strap-on crampons, while Hal had a pair of first-generation, twelve-point step-ins.

I was looking straight ahead, right at Hal, when he crossed the midpoint of the slide. All of a sudden his downhill foot seemed to slip away from him. He immediately fell down the slide and on to his back. He was gone in an instant, over a sharp drop-off and out of sight. I could hear his body crashing through fallen branches and thudding off boulders for what seemed like an eternity. When the noise halted, I called down to Hal once, and then several more times. No answer. My friend was now alone, hundreds of feet below us, and obviously injured, if not worse, and I had made the decision that led to his predicament. I looked back up and across the slide. Patricia and Allen were safely across the slide; Dorothy was midway and on a higher route than the others had taken. She was grasping a sturdy branch of a tree that had fallen onto the slide, using it like a hand rail. I shouted to my teammates, "Don't climb down there unless you are sure you can do it safely. Try to stay to the side of the slide and off that ice—I don't want anyone else injured." This was followed by, "I'm going down to Carter Notch Hut for help."

The hut is four-tenths of a mile from where we had left our snowshoes, less than a mile from the slide crossing. It was one of two AMC White Mountain huts open throughout the winter then, on a self-service basis. There would be a full-time caretaker at the hut, and he or she would have a radio that could reach the AMC Center in Pinkham Notch. Because it was mid-morning, there was a chance that the caretaker would be away from the hut, but I hoped that would not be the case. I moved down the trail as fast as I possibly could, breaking into a run on the downhill sections and taking long strides on the flats. As I rounded the last little bend uphill toward Carter Notch, the door of the little stone hut came into view. There in the doorway, much to my relief, stood the caretaker, Kevin "Hawk" Methany, shouldering his pack and about to go out for a short hike. I had gotten there just in time.

I explained the scenario to Hawk in as much detail as possible, including the fact that I was an experienced New Hampshire Chapter Leader, hoping that he would make an immediate radio call to Pinkham and get emergency medical and recovery assistance in motion. However, he felt compelled to follow AMC protocol and first reach the victim, to determine the extent of the injuries and access the accident site, before requesting assistance. We headed out immediately, with Hawk in the lead and moving seemingly faster uphill than I had come downhill. Hawk decided that we should go only a short way up the Wildcat Ridge Trail, then bushwhack toward the bottom of the slide, where Hal was. This would be a rather arduous bushwhack, but certainly safer than working from the top of the icy slide.

We stepped off the trail and found ourselves in hip-deep powder. The thick spruce trees had shielded the snow surface from much of the freezing rain and there was only a thin icy crust in this section of the forest. Hawk was able to proceed at an amazingly fast rate, but even with him breaking trail, I was finding it hard to keep up. After a short distance I suggested it would make more sense for me to continue up the trail to the top of the slide, where I could rally the rest of my group and get them down to the route Hawk was now breaking. He quickly agreed, and I hiked back to the slide crossing.

When I returned, Allen was still on the far side and Dorothy was still in the middle, clutching the same tree branch. Patricia had maneuvered her way carefully down the slide on her eight-point crampons and was administering first aid to Hal, somewhere out of sight but within voice range. I shouted down to Patricia and asked her about Hal's condition. In a very controlled voice, she stated that he had injured his shoulder and had a cut on his head that she had dressed and stopped from bleeding. She said he was awake, sitting up, but not able to travel under his own power yet. I asked her if they would be okay for a while and she said yes. The next order of business was to get Dorothy and Allen safely back to the downhill side of the slide. Having observed Hal's fall, and after standing out on the slide holding onto a branch for over half an hour, Dorothy had lost confidence to cross back to the trail. I walked out on the slide, just downhill from her position, and assured her that I would be able to block her fall if she slipped on the ice. Just then, Hawk, who had given up on his long bushwhack, arrived at the slide too. Together, we convinced Dorothy that she could safely turn her body around and get back to the trail. Hawk stepped out a few paces, took her hand, and coaxed her off the ice. After Dorothy cleared the slide, Allen crossed back to our side using the downed tree as a handrail.

Patricia, after courageously negotiating what had become a technical ice descent in eight-point crampons and tending to Hal alone for more than an hour, was anxious to get help and see some progress made. When I called down this time, her voice did not express the same calm, patient demeanor. She said Hal was still all right but asked, "When are you going to get your ass down here?" This was no time to share the litany of problems I had just faced; she justifiably felt like she was dealing with Hal's survival all by herself. I got the message. Allen had the only ice ax in our party; I borrowed it and headed down the slide, at times facing in on my front points. Hawk led Dorothy and Allen through the deep snow in the woods, on a steeper and much shorter route than he had taken earlier.

When I got to Patricia and Hal, he was awake and alert, but his face had been badly battered. His most obvious injury was a severe laceration on the forehead that Patricia had dressed with a sanitary napkin. That dressing was now soaked through with blood and he had several less serious cuts on his badly swollen face as well. The right side of his torso, including his shoulder, was in significant pain and he could not use his right arm. I thought he had separated his right shoulder and perhaps broken his collarbone. His lower extremities seemed okay, and Patricia had put warm clothing on him and had him sitting up on a foam pad. Since the bleeding had largely stopped, I left the sanitary napkin on his major wound and placed an army field dressing over it, securely tying it in place. Then I fashioned a sling from Hal's fleece jacket. At that point Hawk joined us, quickly examined Hal, and made the radio call to Pinkham to request help.

Since Hal had the use of both of his legs, we thought it best to try to get him to start moving down the mountain in some manner, as quickly as possible. He was still on the slide, on a relatively flat section. It was icy where we were located and there was a steep drop-off just below us. Hawk had scouted the route below and thought it would be best to angle off the slide to the left as we faced downhill, then into the woods, where it was not as icy. One of Hal's crampons had remained on his boot, but the other one had come off during his fall. Patricia had recovered it when she descended the slide. In fact, she had recovered all of the equipment that had fallen off Hal, including his broken glasses and a missing lens.

Unfortunately the crampon Patty found was broken and could not be repaired. The wire bale that went over the toe portion of the boot had been pulled through a hole on the crampon's side plate. (This was an early step-in crampon which had several design flaws that have since been rectified. The wire bale had been held in place merely by bending the wire back inside the mounting hole. Later versions have flattened ends that are virtually impossible to pull back through the hole. His crampons also lacked the strap that runs from the front wire bale around the ankle and through the rear binding latch, to hold it firmly in place when the strap is tightened properly.) When we examined the broken crampon, it appeared that the torque Hal had applied to the wire bale as he stepped down firmly on hard ice while standing perpendicular to the fall line had caused the binding system to fail. This had been the primary reason for his fall.

Initially we moved at a very slow and deliberate pace. Hal stayed in a sitting position, and would move one foot at a time, repositioning his cramponed boot himself, then sliding the other boot down and against my firmly planted boot. After 30 minutes we had moved several hundred feet off the slide and onto safer terrain, so Hawk went back to the hut to rally some folks to assist us. At this point, Hal was willing to try to walk with some assistance. Just moving a short distance had done wonders for his spirits; he began to feel like we might actually be able to get him out of this peril. With assistance from at least one other person, we helped Hal to his feet. Hal was close to my height, but about 90 pounds lighter. We decided that he would put his "good" left arm around my shoulder, while I wrapped my right arm around his back and latched firmly on to his belt. We moved our inside legs as one, together, and caught up with our outside legs, completing about one half-step of normal distance for every two strides. It wasn't fast, but it seemed like light speed compared to the rate we'd been moving previously.

This process was extremely difficult and very painful for Hal, and we made frequent rest stops. Additionally, the forest undergrowth had gotten considerably thicker and the going was more difficult. Patricia, Allen, and Dorothy, already burdened by the additional weight of both Hal's and my gear, had to go ahead of us, breaking trail and knocking away dead pine branches that blocked our route. After an hour or so, Hal was totally spent and needed to rest for a longer period. We decided to wait in place until more help and a rescue sled could arrive. It was getting late in the day, almost dusk, and darker in the deep woods where we were now located. I looked at my watch—it was 4:00 p.m. and we had moved less than half a mile.

Fortunately, the rescue team from Pinkham arrived in ten minutes, followed by Hawk and several overnight guests he'd recruited from Carter Notch Hut. The leader of the rescue team was a full-time AMC employee and Wilderness EMT named Chris Eaton. Chris had brought several young, sturdy-looking, and seasoned volunteers who appeared quite up to the task. But Hawk's Carter Notch guests looked like the sort of folks who viewed a winter hike up the moderate Nineteen-Mile Brook Trail as an arduous, once-in-a-lifetime undertaking. At that point we welcomed them all; we were going to need a lot of help to get Hal out to the trailhead.

Chris was painstakingly meticulous about placing Hal in the rescue sled and preparing him for the journey out. Although at the time it seemed excessively cautious to me, I was soon to become aware of why Chris had exercised so much care. This was not going to be a simple matter of twelve people pulling a sled through the woods to the Nineteen-Mile Brook Trail and then out to the trailhead. For starters, we still had several very steep pitches to descend. The pine trees were close together, creating thick underbrush of dead pine branches. There were many downed trees and limbs and 6 inches of powder snow on top of a fairly thick ice glaze. The ice would hold your weight most of the time; every eight or ten steps, however, we would break through and posthole into another foot or more of snow.

By the time Chris had Hal ready to go, it was after five o'clock and getting dark. In half an hour, we would require headlamps to travel safely. We encountered the steepest sections first. On each, Chris, who was wearing a harness, would connect himself to a sturdy tree and tension belay a long section of webbing attached to the sled through a figure eight on his harness, while a couple of us steadied the sled from the bottom. After three or four pitches like this, the slope became gradual enough to control the sled by using the three straps located on each side, along with the straps on the front and rear of the sled. At least two people were required to stay downhill of the sled, breaking dead branches off trees to make enough room for the sled to travel through. In numerous places the sled had to be picked up and passed over downed trees and limbs. I assumed that all this jerking and jostling was tough on Hal; however, you never would have known it from him! He remained calm and positive throughout the ordeal. After 2 hours of helping us struggle through the dark woods, Hawk had to leave to attend to evening chores at the hut, where thirty overnight guests were eagerly awaiting his return; some of his volunteers departed with him. Although the most demanding and dangerous part of the day was behind us, we literally were not out of the woods yet. After 30 more minutes of dragging and hoisting the sled through thick forest, we finally reached the Nineteen-Mile Brook Trail. A couple of volunteers from Pinkham had walked up the trail to assist us with the sled, and to the joy and amazement of all of us, they had hot soup on a Whisperlite stove and were almost ready to serve us. Unfortunately, I didn't have time to enjoy any; my snowshoes were half a mile back uphill at the trail intersection.

The walk back up to the Wildcat Ridge Trail turned out to be cathartic for me. For the first time all day, I no longer felt responsible for anything but my own well-being. I allowed myself to feel confident that Hal would be okay and that the rest of the trip out would be easy and relatively routine. I knew that I should have been more assertively cautious when we approached the slide; for one, I should have been in the front, where I could have personally assessed the conditions. Instead, I trusted the collective wisdom of my hiking partners. That seemed reasonable enough, when you consider that all were experienced and that Hal and Patricia had winter hiking experience comparable to mine. However, all had trusted me as the leader and the decision, ultimately my decision, had not been a good one. I determined that I would come back to Wildcat A and climb to the summit, using methods that would effectively mitigate the danger of crossing the slide, regardless of its condition.

Throughout the day Patricia had shown incredible character and competence, first in down-climbing that difficult slide and administering first aid and emotional support to Hal, then later by giving her physical all while manhandling that sled out to the trail. Allen and Dorothy had been helpful, but not totally committed to a successful outcome. They were now heading home ahead of the rescue party to take care of personal issues. Patricia and I were determined to see this thing through to the end, however, the end being Hal safely at the hospital and on his way to recovery. I know, absolutely, that Hal would have done the same for one of us, or any of his hiking companions. This sense of dedication to one's companions is deeply embedded in the mountaineering ethos; acquiring it is a non-negotiable rite of passage in becoming a genuine member of the community.

When I got to the intersection of the Wildcat Ridge Trail, I strapped Patricia's snowshoes to my pack and mine to my feet, then started back downhill at a slow jog, something I frequently did while wearing snowshoes on a moderate trail. When I caught up to Hal and the rescue party, I saw that they'd moved a lot faster than we had been able to do through the woods; however, they had not covered as much distance as I'd thought or hoped they would have. We had enough people to pull the sled, but no longer enough to carry all the excess gear or to provide an occasional break to anyone. Of the volunteers now remaining, Chris Eaton and the three young people who'd accompanied him from Pinkham had been at it for over 5 hours, while Patricia and I had been on our feet for more than 10 hours! The two volunteers who had met us at the Nineteen-Mile Brook Trail made a total of eight, the optimal number of people needed to pull the sled.

Even though the Nineteen-Mile Brook Trail had been thoroughly broken out, only the sled could fit in the snowshoe track. The volunteers pulling straps from the side of sled were traveling through unbroken snow. The upper trail has sections that are cut perpendicular to the fall line of a fairly steep slope; in these spots, we would have to position volunteers on the downhill side, to hold the sled and keep it from sliding sideways down the slope and into the brook. After an hour, we had covered less than 1 mile of the 3 miles to the trailhead. We were all dealing with fatigue and requiring breaks more frequently. As we approached the intersection with the Carter Dome Trail, we heard voices, and soon we were in the company of a larger rescue party, consisting of members of local volunteer mountain rescue organizations and several New Hampshire Fish and Game officers.

The new rescue party took control of pulling the sled, while Chris continued to maintain responsibility for the primary care of Hal. Some of the young volunteers that had come up from Pinkham earlier continued to take turns on the sled, but Patricia and I decided to shuffle along behind. Considering our level of exhaustion, taking a turn on the sled only would have slowed the process. The combined team covered the remaining 1.9 miles in slightly more than an hour. Hal continued to endure his ordeal with good humor and great appreciation for all the folks who were helping with the rescue. He didn't complain about anything, even when one of the Fish and Game officers tripped on a sled strap and fell onto his chest. As we approached the trailhead, Chris mentioned to Hal that we were "almost home." Hal jokingly responded, "Okay, you can let me out of the sled, I'll walk the rest of the way." After a moment of silence, Chris said, "Hal, if you get out of that sled now, you are going to definitely need it; some of these people are likely to break both your legs."

At the trailhead, Hal was quickly transferred to a gurney and put in the back of the waiting ambulance. He had fallen at approximately 10:30 that morning; now it was nearly midnight. Patricia and I drove to the Berlin hospital to check on Hal. He had already been examined and treatment had begun when we were allowed to see him. Hal's head wounds had been stitched and dressed. His face was still swollen but he had been cleaned up and was beginning to look like himself again. He had sustained a concussion and had bruises and abrasions all over his body, but his only truly serious injuries were broken ribs and a punctured lung. Hal was very slender and a dedicated practitioner of yoga. These factors lessened the force of his impacts and increased the resiliency of his body—and I believe they both contributed to his quick and full recovery. (He would be out hiking again in the spring.) With the knowledge that he had no life-threatening or long-term injuries, we were able to share a few laughs with Hal about the humorous things that had occurred that day. After a short visit we departed for a well-earned, half-night's sleep.

CLIFF NOTE At least two unusual conditions contributed to this accident: a pair of crampons with a design flaw, and the remnants of an unprecedented ice storm. Seven years later, however, another accident occurred in the same spot—near an AMC hut that is open in the winter. A permanent cable could ensure safe traverse across this well-traveled, inherently dangerous slide.

The next morning we drove back to the trailhead to move Hal's car to the hospital, then stopped at an optometrist's office to have the lenses of Hal's glasses remounted in frames. He remained in the hospital for about a week while his lung healed and re-inflated. Two weeks later I returned to Wildcat A with Patricia and a friend. We brought a static rope, used to fix lines in mountaineering, and some climbing slings and hardware. We belayed one team member across the slide to secure it on the far side and create a rope traverse. Then each of us crossed the slide, securely clipped into the rope traverse. I have repeated this process on several AMC hikes I've led, even using it one time when the snow was deep and soft enough to have easily allowed self-arrest.

Hal and I both stayed active in the AMC White Mountains community, but our interests diverged. He got into rock climbing and eventually did most of his hiking mid-week, when I was at work. I continued to hike weekends and got into doing and then teaching mountaineering and glacier travel. I'll always remember him as a good friend and a reliable hiking companion, and I'll always be thankful that he was not more seriously injured during that now infamous fall.

MARJORIE LAPAN DRAKE

Rescue on Hal's Slide

On January 8, 2005, a group of friends met to hike the Wildcat Ridge. Although this trip was not an official Appalachian Mountain Club hike, three of the participants—Mike Woesnner, Doug Hunt, and I—were AMC trip leaders. Others on the hike were Joe Courcy, Jean Williamson, and Bill Bartsch. We spotted cars at Wildcat Ski area and hiked in bare boots up the Nineteen-Mile Brook Trail to the Wildcat Ridge Trail. We met a group of hikers from Maine who were also planning to hike the ridge. Although the trail was very icy, Doug noticed some of them wearing only Microspikes instead of crampons and cautioned them about a section of trail on the ridge that has a steep slide. That section became known by many as "Hal's Slide" after a fall in 1998 which left a hiker significantly injured.

As we approached Hal's Slide we heard someone yell, followed by a lot of commotion. Word quickly traveled down the trail that someone had fallen on the slide. Shortly thereafter, two women from the Maine group came back down the trail to get help at the Carter Notch Hut. They told us that a man from their group had fallen with his dog, and that he had yelled to them that he was injured and couldn't climb back up.

We quickly realized our plans had changed. Thinking first of the safety of our own group, we all agreed that Joe and Jean should hike back to the parking lot, while the rest of us would bushwhack to the injured hiker. There was a tremendous amount of undergrowth, making travel extremely slow and difficult. By the time we reached Carl N., the fallen hiker, a group from New York who'd been hiking ahead of the Maine group had climbed down from the opposite side of the slide and were attending to his injuries. Among that group were a surgeon, an anesthesiologist, and a physical therapist. Carl was conscious, alert, and able to explain where he was hurt. The New York group had applied a splint to Carl's leg, put coats and a hat on him, and was giving him something hot to drink. When my group arrived, we all noticed right away that Carl was sitting directly on the snow. One of the first things we are trained to do when coming upon an accident scene—regardless of the time of year, but especially in winter—is to get something between the injured party and the ground. We got our ground pads under him and helped to get him into a bivy sack. Shortly thereafter,

Marjorie comforting Carl at base of Hal's Slide on Wildcat A.
Photo by Douglas W. Hunt

the hut master from Carter Notch Hut arrived with a litter. It took several hours to carry the litter through the thick brush back to the trail.

Once on the trail, we were able to slide the litter most of the way back to the trailhead, so the New York group hiked to the hut, where they planned to spend the night. This left the hut master, my group, and one man that had been hiking with Carl to finish the carry. Eventually we were also joined by two workers from Pinkham Notch, who had responded to assist with the carry. There are some places where the trail is very close to a bank that drops sharply to the river. At these places, the hut master would tend the front of the litter and I would tend the back, while the rest of the group climbed over the bank to guide the litter across. We arrived at the trailhead at 6:00 p.m. to a waiting ambulance and hot coffee.

Carl was transported to the hospital, where he was treated for multiple leg fractures. After the accident, there was much speculation among the hiking community regarding the details of Carl's fall. Many people blamed the dog, but I had spent some time talking with Carl—both at the scene and during the carry. According to him, the fall was a result of a crampon getting snagged in the snow and ice, causing him to loose his footing and stumble. Prior to crossing the slide, Carl had put his dog on the leash. As a result, he pulled the dog down with him when he fell. Fortunately, the dog was not hurt in the fall. Carl was also very fortunate that several hikers with both medical and rescue training were close by when he fell. This serves as a reminder to always be prepared for the worst when you are out enjoying the mountains.

DOUGLAS W. HUNT

Hiker and Dog Fall on Wildcat Slide

We'd planned a traverse of the Wildcats on this cool and icy January. Our trip was not a scheduled Appalachian Mountain Club hike but a bootleg hike among friends, organized by AMC leader Marjorie LaPan Drake. At the Wildcat Ridge Trail, we put our crampons on; there was some new snow but it was not packed enough and the trail was very icy. At this junction, Bill and I met two hiking groups from Maine and New York State while waiting on the rest of our group (we never leave a trail junction until our entire group has arrived); these groups were doing the same traverse. I spoke to the Maine group about inadequate crampons—they were not using full crampons, but an older form of Microspikes. I was also concerned that they were traveling with a dog, knowing about the slide that would be crossed. I had crossed this slide numerous times and had heard of Hal R.'s experience seven years before. He had slid down the slide and was hurt quite badly; since then it has become known as Hal's Slide.

As we were climbing, we heard a yell, then learned that a guy from the Maine group had fallen down Hal's Slide, along with his dog. While women from this group descended to the Carter Notch Hut, looking for help, we bushwhacked in to assist with the rescue. By the time we arrived, Carl was already being assisted by several doctors in the New York group who were trained in first aid, but I was concerned that they had not placed Carl on a ground pad to keep him free from hypothermia; he was still lying directly on the snow. We placed our ground pad under him until help arrived, then got him on a sled to take him out of the wilderness. Another concern for our own group was an older member; we needed to care for her and make sure she was not getting too cold. Joe volunteered to take her out; reminding us of the importance, for winter travel, of making sure that your group is large enough to handle trail emergencies. Joe had nice hot coffee ready for us when we finally arrived back at the trailhead.

Marjorie's leadership skills were well noted during this successful rescue. One of the photos shows Marjorie's wonderful bedside manner in keeping the patient responsive, and I thank the AMC's New Hampshire Chapter for the great training they provide to their leaders. We also were very thankful for the experienced hiking group from New York, which undertook the medical responsibilities of the rescue; for the Carter hut master's quick response, team leadership, and direction; and for the many that assisted from the Pinkham squad. One thing that really stood out about the young hut master was how he challenged the judgment of the orthopedic surgeon, who was withholding water to ensure that Carl would be ready for surgery. The hut master stated quite forcibly that this is not how we handle wilderness first aid; in the backcountry, we must make sure that the injured person is adequately hydrated.

We were able to get Carl down safely, despite his severely broken leg, and on to the Gorham hospital. Carl was fortunate indeed to have two other hiking groups in the same area at the same time, plus a hut nearby for additional assistance. This episode serves as a reminder: when conditions are extremely icy, make sure you carry proper winter gear and first-aid supplies. Marjorie's group was well supplied to assist this fallen hiker.

DAVID SCOTT WHITE

Wild Days on the Wildcats

On the day that Carl fell down Hal's Slide—January 8, 2005—Carol and I were approaching the Wildcat Range from the ski area, because Carol considered the slide on Wildcat A potentially dangerous. Conditions were incredibly icy that day and we finally turned back between Wildcat D and C. Returning to Gorham we saw many rescue vehicles and ambulances at the Nineteen-Mile Brook trailhead and, remembering how icy the day had been, Carol said, "I bet someone fell down Hal's Slide!" Researching the history of this treacherous place, she communicated with the authors in this section—Marjorie, Doug, and Keith—who kindly agreed to write about these accidents.

On an earlier approach to the Wildcats, we *had* taken the Nineteen-Mile Brook Trail. It was –7 degrees Fahrenheit, mid-February 2003. Though the snow was very deep, there was a potentially hazardous icy crust on Wildcat that made this steep slide look dangerous. Carol refused to cross, and insisted that I put on full crampons to do so, since my old snowshoes had inadequate crampons.[15] Losing one's footing, she felt, could result in injury or worse; in fact, she thought that a cable should be fixed there to ensure safe crossings. (We did not yet know about Hal's accident in 1998.) She turned back, saying she would meet me at the other end of the Wildcat traverse. "Be careful on the summit edge," she warned. After a difficult climb to Wildcat A, I followed her advice and did not venture out on a cornice for a photo of the hut, hundreds of feet below. By the time I reached the views near Wildcat C, my camera would not open because of the frigid temperature.

At Wildcat D at 4:00 p.m., I met a pair of hikers going the other way— and only one of them had a flashlight! "Are we close to the hut?" they asked. They chose not to believe that I had left Wildcat A around noon, but did say it had taken them hours to ascend to Wildcat E from Route 16, postholing in deep snow. They had a reservation at the Carter Notch Hut and were determined to get there. I described the range still ahead of

Failure to turn back is a common mistake for hikers. Getting to a hut where you have a reservation is a pleasant ambition, but not a reason to put yourself in a dangerous situation. Fatigue, unexpected conditions, and inadequate time are all sound reasons to turn back. Consult a topographic map before choosing a route, so you'll be familiar with the terrain you'll encounter. Traversing the Wildcat Ridge to the Carter Notch Hut may seem like a reasonable goal on paper; but when you are confronted with very deep snow, on steep terrain with many ups and downs, in subzero temperatures, and are approaching dusk with only one flashlight, you should turn around. Those hikers wanted to see if they could make it, perhaps thinking that, since Dave had already broken trail, the route couldn't be that hard. One can only imagine their chagrin when they finally turned back, at 9:30 p.m.

them—the AMC *Guide* warns specifically about the many ups and downs, and notes that hikers with "heavy packs should allow substantial extra time." I shook my head about their chances, but they continued on in spite of my warnings. When I reached the precipitous descent to Route 16, I switched into crampons. Later, I learned that my headlamp shining on the dark mountainside gave Carol hope that I was still moving. We drove to the Pinkham Notch Visitor Center to send word to the hut that two hikers were pushing on without adequate gear. The next day we drove back to find out what had happened—the two finally decided to turn back. My comments may have been the deciding factor in a very wise decision.

PART IV

Dangers of Water in the Mountains

The first story describes Laura and Guy Waterman's
adventures in New Hampshire's Waterville Valley,
including an outline of the many perils of rain in winter.
The hazards of river crossings are noted next and, finally,
the special challenges presented by Adirondack passes,
lakes, brooks, and peaks in winter. In that region, about
twenty of the highest peaks are untrailed.

LAURA WATERMAN

Waterfilled
In Which We Nearly Drown

There might be nothing more dreaded by winter hikers than heavy rain. Certainly there is nothing more potentially dangerous. *Hypothermia weather,* we called it. Streams that were easily stomped across on snowshoes become impassable. Keeping gear dry is essential—and nearly impossible. Winter rains can turn that 3-foot snowpack to the consistency of mashed potatoes, wreaking havoc with your hiking times. Your backpack gains pounds from your saturated equipment. In wet situations, tempers flare, depression sets in, and your sense of humor somehow evaporates. It's hard to keep your equanimity. Perhaps nothing tests the spirits of a party more than winter rains. Yet it rains in our Northeast mountains every month of the year. Rain in January is not a rare event. A forest ranger we knew always said, "If it starts to rain in winter, get out of the mountains. Crazy things can happen." Guy and I made two trips into Waterville Valley, in the White Mountains, that were as rain-soaked as trips could get—both in January. Forever after, Waterville became for us the Waterfilled Valley.

On January 22 and 23, 1983, we made the first trip with our good friend Ned Therrien, who worked for the White Mountain National Forest and was about as tough and capable and fun to be with in the mountains as anyone you could find. He'd cut his teeth on river trips in northern Canada that were long, buggy, and wet. The forecast for our three-day January jaunt was for rain in the flatlands and snow up high, so we were optimistic for snow. Our plan was to climb North Tripyramid by way of the slide, a long broad scar down the entire north face of the mountain; it was caused by heavy rains in August 1885, which exposed a great deal of bedrock, and is visible from a long distance. The North Tripyramid slide is among the steepest in the White Mountains; facing northwest, it forms ice early and holds it late into the spring. Guy and I prized this slide for its magnificent views, steepness, and exposure.[16] It was broad enough that we could select routes which kept the steepness at a reasonable angle—that thin line which weaves between comfortable and exhilarating, without crossing into fear.

By their nature, slides are hard to access, with very steep terrain, often requiring bushwhacks to reach. For those reasons they can be great places to be. We found them an incomparable way to climb a mountain.

The first day we dashed up Mount Tecumseh and then shouldered our big packs with our camping gear. We mushed up the Livermore Road, then cut off-trail toward the stream that drains the slide on North Tripyramid, and set up our camp. We ate the dinner Ned had brought, with moonlight shining in the tent door. All seemed serene; we spent a cozy night.

The morning temperature read a suitably cold 11 degrees when we left the tent and it didn't take us long to reach the bottom of the slide. We were equipped with crampons, ice axes, and snowshoes; we didn't need a rope. We were changing into crampons at the slide's base when we noticed drops on our packs. "This isn't snow!" Ned exclaimed. I held out my sleeve and the drops soaked into my wind gear; they were not light and fluffy and white.

"The temperature couldn't have risen 20 degrees in the last hour!" I protested.

We started up. When we got high enough to see the Osceolas—or where the Osceolas should have been—the sky was very black and the clouds were making a rapid beeline for us. It began to drizzle harder—time to don rain gear! Then Guy and I remembered that we'd left ours in the tent. Ned had left his at home! We continued up. It's not possible to explain these things. No one wanted to turn around. The steep rock slabs became glazed from the freezing rain, but we were wearing crampons so everything seemed fine. We had ascended more than halfway up the slide when it bore in upon us that we were more than a little damp. This forced a very difficult decision—we must turn around.

Our plan had been to gain the summit by a short bushwhack, then descend by the slide or the more gentle Scaur Ridge Trail, depending on the snow and ice we encountered. Mid-January rain had left much exposed rock, which can dull crampons quickly. We had to be careful of our footing because the spaces between the rocks were not filled in with snow. This had forced us to move slowly. As a friend once said at a similar point on a climb, where prudence also was advised, *The mountains will always be there.* Hypothermia is a possibility in such conditions!

We opted not to retrace our route down the steep slide on icy, glazed bare rock, without adequate snow to fill in the crevices—that was a recipe for a sprained ankle. Instead we traversed over to the woods, where the snow was deep, requiring snowshoes. The stunted spruce and fir at 3,500 feet grew *very* densely and we had to push our way through with our heavy wooden snowshoes. Snow was heaped on every bough and, as we struggled steeply downhill, each branch and twig unloaded itself on our heads and down our necks. Wet snow crammed itself between our packs and our backs, then soaked in. We had not a dry thread among the three of us when we reached the tent.

"Let's hole up and see what the weather brings tomorrow," I said. But Guy and Ned pointed out that the forecast had been wrong: it was raining, not snowing. We were soaked, and it was impossible to dry our gear. It was time to retreat! Guy and I crawled into the tent and stripped, donning a dry layer and our blessed rain gear. Ned remained in his saturated clothing and began moving very fast—stuffing his sleeping bag, pulling up stakes, and packing. He shared cookies laced with chocolate and caramel that his wife Jean had made. We ate them all. We didn't mention hypothermia. The trees were now firmly coated with ice. Livermore Road, which had been hard-packed by skiers, was as slick as a skating rink and running with water. I would have been better off in crampons but, rather than carry the heavy wooden snowshoes, I left them on. Ned and Guy wore neither snowshoes nor crampons but chose to slide, in their surefooted way, down the road. Ned set a brisk pace and kept up our soggy spirits by singing canoeing songs from his river trips, appropriate for our very wet slog. Then he started telling stories about Far North river trips, stories that all featured rain and bugs. I don't know how he had the energy for it. The way my feet were feeling—pounding under my heavy pack, snowshoes clattering on unyielding ice—almost made me long to be in a buggy place. Finally we reached the car. I climbed in, making a pool of water in the back seat. Ned asked us to stop at a gas station as we were leaving Waterville. "I called Jean," he said, as Guy started the motor. "She says she'll leave the dryer door open."

The second trip, from January 24 to 27, 1986, was just Guy and me. We had discovered how easy it was to haul loads on a sled on a flat-ish approach trail. So that's what we did—light day packs on our backs, heavy gear on the sleds—for the long walk on the Livermore Road, then another half-mile up to Cold Brook, where we set up camp. On the uphill side. We strung up a big blue tarp to protect our leaky fly and made ourselves cozy. The temperature read 2 degrees. We called our camp Fort Tripyramid.

When we awoke the next morning, we decided to make the day our big one, as the forecast was less good for the following day. The plan was to ascend Whiteface Mountain and, on the return, take in both South and

Middle Tripyramid. As the snow was firm, the conditions would be fast. We wore only boots; there was no need to don snowshoes, though we carried them. As we were coming onto the summit of Whiteface, we met a party from the AMC's Worcester Chapter, some of whom we knew, and chatted briefly; the mountains can seem very neighborly. But with snow falling and temperatures in the single figures, no one hung around for long. On our way along the ridge between South and Middle Tripyramid, we encountered moose tracks so large and deep that they were a problem to keep from falling into! We returned to South Peak and descended the slide back to Fort Tripyramid.

It snowed all night; we could hear the tarp shedding it. At 6:00 a.m. the snow changed to rain. We decided to spend the day holed up, hoping it would clear by evening and get cold, in which case we could continue our climbs. It rained steadily all day, though we spent it pleasantly enough by reading, eating, drinking hot drinks, snoozing, chatting, and playing the alphabet game. Each person writes the alphabet vertically, accompanied by a quotation, also written vertically. Beginning with the letter *A* and the first letter of the quotation, you have to come up with the initials of a famous person; the person who can list the most names in 15 minutes wins. We also experimented with various forms of the "Everest position," as we called the pose one adopts when forced into inactivity in a tent, such as holding book over head while lying on back. The temperature sat on 38 degrees all day.

By nightfall we were worried about Cold Brook and the location of our camp. We had pitched our tent well up on the bank, but the steady rain was causing the stream to melt and rise. We went to sleep both with the sound of rain and the more troublesome sound of Cold Brook, now only 4 or 5 feet away and roaring. We hoped we wouldn't have to evacuate in the darkness. I felt anxious and packed up some gear, and had my boots, rain pants, and jacket handy. So did Guy. We awoke at 5:30 to rain. When it became light enough to see, we realized that Cold Brook had risen to within 2 or 3 feet of our tent, with the lines from the tarp in the water.

High time to retreat! We packed up inside the tent, careful to keep dry things well bagged. The problem had become how to negotiate the stream crossings, beginning with Cold Brook. We decided to ferry the loads. About a quarter-mile from Fort Tripyramid, we located a low, wide trunk spanning a narrow part of the brook. We both carried our full backpacks to what we had deemed was a suitable spot to cross. We couldn't haul our sleds, as this was a bushwhack, so I returned for the sleds and our lighter packs while Guy prepared the crossing by breaking off branches that would be in the way and adding more logs. It took a good 2 hours to get everything to the trail on the other side. We had made no forward progress—we were still in sight of our camp—but we congratulated ourselves upon working out a method of crossing in fast, high waters.

The rain had eased up. What amazed us—though it probably shouldn't have—was that the streams we had hopped across on the way in had turned into major obstacles. Small streams that had been completely covered by snow and ice—and thus invisible on our way in—had now opened up. Our next crossing was an unnamed stream, though it was noted on the map. I crossed by straddling a log; Guy scampered across. The crossing after that involved walking across one log that led to another slippery log, almost submerged in the stream; I used two ice axes for support. Guy hopped back and forth like a squirrel, as the burden of the repeated ferrying fell to him, including the sleds. The trail was mush. The snow, which had been deep on our way in, had melted, revealing soggy ground. The surrounding woods were dark with wet. Tree trunks, glazed with ice, were not welcoming. We had rarely seen the woods so saturated.

At last we reached the big crossing we were most worried about—Avalanche Brook, which drains the North Tripyramid slide. I'd remembered seeing a large downed birch spanning the brook a few yards down from where we'd crossed on the way in. This was the key. We could get onto its top branches and move to the main trunk. This we straddled, and all would have been pretty straightforward except for having to get around a big branch, broken off several feet up and sticking straight as a bayonet at anyone foolish enough to attempt a crossing. It was not rotten and could not be dislodged. It made a good handhold—requiring careful balance—but there were *no* handholds on the other side.

The brook below us was raging very fast and noisy; Guy and I had to shout. We shouted *If you slip, you'll still have a chance*—it was important to believe that, to build courage. But we knew we would not have survived. Just downstream, Avalanche Brook is forced through a narrow rock-strewn gorge, pretty in summer but frightful in this torrential high water. A slip off this wet log would have washed you—that is, your body—all the way down to the Mad River. I was good for one trip across, but Guy made repeated carries, becoming somewhat more confident with each one. After many anxious minutes, he finally had our heavy sleds and packs safely on the other side and we gave each other grateful, joyous hugs.

The 2.25 miles down the Livermore Road were easily dispatched in 1 hour and 40 minutes. In Waterville we ran into a friendly cop who told us that this storm, which had begun with 6 inches of fresh snow, had ended with 3 inches of heavy rain. Strangely, this water-filled trip was satisfying, an experience that felt like a success and not a failure. We had both felt anxiety—and there was real danger with that Avalanche Brook crossing—but with them came exhilaration. Looking back at a significant triumph over adversity, however, can lead you to downplay the risks.

Broken Compass

"Diane, I don't think we should try to cross," I said, feeling sick.

Amy nodded in agreement. "I don't want to cross here, either," she said quietly.

"No, no. We cannot cross here," Diane agreed.

We stood in the wilderness with a raging river on one side, miles of dense forest surrounding us, and one single trail leading back the way we had come. Uphill, through miles of old, soggy snow to the Tripyramids. We were tired, my knee ached, and it was almost dark. We stared across the river at the trail on the other side. Maybe, in summer, this trail would be pleasant and inviting, and crossing this section of river would mean hopping from one boulder to another. But now, the river was at least 4 feet deep, with angry spring meltwater thundering down the mountain. We had no ropes and absolutely no experience with river crossings like this.

I was excited about the first hike of the season. "Let's bring snowshoes and Microspikes," I e-mailed Amy and Diane. "I'm bringing my water shoes, too. There are a few stream crossings." I was peakbagging and had never hiked the Tripyramids. The plan was to hike up the Pine Bend Brook trail, bag both summits, and then head back on the same trail.

We arrived at the trailhead after 9:00 a.m., which felt closer to noon. It was hot and humid, unusual for so early in the morning, especially since it was only April. Blissfully unconcerned with time, we packed up our gear and hit the trail. Two hours later, I was on the trail in my Crocs, pant legs rolled up to mid-calf, carrying my boots over my shoulder and my snowshoes strapped to my pack. I tiptoed through moose scat, sprinkled on the snow-packed trail like a spilled box of malted milk balls. The stream crossings were minor enough—jumping from rock to rock, wading through, or walking upstream for a narrower crossing. Diane was patient, waiting for Amy and me to decide how we wanted to cross the streams. We were like two princesses, not sure if we should cross here, or maybe over there, delicately picking our way over, laughing, sighing with relief when we crossed a stream that was merely a few inches deep. Diane plowed ahead of us, having thirty more years of hiking experience under her boots. But, then again, she was fast on a bad day, too.

Our pace came to a halt when we hit the monorail, the remnants of a packed snowshoe trail. (Snow gets packed down from regular snowshoe traffic; during a thaw, the surrounding unpacked snow melts considerably faster, leaving the raised "monorail.") Postholing in several feet of mush was slow and tedious, sapping our strength and good moods. Diane could have gone ahead, reached the summit, then come back for us, but instead she waited. Hiking became a rhythm; step, step, sink. Step, step, sink. Amy was struggling. Either she was carrying too much in her pack, or her recent surrender to her nicotine addiction had caught up with her. Whatever it was, she weighed about the same as Diane and me, especially with our heavy backpacks, and we couldn't figure out why she kept falling in.

"Are you carrying rocks in your pockets?" I asked Amy, hoping humor would crack her frustration.

"Ah, not quite," Amy replied tersely, wiping strands of sweaty hair out of her face.

Diane tried to show Amy how to snowshoe on the monorail without falling in. "Here, you just do this," she said in her Austrian accent. She took one step forward slowly, waiting before she put all her weight on it. It held, and she took another slow step forward with the other foot. It held too. The next step didn't and she fell in. "Just don't go so quick, and wait before you move the other foot," she said.

Amy did exactly as Diane instructed. She took one step forward without putting her weight on that foot. Diane and I held our breaths. Good, she was still upright. She slowly moved her weight forward, and picked up her back foot. We exhaled, and she promptly postholed. "Mother fucker," was Amy's response as she fought to get out of the hole. Diane gave a sympathetic grunt. "Here, follow me," I said after Amy composed herself. I gave her the exact same instructions as Diane, somehow thinking that it might help. Amy watched me go through the motions, staying upright on the monorail. I took one step forward, then another. And another. Amy took a half step forward and promptly postholed.

"Shit," was her response.

"Try holding your breath," I said, sheepishly. Amy didn't respond. Neither did Diane.

"If anything, this is going to be a stimulating hike," I said as we took a break, trying to be positive.

"Yeah, real stimulating," Amy grumbled.

"Stimulating," repeated Diane, eyebrows raised. Perhaps, in her native Austria, they don't often refer to hikes as stimulating. Crazy American.

We continued up the trail without speaking. *Maybe this wasn't such a good idea,* I thought. *Maybe we should have waited until after the spring melt.* I struggled to keep up with Diane and provide encouragement to Amy, who was cursing everyone and everything. At the top of the valley, a snow bridge was the last crossing over the stream. It was minor, but I get freaked out at the weirdest things. Like I'm afraid of heights, but not all heights bother me. This snow bridge was freaking me out because I knew that Amy, on a midwinter hike with several feet of snowfall, had fallen through a snow bridge and gotten stuck under a rock in the stream. Luckily, she had been part of a large group and the guide had pulled her out. As she was postholing up this trail, she had been reminding me of how much she hated monorails and snow bridges. Plus, I had read the book *The Last Season,* and knew that the park ranger had died because he fell through a snow bridge into a stream. Of course, the snow bridge I was crossing was about 3 feet high and the stream was about 6 inches deep, but like I said, I get freaked out at the weirdest things. One misstep off the snow bridge and I'd fall in and . . . maybe get my boots wet.

We made it to the summit at 3:30. Looking back, that was very late in the afternoon. But when we had been making plans for the hike, Diane had said offhandedly, "We have plenty of time. Daylight is not an issue." These words kept echoing in my head, every time we postholed: *Daylight is not an issue.* When we had a snack at the false summit: *Daylight is not an issue.* When we stopped to talk to the hikers who went up the slide, in the snow, wearing jeans and sneakers: *Daylight is not an issue.* At the summit, I took off my boots and pants in order to take off my panties—they were soaked from the snow melting off my snowshoes, which were strapped to the base of my pack. I put my pants and boots back on, carefully balancing on one foot at a time, praying that no one would come around the corner while I was standing there, half naked, thinking, *Daylight is not an issue.*

We sat on the rocks at the summit eating our lunches. Slowly, in the amount of time it takes to figure out a calculus problem on a final exam, a very vague thought began to creep into my consciousness. *If it had taken six hours to hike up, how long would it take to hike back down?* Diane proposed taking the Sabbaday Brook trail down the mountain to the Kanc, then hitchhiking back to our car. The upper section of Pine Bend was steep and, on the topo map, Sabbaday didn't look any worse. There were a few more stream crossings, but based on our experience on Pine Bend, we should be able to cross them easily. After all, we had Crocs, so we could just change out of our boots and wade across. No problem.

Diane went down the trail first, followed by me, then Amy. I noticed at one point that there was only one recent set of tracks in the snow—Diane's. But like many things that day, it didn't register until much later. The upper part of Sabbaday was one giant slide down on our snowshoes. Intermittently, we would change into Microspikes, but when we started postholing, we'd stop and put the snowshoes on again. On and off, on and off. I came around the corner onto a straight section of trail. The slope slid steeply off to the right and I could see Diane about twenty paces ahead of me. I turned to see Amy coming around the corner behind me. As I took a step forward, I postholed in with my right leg, and the weight of my pack pulled my body down the slope to the right, back first. My lower leg, encased in a snow cast, remained pointing down the trail.

"Ow, ow, ow!" I cried out, as my knee wrenched under the strain. I unbuckled my pack and slid it off as Amy and Diane shuffled to help me out of the snow. After being helped back up, taking a handful of Motrin, and uttering a few choice words, we continued down the trail. Me limping, Amy postholing, and Diane leading her mangled troops to water.

The snowpack on the trail started to disappear, only to reappear in the shadows. We were getting closer to the base of the mountain and rapidly running out of daylight. Without saying anything out loud, we began walking faster, as if propelled by some Neanderthal instinct to get home to the cave before dark. The trail was now following alongside the stream and we could hear the thunder of the swollen water in the distance.

While hurrying along, trying to beat the saber-toothed tiger, we encountered an unusual stretch of trail. If we'd had more time, I would have stopped to check it out, maybe even take pictures. This 6-foot long, 3-foot wide section of trail was covered from edge to edge with varying ages of moose scat. Some appeared to be recent, like someone had spilled a 5-gallon bucket of Milk Duds, these overlying older, more decomposed scat, which looked like . . . fibrous Milk Duds. This collection of scat was a geologic wonder; recent droppings at the surface, increasing in age with depth. I could just see the archaeologists of the future, excavating this section and proclaiming "These ancient beings pooped in little pellets." How all this scat got there was a wonder in itself. Did moose regularly meet there to discuss wildlife management? Did some of it wash there, transported down the mountain by spring snowmelt? Was there a special type of food just in that one area? While nearly running down the trail, I hadn't seen any special vegetation—just regular trees. What would explain why every moose in the Whites had, at some time or another, been on that section of trail, pooping? I still haven't figured it out.

While driving up that morning, Amy had randomly announced, "I forgot my headlamp." I had replied, "That's okay. I forgot my compass at work." We had both laughed. We hadn't used either on hikes in the Whites in quite a long time.

We eventually reached the stream crossing on Sabbaday. We tried to talk, but the thundering noise of the water rushing over the rocks deafened us. We could see the rocks hiding under a few feet of water flowing way too fast. There was absolutely no way we could skip across these rocks.

We were screwed.

We searched upstream and downstream for a better location to cross. Diane noticed the tree first. It was lying directly across the river, about 6 feet in the air. It was wide enough to hug, but it seemed to be as high as a skyscraper. How could we balance on this? My fear of heights kicked in.

"We can't cross here," I said. I couldn't fathom trying to cross the log standing upright and trying to balance on it with the stream raging underneath. *Shit, shit, shit.*

"We have to. There's no other way," Diane replied, the voice of authority.

"We can bushwhack," I countered.

Amy was quiet, and green.

"Look," I said, pulling out my map and pointing to it. "We can bushwhack down the left side of the stream and pick up the trail again. It crosses the stream several times but ends on the left side."

Diane paused and looked at the map. She looked over at the left bank of the river. It rose at a steep angle from the water, enough of a slope to make the trek challenging, but passable, in my opinion. But, in Diane's opinion, apparently not.

"No," she said. "We need to cross the river."

"Really," I said. "We can just bushwhack. It's steep, but we can do it." I was trying to convince her. Honestly, it didn't look bad, especially compared to getting across that log. She wasn't buying it.

"That's too steep. We need to get back on the trail." She was firm.

I kept trying. "The trail crosses back over," I said, pointing again at the map. "We'll just have to cross the stream again and end up on this side, again."

Amy stood there silently watching us deliberate our fate. Diane wouldn't budge. She was adamant that we needed to cross the stream. I looked over to the other side of the river. The right bank was the same steepness as the left. For some reason, Diane couldn't see it. She knew we couldn't cross the stream, and knew that the log was iffy. But, she wouldn't consider bushwhacking. She didn't see that the right slope was just as steep as the left—and covered in snow. Once we crossed the stream, we'd still need to traverse the bank to get to the trail. On the side we were on, the bank was bare, leaf-covered, getting more sun. We wouldn't have to cross the stream; we could just go across the bank.

I took a deep breath and gave in. We would cross the stream. I knew it was a bad idea, but I gave in to Diane, figuring she knew what she was doing since she had more experience than I did. I was comfortable with bushwhacking and I knew where I was on the map. Following the stream on the left would have been easy. Just keep the stream on our right. Also on the map were some tiny words that struck fear into my heart: *Sabbaday Falls.* They were written in blue, for water, and accompanied by those squiggly lines that indicate a waterfall. Not just a little waterfall, but enough of a waterfall to put it on the map. How high would the water be farther downstream? There were a few more streams entering from the west, all dumping their flows into this brook. And if there was a waterfall, then there was enough of a gradient to cause it. What caused the gradient? Were there huge boulders blocking the streambed, or exposed bedrock, or bedrock ledges? Was the channel narrow, or wide? If it was wide, there'd be less of a chance for a waterfall. How would we cross when we got closer? As much as I didn't want to go through the annoyance of bushwhacking, I did not want to cross the river.

But, I gave in. *Idiot.* We approached the log cautiously, as if it might stand up and bite us. Diane went first. She attempted to stand on it, took one step, then quickly sat on the log and straddled it.

"Undo your pack," I yelled over the roar of the water. She unclipped her pack and inched forward, leaning on her outstretched hands and then scooting her butt forward. After an eternity, she reached the other side. I exhaled.

"Come, come," she called, waving us forward from the other side. She stood in the shallow edge of the stream, ready to grab us as we crossed.

Amy was still green, and still quiet. And oddly calm. I went next, nervous and scared out of my mind. I straddled the log with my poles in my pack, straps unclipped. I inched forward, scratching my legs on the rough bark. *Ohhh, that would really suck,* I thought, when I came to the first knob of what used to be a branch. I came to another knob, inconveniently located at an awkward spot near two other knobs. *Let's see, scratch both legs or get a knob in the crotch.* I chose to scratch both legs. When my feet touched the other side, I was exhilarated. *What a stimulating adventure!* Then Amy crossed and we clapped and congratulated each other, giddy at surviving the river crossing. Thank goodness we had made it to the other side. Now, we just had to scale that bank. The bank was steep, covered in a booby-trapped maze of downed limbs and holes obscured by a foot or two of soppy, melting snow. We slipped, struggled, and pulled ourselves along the bank, following the river.

I found more moose scat on the slope. *How the hell did they get here? How the hell can they be upright enough to poop when I can't even stand up?* While hunched over, clawing at the snow and branches with my hands and feet, trying to keep myself from sliding 20 feet down into the stream, my mind occupied itself with images of mountaineering moose, wearing crampons, mountaineering suits, and goggles, carrying oxygen packs and ice axes, moose with cool European names like Yvon and Pierre, roped together for safety as they rappelled down the slope . . .

Hitting the trail snapped my brain back to reality. Diane and Amy had followed me up the slope and soon arrived at the trail too. Looking back at the trail on the other side of the river, we cheered, celebrating our good fortune and amazing luck, then continued down the trail. For about 50 feet. We were at the river again.

Fuck, fuck, fuck. I knew this was going to happen. We were right back where I thought we'd be. We could look across the brook and see the trail, on the opposite side. The left side, the friggin' side we'd started on. The brook was wider here, and shallow. Pissed off, but unable to utter the words *I fucking told you so* out loud, I walked right through the water. Boots on. No hip-hopping of rocks, nothing delicate now. *Shit.* Amy and Diane followed, silent. Maybe they knew.

We squished down the trail in our wet boots and soon came to the river. Again. I pulled out the map and studied it. Again. Amy had a cigarette. Again. "It looks like we're here, so if we bushwhack, we'd pick up the trail here," I said, pointing to where the trail crossed again to the left side. "Then here, it looks like it's right next to the brook for a while." I showed Diane the map. She glanced at it for a second.

"Look," she said. "The trail is right here. See, the water isn't so high. It'll be fine." We argued a bit more, and I once again gave in. This crossing wasn't as bad as the first, but the water was high, almost to the knee, and it almost pulled Diane under as she crossed first. I went next, and grabbed the end of Diane's hiking pole when she held it out for me. I felt the pull of the water, the instantly weightless feeling of my legs and feet. Then gravity hit and my feet touched gravel on the other side. Amy went next, grabbed the poles we held out for her, and crossed safely. There was no cheering and giddiness this time. We silently resumed our trek down the trail in our soggy boots, watching as dusk faded into nothingness.

It was now dark. We had two headlamps for three people. And I'm afraid of the dark. Diane and her headlamp were far down the trail, moving quickly and deliberately. Amy was in the middle, and I brought up the rear, looking over Amy's shoulder to shed light in front of her as she stumbled down the trail.

"Becky, I can't see. Why won't she slow down?" Amy asked with a weary sigh.

"Diane," I called. "Wait up. Amy can't see."

Diane stopped, but she seemed irritated. When we caught up to her, she started moving again, quickly. As we stumbled and limped down the trail, I tried to think positive thoughts. *Maybe this trail will lead us right to the trailhead, and then everything will be okay. Maybe the map is wrong. Maybe the trailhead is on the right side of the brook.* But deep down I knew it wasn't. I started praying anyway. *Please God, please let there be a bridge.* I knew that on some of the popular trails, there was sometimes a bridge over the river, especially if the river was significant and close to the trailhead. The blue words *Sabbaday Falls* looked touristy on the map. Maybe there'd be a bridge.

Please let there be a bridge. Please, if there is a bridge, I'll never ask for another favor, ever. I'll give up chocolate and I'll eat vegetables all day. For what seemed like miles, I continued limping behind Amy on the trail, leaning to the side to shed light in front of her, repeating over and over my new mantra.

Please let there be a bridge.
Please let there be a bridge.
There wasn't.

There was no bridge and no daylight, just the weak, oddly blue light from our headlamps in the inky dark, barely shining across the water to the trailmarker on the opposite bank. The left bank. The side we wanted to be on. That voice in my head said calmly and deliberately, *It's too dangerous. You'll never forgive yourself if someone dies.* The trail on the other side seemed far away, barely visible in the dim light of my headlamp. Turning my head left and right, I tried to gauge the depth of the river. I couldn't tell. It could be 1 foot deep or 6 feet deep. Even though its width suggested that it couldn't be very deep, there was only one way to tell. And I did not want to risk it. We couldn't cross with only two headlamps and no ropes. Our headlamps were barely lighting up the trail, never mind the river. And if Diane made it across and I stayed on the bank and we both shined our lights into the river, Amy would be crossing in near-total darkness. *What if she got swept away? How would we find her?* Diane started to cross.

"Whoa, Diane. Wait," I grabbed her arm.

"We don't know how deep this is, and the water could pull us downstream." I yelled so she could hear me.

"We have to cross," she yelled back. "The trail is on the other side." It was then I realized a very important thing. Diane needed a trail. She needed a trail like elephants need peanuts. Like I need chocolate. That wasn't a bad thing, necessarily. When I first started hiking, I needed a trail too. I still prefer to use a trail. I don't enjoy bushwhacking, but geology classes and fieldwork had made me comfortable navigating off trail. When doing either of those, there was never an option to use a trail. But Diane couldn't go off trail. That wasn't something she did. It wasn't wrong, she just needed to be on the trail. Needed it like heroin.

"I know," I said. I too wanted to be on the other side, on the trail, heading home. But, more than that, I wanted all of us to live through this. Diane looked perplexed.

"Wait, let's just talk this through," I said, moving away from the deafening thunder of the fast-flowing water. We stood up on the bank where we could hear each other speak. It was warm, dark, and the trees were huddled around us. Our options were to camp out overnight at that location, then at first light attempt to cross if it looked safe enough. We had enough to spend the night; layers, rain gear, plenty of food, emergency shelter, waterproof matches, and an unlimited supply of fresh water only steps away. Or we could bushwhack out. Like any good democratic gathering, we put it to a vote.

Amy was quick to offer her opinion. "I say we camp out here."

I was impressed. This was coming from a woman who, when sleeping in the car at a trailhead, was afraid to pee outside the car for fear of meeting a bear. Then again, there was that time in Acadia when we had wandered down a trail at dusk, intently searching for the bear someone else had just seen, until we realized the absurdity of the situation and ran back out of the woods, scared.

Diane said, "But we all have to be at work in the morning. I can't camp out. I think we should cross the river and follow the trail to the parking lot."

I said, "It's just too dangerous. We don't know how deep it is, and we only have two headlamps. I vote we bushwhack down to the Kanc."

Amy nodded. She was okay with bushwhacking. She just didn't want to cross the river and she was prepared to fight. Diane was outnumbered. I realized, for the second time that day, that I had forgotten my compass at work. Diane dug around in her bag and produced a small, well-worn compass, and her maps. Her compass didn't have a declination adjustment. How would I be able to use it? I was accustomed to geologic compasses, with declination and inclination and mirrors and all sorts of fancy stuff. I pulled out my maps.

"See, this is where the trail goes," I said for the millionth time that day, pointing to the left of the brook on the map. "And this is where we are," I said, pointing to the right. "We just need to bushwhack about an inch to the north and we should hit the Kanc."

Diane put on her reading glasses, for the first time that day. "Isn't the falls over here?" she asked, pointing to her map.

"No," I replied, shocked at the realization that she hadn't seen the maps earlier. Without her reading glasses, the maps would have been nothing but a blur. "It's just the words in blue on that side of the trail. The brook is on this side."

"Oh." She was quiet. "I didn't really look at the map before."

I could have strangled her. That was it. It was now all up to me. I had the map, the compass, and I really wanted to get out of the woods. We headed off and immediately picked up an old cart path. As we were following it, it seemed like it was bending too far east. I stopped to take a reading. According to this Cracker Jack compass, we should head forward almost 180 degrees from where we were. Almost back the way we had come. This made no sense. I was tired, getting worried, and very frustrated. I could no longer hear the water and I didn't feel comfortable navigating with Diane's compass. *My god, it doesn't even have declination!* To reassure my anxiety, I wanted to use the brook for navigation, so I told Amy and Diane the compass wasn't working right.

"We need to head back to the river and follow it downstream," I said.

"What?" asked Diane.

"The compass . . . I think it's broken," I said, shaking my head. Diane exhaled in annoyance. Some genius I had turned out to be. We moved closer to the brook. In the darkness, I could hear it pounding, and immediately felt reassured. *We'll just keep this on our left.* But Diane's headlamp was far ahead of us, sinking into a huge valley. Amy and I were together, sliding down the slope on our butts, my headlamp illuminating the ground in front of us.

"Where is she going?" I wondered aloud. We stopped our sliding.

"I don't know. Is she going to the river?" asked Amy. We were both perplexed.

"Maybe. But why? We can hear it from here. We don't need to be next to the river, just close enough to hear it and use it to navigate."

"That means if we slide down this hill, then we need to climb back up," Amy said, exhausted.

"Yeah, let's just wait here. She shouldn't be getting so far ahead of us." Diane's headlamp danced in the darkness, then turned toward us. Then turned again toward the river. Then, turned again toward us and grew larger. She was angry.

"Why are you waiting up here? Why didn't you follow me?" she asked us, struggling to remain upright on the slope.

"Diane," I took a breath. "We need to be close enough to the river to hear it. We don't need to be right next to it. We won't be able to hear each other talk if we're too close."

"But you're the one who wants to be next to the river," she said, angry.

"I know," I replied. "We just need to go in this direction," I said, gesturing to the north, "while keeping the brook to our left."

"But, it's not flowing that way," she said, pointing to the north.

"What?" Amy and I said in unison, confused.

"The river is flowing the other way," Diane said, gesturing to the south. Amy and I looked at each other. There was no way we had gotten completely turned around. Even with a supposedly broken compass, the topography wouldn't allow it. We hadn't gone uphill, just downhill. It seemed like Diane had suddenly, without warning, gone nuts. "Diane," I tried a reassuring voice. "We just need to be close enough to hear the river. We don't have to be right next to it." I spoke calmly, patiently.

"But you said the compass is broken and we need to follow the river," she argued.

"Yes, I know. But it's too loud next to the river. If we follow it from up here, we'll be okay," I replied. "Do you think we can hear it if we go north from there?" I asked, pointing to the top of the slope we were perched on. Diane thought for a minute, then nodded reluctantly and started up the hill. As we turned to crawl back up the hill, I caught Amy's eye. She and I exchanged words without speaking. *What the hell was that?*

It was rough going in the woods, up and down hills, through feeder streams in ravines, under and over mazes of downed trees. We walked directly through streams, not bothering to step on rocks, and clawed our way up embankments on the other side. We were already wet, already sweaty, and plenty warm enough. The trees were close together, prefer-ring the familiar company of others. *How do moose move through here without getting their antlers caught up in the trees?* Branches groped at my legs, scratching and picking at my skin through the thin nylon. *I wonder if there's one out there looking at me? Probably not. I'd smell them if they were.* Countless times, I walked between trees with my arms up, protecting my face with my forearms, only to emerge on the other side with tiny drops of blood oozing from new scratches. Cobwebs made lines on my eyeglasses and pulled at the skin on my face. Periodically, we took breaks so I could check the map and take a compass reading.

"I really hope Dave doesn't call search and rescue," Amy said, between puffs of her cigarette. I thought about that too. "Yeah, I hope Paul doesn't call either. Does Dave know what trail we're on? I didn't tell Paul which trail," I said, looking to the side to shine light in front of Amy.

"No, I didn't tell him what mountain we were going up," she replied.

"I hope no one calls search and rescue. That would be so embarrassing. We're not lost, we're just . . ."

"Delayed." Diane finished my sentence.

"Right on. We're delayed," I said, smiling.

After several hours of scratches and slopes, my good cheer vanished. Overwhelmed, tired and thirsty, I broke down crying.

"Rebecca, what's wrong?" Diane was by my side, her sanity back.

"I'm so sorry. I'm sorry," I cried.

"What for? Why are you sorry?" Amy was next to me too. "I'm sorry I got us in this mess. I'm sorry we ended up here. This hike was my idea." Head in my hands, I was spent. I felt like an incompetent fool.

"Well, it was my idea to take this trail," countered Diane. We sat in a gully, surrounded by boulders, and talked. We worried out loud how our families would be concerned about us, how they were probably calling the rangers or state police by now. We all hoped, as we did earlier, that they wouldn't call search and rescue. That would be embarrassing. We were, after all, just delayed. The idea of camping out was brought up again, except we all needed to be at work in a few hours, and we had no cell service to call our jobs or families. My mind became busy again. *Sure, let's camp out. Then in an hour or two, we'll hear this loud noise, then see headlights and realize we camped ten feet from the Kanc, and had no idea because we couldn't see it. Won't we feel like idiots then?* We kept on walking.

The terrain had flattened out, though the trees were still scratching and poking. I had long ago run out of water, but I didn't want to deal with trying to get more. While walking in resigned silence, I looked up and saw a mirage, a weirdly reflective, linear object floating about three feet off the ground at the far end of my light. I stopped, puzzled. Amy and Diane bumped into me.

"What?" they asked in unison.

I stared at the floating thing, cocking my head from left to right to shine my light on it at different angles. *What the hell is this?* Then, slowly, like trying to swim across a lake full of nearly frozen maple syrup, I realized what it was.

"The road!" I yelled and ran forward. I have never been so happy to see asphalt. We hugged each other on the road, happy, tired, joyful and relieved. Now we just needed to walk back to the car. No sweat, considering what we had just bushwhacked through. We saw the headlights coming at us, and before I had time to react, Diane instinctively stuck out her thumb. The car pulled over. If it had been up to me, I'd have walked back to the car. Enough living on the edge for one day, thank you. The SUV pulled over and Diane went to the window. She talked with the driver while Amy and I hung back, timid. We climbed into the back seat, squished together, with our heavy packs balanced on our legs, profusely thanked the driver and

CLIFF NOTE It is risky to descend by an unfamiliar route, especially when the new route involves many river crossings in a season of high water. Know your routes and options very well. When mountain snow melts, challenging brook crossings can become hazardous. Many backcountry river crossings are not bridged, requiring care to cross safely even at low water levels. With the extra flow from snowmelt, plus more water from spring rains, some crossings may become difficult or impossible to negotiate safely. In this situation, with multiple crossings of the same brook, bushwhacking to avoid crossings can be a good idea.

It certainly was when we and our friends Wanda and Marty hiked to North and South Twin Mountains, on a trail that crossed the Little River three times. The day began with beautiful weather. Hours later, we descended to find the Little River was not as small as it had been earlier. There was a thunderstorm right over us as we crossed to the east bank. The AMC *White Mountain Guide* notes that the remaining two crossings are the more dangerous ones in high water, and that they can be avoided by staying on the east bank. We took that advice, bushwhacking in a downpour—complete with lightning and deafening thunder—while the storm continued most of the 1.9 miles back to the trailhead. It is good to know your options.

the woman in the passenger seat and apologized to the dog who's comfy bed we disturbed by sitting in it. It took a few minutes to drive to the car. The driver looked at us in the rearview mirror.

"I'm glad I stopped for you guys," she said. "You never know what kind of people are out on this stretch of road at this time of night."

I am incredibly thankful for the kindness of strangers.

Several days later, I found Diane's compass tucked into my boot. When unpacking the car in my driveway on Monday morning, someone must have slipped it into my boot instead of hers. I e-mailed her and she told me to just throw it out, since it was broken. Even in the middle of the woods and the middle of the crisis, I knew it was impossible to have a broken compass. I knew it was just my perception in the woods that had been off. I took her compass, lined it up with mine and it worked, just like I thought it would. Both needles pointed to exactly the same north, then swung around in unison as I twirled in a circle. Yep. Not broken.

LEONARD H. GRUBBS

A Bridge to Safety?

After a full week of mild weather and rain in February, our long-scheduled hike involved crossing a significant river. Ordinarily, midwinter is the best time to schedule this hike, because the river is frozen enough to find good crossings. Today, though, we decided to attempt the crossing a mile upstream, where the river was narrower, and we found an ice bridge that held. The hike involved an extensive bushwhack on the other side, but we reached the summit at a relatively early hour with several strong trail-breakers, so we decided that we would bushwhack to a second nearby peak. It was a great decision, taking only one hour.

We could now retrace, climbing some 400 feet back up the first peak, then down the other side on our broken trail to the safe crossing; or we could descend from the second peak, proceeding more directly down while also avoiding the re-climb. We opted for the latter, hoping that another safe crossing would be found a mile downstream, even though we had been pessimistic about it originally. We set our compasses and, after some time, realized with chagrin that we were descending into the wrong valley, a route that would push our crossing even farther downstream. Again, hope triumphed over reason and we elected not to retrace our steps, thereby avoiding another ascent and additional miles.

We reached the river at five o'clock; all we saw was open water. It was zero degrees and night was imminent. A scouting party finally found a small ice crossing and the hike leader carefully walked out about 10 feet. With a loud crack, the ice suddenly broke and he fell in up to his chest, with his snow-shoes and ice ax. He somehow managed to find strong enough ice, rolled onto it, and got back to shore, but now hypothermia and frostbite were rearing their ugly heads. He quickly stripped off all his clothes in the frigid air and changed into dry ones, while another brave person tested some ice nearby, locating a safe crossing just as dark was becoming complete.

The first part of our substantial bushwhack back to civilization required us to hike a mile back up the river. We stopped periodically to put the leader's cold feet onto bare bodies, warming them up enough to evade frostbite.

It was difficult for everyone to tarry in the subzero temperatures, where not moving meant quick loss of body heat and painfully cold extremities. The bushwhack away from the river in the pitch-dark was onerous, involving route-finding and slow going over much snow-covered blowdown and thick forest. On the river bottom rests a good ice ax, and in the minds of several hikers is lodged a lesson about winter thaws.

CAROL STONE WHITE

AND DAVID SCOTT WHITE

Icy Passage through Iroquois Pass

During an extended January thaw, we decided to climb our first remote, trailless peak: 4,360-foot Mount Marshall, named after Wilderness Society co-founder Bob Marshall. It seemed like a good idea to do this long bushwhack trip in relatively warm weather, and we checked out what the mountains would be like in such conditions by climbing over Big Slide Mountain to the Johns Brook valley. There wasn't much standing water, even in the notoriously muddy spots; brooks were fast, but not flooded. So off we went in a murky 50 degrees for our 14-mile round-trip to Mount Marshall. The first tributary rushing down to Indian Pass Brook was high, but it was possible to cross on rocks; the second tributary had rapids and was swollen over its banks. We scouted up the steep bank for a possible crossing and saw two young men descending.

"We're packin' out today," they reported. "Conditions are bad! There's blowdown upstream."

We hiked up to look at the possible crossing: a big log all the way across. We shimmied over; it was doable, but the rushing water, roaring just inches below our boots, was unnerving. From the high-water trail, we decided to bushwhack the south face of Iroquois Peak rather than lose ascent to the soggy lowlands to reach the Iroquois Pass Trail. We hoped to intersect the trail well before the pass. Blowdowns and snow-buried stunted evergreens caused us to posthole up to our knees in soft snow. When the mountainside steepened, becoming nearly vertical below us, we were forced to climb and clamber around great rock outcrops to find more level terrain, where staying upright would be possible as we slabbed the steep slope. We searched for any passage through claustrophobic forest, where heavy hunks of snow plopped repeatedly onto our heads from evergreen branches, seeping into our hoods and melting down our necks. After Dave jumped off a huge fallen tree into deep snow, I sat resting and wondered, *Is this the turnaround spot? We won't get to Marshall and back in these conditions, and we don't dare return through this trackless forest in the dark.* But a brief review of what retreat meant persuaded us to continue. The trail could not be far ahead, and on the other side of Iroquois Pass was the Interior Outpost down at Lake Colden, where a ranger is available. From the pass it would be 7 miles back, down a steep 1,000 feet to Lake Colden, then over the Honey-I-shrunk the-kids-size boulders lining Avalanche Lake.

Finally Dave yelled, "We're on the trail! But it's good news and bad news—it's under a foot of water." *So what?* Our bodies and feet were already soaked with sweat and melt, it was reasonably warm, and we were generating tremendous heat. *Just plow through it and get down.* But after slipping off a submerged rock into knee-deep slush, I realized with a sinking heart that our progress would be slow. We'd have to struggle to keep our balance and not topple into the icy slush. Now I was frightened. The thick evergreen forest surrounding the trail would be hard to walk through with snowshoes, so we continued carefully through the water, unable to see our feet. Occasionally we stumbled off something and went into the icy water up to our hips. Our progress was glacial—we couldn't risk falling in altogether! At some point I realized that I couldn't feel my feet and jumped out of the water, fighting off panic. *Now we've gotten ourselves into real trouble.* Thoughts of permanent consequences raced through my mind—even survival itself. *We'll have to bushwhack 1,000 feet down to Lake Colden; it will get dark; we'll reach the top of an icy cliff that cannot be descended and we'll search through impenetrable forest for a way down, postholing and breaking an ankle—*

"We've got to eat something." Dave slung his heavy pack through balsam branches to the ground. *We have only two and a half hours more of daylight,* I thought. But not eating or drinking enough would be a mistake; we could get exhausted, dehydrated, and unwittingly become hypothermic. I can still remember that lunch; it was hard to choke down a sandwich with a churning stomach. After a few minutes, though, I began feeling my feet again! We realized with tremendous relief that the temperature was high enough to keep our feet warm—if we stayed out of the slush. *Okay! It might take hours, but we can get out of here in one piece.* We got moving again, trying in vain not to fall off the slippery, water-covered wooden planks which appeared farther along the pass. Soon the trail veered down to the left and—the deep slush was gone! The brook crossings on the descent were manageable. We made it to the Interior Outpost by 3:15, and the ranger let us in to finish our lunch.

"I'm beginning to wonder whether having the Winter 46 as a goal is a good idea," I ventured. "People can get into real trouble."

"I think climbing these peaks is more dangerous in other seasons!" he said. "People think it's hot and don't know that the summit of Marcy can be cold and windy in *any* season and that torrential rainstorms blow in quickly on the nicest days. They climb unprepared for cold and wet, hiking in cotton that can make you hypothermic in those conditions, with little extra gear; they don't know that it takes hours even to descend and they don't bring flashlights for each person, if any! They don't bring enough water or food. At least in winter, people know that they have to bring gear for all contingencies."

Just three months earlier, Dave and I had been helicoptered to this Interior Outpost to search for a psychiatrist from Ithaca who vanished after hiking into the High Peaks. With a former Marine and a ranger, we grabbed our gear, jumped off the helicopter, and each chose one of the dozen bare beds. We received a briefing on the search strategy; first, we would explore drainages and cliffs west of Lake Colden. We studied a map of drainages from the MacIntyre Range, our next assignment, and suggested a search down to Shepherd's Tooth, south of Iroquois Peak. Another search group would explore the Iroquois Pass area; years ago a plane had crashed in trackless forest between the pass and Mount Marshall—this place might have been of interest to the missing hiker.

The rangers cooked a pasta dinner and we all climbed into sleeping bags. The next morning we headed up one of the steepest trails in the Adirondacks, from Lake Colden to the south base of Algonquin Peak in the MacIntyre Range. Balsam and spruce were so thick off the ridge that it was difficult to imagine a hiker choosing to descend by bushwhacking, but we remembered the sudden cold that blew in two weeks ago, when this man disappeared; he might have wanted to get out of the wind, then twisted an ankle in the undergrowth. We fanned out and bushwhacked steeply down, calling his name constantly. Hours later, scratched and filthy, we arrived at the outpost with no news. The search continued for many more days and ended with one slight clue—some hikers had talked to a lone man near Scott Clearing—but the missing psychiatrist was never found.

After finishing our lunch at the Interior Outpost and realizing that we still had 5.7 miles to go, we asked the ranger, "Is it safe to walk across Avalanche Lake after this long thaw?"

"I skied across a couple of days ago, but it would be safer now to go over the trail," he advised.

So, we'd have to take off our snowshoes and scramble down a 15-foot, possibly icy ladder, along with several other ladders over the gigantic boulders that are scattered for half a mile along Avalanche Lake. When we first began hiking, we had worn jeans on a trek up to this lake on a warm April day. Five miles later, at an elevation of 3,000 feet, we found that we had hiked back into winter. We met a man and his teenage daughter who told us they were camping nearby and had just descended from Mount Marcy.

"It's my favorite time to camp," the man said. Looking Dave over, he added, "If you fall in this lake, you're a dead man."

"What?"

"Don't wear cotton in the winter. It stays wet and cold and you'll freeze before you can get back. Wool stays warm."

Avalanche Lake.
Photo by David White

I think of this episode as we start out in our *wool* from the Interior Outpost to Avalanche Lake. Lesson learned. The climb to the lake brings us to a boardwalk nailed to the cliff of Avalanche Mountain. Below, the unfrozen edges of the lake lap at the vertical rock. We carefully test the boardwalk, taking extra care on slippery wood; when wet, wood can be at least as slippery as rock is. Prior to these boardwalks being built, one had to wade through these sections. Nineteenth-century guides would carry their parties piggyback. One brave young woman, Matilda, was wearing a long skirt that was precariously close to the water. "Hitch up, Matilda!" her companion said, and that became the name of these boardwalks.

Across the lake from this spot, you get a closer look at the Trap Dike, a deep cleft caused by the differential erosion of the gabbro rock intruded into the anorthosite granite. Some hikers ascend this very steep place, then crawl onto the open slide near the summit, a dangerous route. One woman climbed a long way up, then panicked after looking down; she couldn't bring herself to go up or down and had to be helicoptered out. Some people even climb the Trap Dike in winter; more than one have fallen to their deaths. In September 2011, a college student was leading a group of seven on an ascent of the Trap Dike, in rainy weather. He was helping two others at a precipitous place when he lost his footing and fell 25 feet, dying almost instantly from a head injury.

Once past Avalanche Lake, we climbed to Avalanche Pass, an awesome area winding through rock cliffs, where we again found the trail completely under water. Water must collect in passes! Sloshing through, we still had 3.7 more miles and 900 vertical feet to descend to the trailhead, which we reached well after dark, weary and a bit wiser.

As a splurge for our thirtieth anniversary, we stayed in a Lake Placid motel with a hot tub. In January, we were able to walk comfortably across the parking lot in bathing suits.

MARTA BOLTON QUILLIAM

A Nice Day Becomes an Ice Day

After hiking 7.5 miles to Uphill Lean-to, we split up with two of the guys; they want to climb Cliff Mountain. Our bushwhack with snowshoes up 4,606-foot Mount Redfield, the second-highest trailless peak in the Adirondacks, is difficult, through thick trees, so we opt to ascend via frozen Uphill Brook as far as we can. I am now in the lead, breaking trail up the snow-covered brook and trying to be cautious. We come upon a frozen waterfall, hidden underneath snow, looking like nothing more hazardous than a steep climb. I get to its base and suddenly—*crack, snapple, pop*—I'm floating on a sheet of ice. Tom reaches out to grab me but somehow I slide off and go down into the freezing water. I'm now up to my waist in water, not even touching bottom, screaming for help, in danger of going under the ice and drowning or—at the very least—getting completely soaked on this very cold day.

Tom tries to pull me out, but only gets a grip on my coat. This keeps me from going in any deeper. He is worried that the ice might break under him, as well, if he gets any closer. Mike and Joe snowshoe down the steep bank to help; by distributing their weight to get better leverage, the three men are finally able to pull me out and back onto firm ice—it takes *all* of them to rescue me from the icy waters. We bushwhack up the bank, find a clearing, get dry socks on my feet, then put plastic bags over them before putting my boots back on. I don't want to ruin this hike for the others and urge us to continue. The men keep asking me how I'm doing. Because I desperately want to push ahead, I say that I'm okay and hope for the best. But within 10 minutes, my feet are feeling like two iceboxes. I cry silently to myself—my feet are so frozen—and I worry. Finally I have to admit that it isn't working—the fresh socks are already wet and the boots are very cold. We turn around and descend to Uphill Lean-to as quickly as possible.

I lie down in the lean-to while Tom and Joe remove my frozen snowshoes, boots, and wet-again socks, put me in a space blanket, then rest my frozen feet under their jackets on their bare chests. Mike gathers wood for a fire. It takes 20 minutes before my feet feel better, but meanwhile my body temperature is dropping from inactivity, increasing the danger of both frostbite and hypothermia. I go into a shiver even though I'm wrapped in the space blanket to preserve body heat. Before Mike can get a fire going, we all agree that I have to get moving to increase my circulation. The men put dry socks on my feet—our only concern is to get out the 7.5 miles as quickly as possible. Luckily I run into a friend at Marcy Dam; I don't hesitate to ask for dry socks, which she has. I feel like the Dry Wool Socks Thief.

Now I always carry more pairs of wool socks with me—another lesson of winter hiking. I received mild frostbite to my toes.

CLIFF NOTE Tony Goodwin writes in *Guide to Adirondack Trails: High Peaks Region,* "It is imperative that persons travel in groups of not less than four and be outfitted properly when winter conditions prevail." Climbing the high peaks in winter requires a team effort in most cases—for breaking trail, climbing cliffs, sharing advice, ensuring safety, and keeping spirits high. Strong friendships are forged in these shared experiences. For example, consider this bizarre incident: while camping with a large group, Jo and Cindie pitched their tent in what looked like a snow-covered meadow—but was actually the snow- and ice-covered Opalescent River. When Jo left the tent to answer the call of nature, her headlamp conked out and she fell through the ice up to her waist. Cindie heard a faint call and struggled out of her sleeping bag. She found Jo, helped her back to the tent, then stripped the clothes off Jo's lobster-red body. The two friends didn't sleep much after that, imagining their tent breaking through the ice.

Addendum

When your editor received Marta's story for *Women with Altitude: Challenging the Adirondack High Peaks in Winter,* I realized with a chill that Marta's accident happened on the day before my husband and I had climbed the same Uphill Brook. We asked ourselves: *Was that brook ice weakened? Could Dave, alone, have gotten me out of that water if I had broken through? Or I, him? Without both of us falling in?* A situation like that—many miles into the wilderness, on a trailless peak—could have been deadly. Dave and I had camped 5.7 miles from the trailhead at Lake Colden to climb Mount Redfield. The blistering cold of that weekend might have saved our lives because it froze Uphill Brook solid (perhaps).

Just eight days previously, while climbing in the three-peak Seward Range, Dave had jumped several feet off a small frozen waterfall on Calkins Brook and encountered only several layers of ice at its base. Because of this experience, we'd mistakenly assumed that the brooks were solidly frozen in midwinter, as the high lakes were. (The week before, when we'd climbed nearby Seymour Mountain, the temperature had been –20 degrees, surely freezing all water in the High Peaks solid!)

We ascended Uphill Brook, knowing nothing about Marta's accident, and saw no hole in the ice as we approached the frozen waterfall. Could the hole created by her struggle—which must have been relatively large—completely refrozen? Perhaps, but running brook water doesn't refreeze as quickly as lake water does.

Another person, on another day, learned that lesson when he broke through the ice at this same spot. The stream level had dropped during a hard freeze, leaving two thin layers of ice, with air space between them, and an open pool below. He went in above his knees but did not touch bottom. He knew that he could be forced under the ice, and that he needed to spread his weight over a greater area to get out. He threw his pack as far as he could, holding on to its straps; though snowshoes hindered his mobility and he couldn't easily lift out either foot, he lined up his snowshoes, shifted his weight to the pack, and somehow propelled himself up and out. This waterfall should be well known by now: three people fell in there one December 21. Perhaps the brook had not frozen sufficiently, or maybe the ten people in that party had weakened the ice (when Dave fell through Panther Brook the following month, four people had crossed before him).

Climbing unscathed out of Uphill Brook, the day after Marta's frightening submersion, we saw snowshoe tracks that soon stopped and wondered why. We continued up Redfield, with Dave breaking trail in knee-deep powder, often becoming mired in spruce traps up to his chest. In spite of the rigor of this ascent, he was glad to reach the summit. When he finally found the elusive canister—a can attached above shoulder height on a summit tree—it was level with the snow.[17] From the journal inside, he discovered that no one had reached the summit since Wayne Ratowski, a hiking legend, on January 2.

CAROL STONE WHITE
AND DAVID SCOTT WHITE

Frostbite!

We had one more weekend to complete our climbs of the Winter 46. This would require hiking three peaks in the Santanoni Range and two mountains in the Dix Range. Whether we finished or not would depend on the weather—we thought.

On March 15 we hauled our gear-laden sleds along an icy road for a mile, reaching a narrow bridge, open on one side. This plank was piled with hard snow and our sleds threatened to slide off into the river. On the other side, we were greeted by a tall, ice-encased ladder. Dave clutched a heavy sled under one arm, gripped the slippery railing with his free hand, and ascended the narrow steps in his large snowshoes. I tried not to think about getting back down on our way out.

We were heading for a lean-to, 4.6 miles and 1,200 feet up a trail pocked with countless thawed and refrozen postholes. Slushy drainages tipped over our sleds, our bungee-corded gear sometimes pitching off into half-frozen mud. After setting up our tent and changing out of sweaty clothes, we met three friends for dinner at their snow kitchen. The next morning, a fourth friend joined us. Ascending Panther Brook was magical: the waterfalls that plunged from high cliffs into the creek bed had become solidly frozen icefalls, shining in the rising sun. Shadows of great conifers created art along the eerily silent, ice-covered brook. It was a real treat to experience this route on ice. A spectacular day!

As we climbed the frozen cascades, I heard a shout from John. "Dave has fallen through the ice!"

When I reached the scene, John was saying, "Get those boots off and change your socks." Dave had been in the icy water up to his knees and it had taken some time to haul himself out.

"I've got bread bags," Dick offered. (Dry socks don't help if you put your feet back into wet boots.) But Dave doesn't want to lose time by changing socks.

"If I hike fast, I'll be okay," Dave replied, unperturbed. "That'll keep

Carol White ascending Panther Brook on Santanoni Peak.
Photo by David White

my feet warm and it's supposed to warm up some anyway. I don't want to stop now."

Since urging him to change was of no avail, we left the brook and began bushwhacking through thick forest. I saw Dave later on the summit of 4,607-foot Santanoni Peak, the second-highest trailless mountain in the Adirondack High Peaks. The warming weather had not materialized—it was 8 degrees Fahrenheit and a fearsome wind made for a subzero wind-chill. Still, we lingered on this beautiful summit. Because the stunted trees were totally buried with snow, it was like being on an open peak. Then we took the long ridge to Couchsachraga Peak, a 3-hour round-trip. Couchie's tree-covered summit, also buried under many feet of sparkling snow, of-fered 360-degree views as well. Dan Barski, who wrote "Agony and Ecstasy: The Dixes in Winter" for *Adirondac* magazine, was also there. I told him that, after Panther Peak, Dix and Hough would be our only remaining win-ter climbs, and asked if he had any advice. Dan talked about a harrowing adventure, backpacking 3,200 feet up Dix with a bad cold, and described how he had dropped off the Beckhorn toward Hough and nearly got swal-lowed by spruce holes, forcing retreat.

By three o'clock we're on Panther, blown away by awesome views, not fearsome wind. Descending the range, we exited Panther Brook early to avoid breaking through again. Dave's feet felt fine—though, in retrospect, he thinks perhaps they were numb. We decided to break camp and descend. Because it was completely dark when we reached the large vertical ladder, Dave kicked steps into the steep snowbank and backed down, carrying each sled. The snow on the road had melted. "Let's leave the sleds here—I'll drive in," Dave said, leaving me behind. Hiking alone, I noted some icy sections and imagined being unable to drive up these pitches.

Dave was worried that if we drove fast enough to make it up some icy sections, we might get mired in a snowbank.

He had also started noticing his feet—they hurt now, as if the tops of all his toes had blisters. Hurrying, he fell several times on the ice. He tried to remove his boots at the car, but he could not get them off. *I'll take them off after they warm up*, he thought, but they were frozen onto his feet.

"It's late, why don't we grab some fast food?" I suggested.

"I'm in the mood for a big dinner!" Dave enthused. "Let's go to a good restaurant after we clean up." After a freeze-dried dinner last night—and peanut butter and jelly sandwiches with ice water today—I too was ready to eat vast quantities of hot food.

At Dun Roamin Motel, Dave tried again to remove his boots, then went into the bathroom for many minutes. (Later he would tell a reporter, "I tried to take my boot off and it was frozen to my foot. I didn't tell Carol what was happening at first. I finally got it loose and there was ice at the end of my sock.")

"It's late—should I bring in something?" I suggested through the door.

"Yes, go out and get something."

Now I was nervous. He had been in there a long time—and why didn't he want to go out anymore?

"Are you okay?" I asked.

"I don't think so."

I drove to Schroon Lake and found hot subs. Dave was in bed when I returned. I sat on the other bed, wolfing down a sandwich. His remained uneaten.

"Don't you want your sub?"

"Nope—I really just want to go to sleep," he said quietly.

To complete the Winter 46, hikers must reach the summits in calendar winter. We had three more days. "Can we do Dix and Hough tomorrow?"

CLIFF NOTE In freezing weather, cold wet feet cannot be kept warm by hiking fast. If your feet get wet, place plastic bags over dry wool socks before putting your boots back on. At the first sign of numbness, attend to your feet and change socks again. (If your toes are painfully cold, that can be useful information—at least you still have some circulation.) Getting wet feet can result in frostbite that affects deeper layers of tissue. Deep frostbite can even freeze muscle and bone, requiring professional treatment and care. Although healing can be complete, the affected area can be susceptible to recurrence. Dave and Carol finished the Adirondack Winter 46 the next year, and climbed the forty-eight highest White Mountain peaks in winter as well. Dave's big toes become calloused and white at their tips during winter.

"We're not going to finish this year—I've got frostbite."

Dave had brought loose-fitting Sorels, luckily. He was already wearing them when I woke up. "I'm going to pay for these bloody sheets," he frowned. "I doubt they're cleanable." He wouldn't let me see his feet.

"We've got to find a doctor!" I said, very alarmed.

After we explained the bloody sheets to the motel owner, he said, "We'll get 'em clean, that's all right—there's not much we can't get cleaned up!"

We drove home and Dave saw a doctor the next morning. "He says I have good circulation and will be okay!" But he wouldn't let me see his feet for another two weeks.

Then, one night, he let me watch him pull off his socks. His toes all looked like black cracked plastic, a bodily injury so horrifying that I didn't even think of taking a picture, though I should have. Three weeks later, we were manning the winter information table at an Adirondack Mountain Club open house. Dave was wearing the loose-fitting Sorels. When women with children came by, he asked if they would like to see his feet. After an awed silence, a mother would often say, "Listen to me when I say to come in!"

PART V

Animal and Avian Behavior

In the northeastern United States, large mammals
are seldom aggressive or hostile toward humans.
My husband and I have had extensive personal
experience with both moose and bear on the trails.
Threatening episodes, like the one described in "On
the Horns of a Dilemma," are extremely rare. We have
heard, however, that moose can be testy during the
fall rut, and it is true that black bears have learned to
bluff charge to get hikers' food. Caution around wild
animals is always essential, of course, and female
bears with cubs can be especially unpredictable.

JOHN HARTFORD

On the Horns of a Dilemma

Marcia and I had been planning to climb the Bonds, but the forecast for the higher summits predicted an approaching warm front, with winds increasing to the 75–90 mph range. Since the Bonds have substantial exposure above tree line, we decided on 4,260-foot Zealand Mountain, which is mostly beneath tree line. This hike is one of the most grueling of the forty-eight White Mountain 4,000-footers, as the easy road access of summer is replaced by a 19-mile marathon in winter. When we reached the trailhead at 6:30 a.m., the temperature was –8 degrees Fahrenheit. By the end of our hike, the temperature would be 41 degrees, the greatest temperature swing that I've experienced in a single day.[18]

We were soon moving quickly on the Zealand trail, feeling good. We started seeing moose tracks, not an uncommon sight, and soon came across some moose scat. Marcia was leading and we were both keeping an eye to the woods, in hopes of catching a glimpse of the great creature. We had both seen one in the distance, on a hike of Mount Carrigain two years before, but that was our only previous sighting. Then, as Marcia turned a corner, we came face to face with a big bull moose. He was standing right on the trail. We stood dead still, then quietly dug out our cameras for a once-in-a-lifetime shot. After taking several pictures, we were ready to move on. I told Marcia to go ahead and shoo the beast away.

But he didn't shoo. What do you do when your path is blocked by a 1,200-pound moose? I must admit that I didn't know. We tried yelling, "Shoo, moose!" We waved our poles and generally acted like primates. No effect at all. This standoff lasted about 20 minutes. The trail was packed down and very easy to walk on; the moose had no intention of leaving it. We thought of bushwhacking our way around the moose but this was a tricky option. Stepping into the deep snow, just off the trail, meant we would sink down 3 or 4 feet, even in our snowshoes. If the moose came at us in that deep snow, we'd be in trouble. We discussed climbing the trees just off the trail, should we need to. As the moose was not giving ground, we could see few options.

My husband David and I have encountered moose on the trails several times. Our presence doesn't usually alarm them, unlike most other denizens of the forest who move away when approached. Moose look at us, aware of our human presence, but unafraid. In September, on Maine's North Brother Mountain, we saw a moose ahead of us on the trail; it remained there for many minutes, not moving until Dave exclaimed loudly, "There's some really tasty morsels off the trail!" One December we passed a moose on our ascent to Cabot Mountain in New Hampshire. On our descent we passed it again; it had hardly moved. We saw another moose in Cape Breton one May—this animal was on the trail near a mountaintop. It moved slowly off the trail, but not far, then stood looking at us.

"Let's put on our snowshoes," I said. The packed trail was about 2 feet wide, and we had to crouch down to put on our shoes. As my back was to the moose, I asked Marcia to keep an eye on him.

"I'd turn around if I were you," she said.

I had one snowshoe on when the moose suddenly charged. "Climb the tree!" I shouted. Before I knew what was what, I was halfway up a pine tree, with one snowshoe dangling, while Marcia was up another. The moose stopped a few yards from us, which gave me time to climb a bit higher and disentangle my snowshoe.

There we were: treed. We looked at each other and broke into laughter at the absurdity of our predicament. But the moose was not going anywhere. We had both left our packs on the trail and Marcia had no gloves on, as she had taken them off to attach her snowshoes. The temperature was still about zero and we had been lightly dressed for hiking, which generates warmth. Unable to move in our pine trees, we were getting cold. After about 10 minutes, I slowly descended the tree and crept toward my pack, ready to race back up the tree if the moose made any movement. I got some extra gloves out and handed them to Marcia, then returned to my perch.

After being treed for about 45 minutes we heard voices coming up the trail. "Hey guys," we yelled, "watch out! There's an angry moose on the trail. You might want to find a tree." In record time they dropped their packs on the trail and climbed trees. The situation was becoming funnier and funnier. The moose now had four of us treed. Marcia sensed that the moose wanted to pass us but was wary of our packs, which were directly on the trail. I felt she had read the situation correctly. So once again I descended and, ever so gingerly, dragged the packs off the trail before returning to my tree.

The moose passed directly below Marcia and me, looking up and eye-balling us. What must he have been thinking? The moose was now between us and the other treed hikers, who were about 30 feet down the trail. Now it seemed that their packs were holding up the moose. Marcia called out, "Can you move your packs off the trail?" The answer came back: "Yes, I think so, but I don't know if I want to get out of the tree." Those were the last words we would hear from them.

It was time to make a move. We were cold and I was getting frustrated. The moose was behind us, if only by a few yards, but the trail ahead was clear. Again, I crept down, readying our packs for a fast departure. When the snowshoes were attached, Marcia descended. We quickly put on our packs and headed up the trail. "Good luck, guys!" I called to the treed hikers, and off we went at a very fast pace toward Zealand. The trail becomes very steep and passes over two false summits. It's a tough climb.

The return hike was long and tiring. When we reached the point of our moose encounter, we took a picture of the area. We told our story when we got to the hut. There were thirty-six people staying there that night and we knew what one topic of conversation was going to be.

Marcia had a problem with her sock that resulted in a blistered big toe. I only found about it because she started hiking slower than I, which doesn't usually happen. I sensed something was wrong and asked if her feet were all right. She didn't lie. She made it out with a bad toe by sheer guts and determination, never complaining. Nineteen miles is a long way to hike in the winter and we were truly spent when we reached the car. We had been hiking nonstop for 12 hours, except for a 10-minute rest at the hut and, of course, that 1-hour break up a tree.

Not long after that day, an official yellow sign was posted, saying loudly, in large letters:

WARNING—HIKERS/SKIERS
An aggressive bull moose is in the area
and has repeatedly charged hikers on the Zealand Falls Trail.

Beware Bear Appetites

Before bear canisters were invented, an experienced backpacker was camping in a lean-to near a trash dump. Unaccountably, he had neglected to bring a rope to hang his food bag. This might have been a good reason to make it a day trip but, having backpacked a long way in, he just hung the bag from a rafter and nervously went to sleep. In the night our friend was startled by a noise. He turned on his flashlight and saw that his food bag was gone; then his light revealed a large black bear in the gloom. He quickly hid in his sleeping bag. Rain was pounding loudly on the lean-to roof, so he couldn't hear what the bear was doing. Unable to return to sleep, he sweated in his bag for what seemed like a long time. When he finally peeked out, the bear was *in* the lean-to. "The last sound I heard before fainting," he said, "was the bear sniffing my sleeping bag!"

The Northeastern black bear is not usually aggressive, as the grizzly or brown bear in the West can be, but they are always hungry. Although they have an omnivorous appetite, they won't touch humans, as strange as this might seem. At popular camping sites, however, they do lose their fear of humans, and can learn to bluff charge to scare campers away from food. The chief thing for campers to know is how to deal with their food. For example, you can rent or purchase a bear canister that will accommodate enough freeze-dried, ultra-packable food for five people over three days, including snacks. Never bring food—or any clothes that you've cooked in—into a tent or lean-to.

Be especially careful not to come between a mother bear and her cubs; the mother will be protective, so slowly back away. We have encountered bears with cubs on two occasions. The first time, we were bushwhacking down to a river, and startled a bear family that probably couldn't hear us approaching. The mother bear lunged away from the water and began whirling around. The two cubs raced quickly up a nearby tree, then the mother ran up the hill.

"Let's just keep moving," I muttered under my breath. We knew that a mother bear might attack if startled or provoked.

"I want to get a look at the cubs!" Dave whispered excitedly. "That circling was kind of ominous, though," he added. After passing the tree, he stopped to confirm that the big bear was still moving away. For a few apprehensive but amusing moments, we watched the cubs clinging to the high branches; one of them even inched a little bit higher. Then, in unison, they quickly climbed down and ran up the hill after mama.

The second time we encountered such a family, we were climbing silently on soft pine needles; again, mama and cubs did not sense that we were coming. Luckily, they were all on the same side of the trail. We stopped, then moved slowly away. As on the previous occasion, the cubs went up a tree and the mother ran off.

We've been told that black bears are shortsighted. If you feel threatened, stand tall and look big. A provoked bear will chomp its jaws and exude a low woofing, growling sound. They have sensitive hearing and a whistle blast might send one scurrying away. Do not panic and run—black bears can run 25 mph, though not for a long distance, and they are excellent climbers. Just slowly back off.[19]

Black bear.
Photo by Paul Misko

Another hiker describes bushwhacking alone off a trailless mountain. Less than 100 yards away, she saw a tall black body standing and looking at her. Then two cute little black heads emerged above the underbrush. The cubs darted away in opposite directions, one only 30 feet from our hiker. The footing was difficult, with slippery, mossy rocks hidden under ferns and nettles. She was forced to move very slowly—which she wanted to do anyway, to avoid alarming the bear. Luckily, this wild and wonderful bear family vanished into the shadows.

Once, when we were measuring trails with a surveying wheel, we hiked into a remote area with grassy paths. Even though our footfalls were quieter than they might have been on rocky trails, we didn't expect to see wildlife because of our clanking wheel. To our surprise, we saw a large bear not far ahead of us. We stopped. The bear looked at us for a few seconds, then ran ahead on the trail we were measuring. We decided to wait a bit and then walk slowly, giving it plenty of space. But when the next junction came into view, the bear was standing there! We stopped again. It peered at us for some very long seconds, while our apprehension grew. The bear knew that we were here in its territory—why hadn't it run away, as black bears usually do? When food or cubs are not an issue, wild bears actively avoid humans. To our immense relief, this big bear finally turned and ran up the hill.

A bear encounter can be frightening to some people and interesting to others. You can learn to increase your chances of seeing a bear, or how to avoid them, depending on your preference. Bears typically know that you're there long before you see them, especially if you are part of a talkative group, and they usually make themselves scarce. To increase the odds of an encounter, try hiking solo, on less popular trails, with prolific berry patches, during midweek. Bears are nocturnal and avoid the heat of midday, so hike on cool, overcast, and breezy days. Bears are sexually active in June and thus less cautious at that time. In late summer and early fall, they want to eat a lot before winter. We know of no documented black bear attacks in the wild, but everyone maintains caution. Bears can be unpredictable, like any wild animal.

On a recent 4.5-mile solo hike up Bearpen Mountain—noted for both berry patches and bear encounters—I saw a large bear print in the mud and fresh bear scat with lots of berry seeds. I met a group at the summit who'd come up a different route; when they saw the print and scat while descending on my route, they couldn't believe I'd kept going. Another hiker on Bearpen described seeing a bear some distance ahead; it walked around the big mud puddles, just as we do. The bear stopped, sniffed, and peered toward our friend; it knew something was there. They looked at each other for some minutes. Finally our friend took a step in the bear's direction and it scampered away.

On a trip to Grandfather Mountain, near the Blue Ridge Parkway, Dave broke his ankle before the ascent began. He was scheduled to lead a hike on our return and, though the doctor wagged his finger and said "no hiking," Dave decided to do a 2-mile round-trip excursion to a quarry wearing his air cast, while I led his 9-mile hike on another mountain. A small bear ran across the trail 50 yards away from him; it's likely that a mother bear was nearby. Meanwhile, far up on the other mountain, a hiker reported excitedly, "There's a bear a hundred yards up the trail!" Our group didn't see that one—they do want to avoid humans—but Dave had led an earlier hike on that same trail when a bear crossed very near them. Bushwhacking up the east face of this peak, on a different hike, we arrived at a plateau at 3,000 feet where the only things missing were three beds and three bowls! Everywhere we saw evidence of bears: claw marks on beech trees, large overturned rocks where grubs are found, mud wallows, and fresh bear scat loaded with berry seeds. Our descent included many miles along an escarpment with waterfalls, where bears come to drink. When darkness fell, I knew that these nocturnal creatures roamed not far away in the forest.

Lake Colden and Marcy Dam, in the Adirondack High Peaks, are places where you will see black bears that have lost their fear of humans. Banging pots and pans can deter bold bruins who hang around such areas. A family with two young boys camped near Marcy Dam, in spite of having been assured that bears were regularly there. The family was advised to eat early and clean up their camp; bears had been charging people at dusk. And indeed, one sizable bear came to their campsite and sniffed their kitchen area, while another checked out their bear canister, some distance away. The family had already moved their cooking dishes off the site; after that first encounter, they removed anything remotely kitchen-related. The next day, after their hike, this family moved their entire camp, although the boys didn't want to. But sleep had evaded the mother almost completely—she could be just as protective of her offspring as her wild counterparts.

Big Thelma was a notoriously bold and resourceful bear who was known to cut peoples' weekends short, not fun when you have hiked far into the wilderness for mountain adventure. As we were setting up our tent after backpacking 8.3 miles to a remote lean-to, Big Thelma succeeded in stealing another man's food bag—even though he had hung it well, many feet up and away from trees. All his provisions for the weekend were gone.

Bears can be amazingly intelligent. One bear marked with yellow tags in the Adirondack High Peaks has even learned how to get into a BearVault canister (it is now being redesigned). Most bears fail to break into these canisters, even after clawing at them for up to an hour.

A friend of ours once hiked 5 miles up to Flowed Lands, near Lake Colden, with his girlfriend. While they were washing their dinner dishes with stream pebbles, a neighboring camper said, "My wife just saw a bear!" The next night, much grunting and snorting was heard when a bear got some young men's food bags, hung too low. One of them said, "I want to pet it!" (Even though cubs can be incredibly cute, you should never approach bears or attempt to feed them.) On our friend's last night at this campsite, he was awakened by rattling pots. The next morning, he found all of their food gone, and the stove too. But it was nice of the bear to leave the coffee.

LEONARD H. GRUBBS

Dog Days in the High Peaks

I take my dog Nigel, a shepherd-lab-chow mix, on some of my hikes. He is a big dog, weighing about 80 pounds, with long, black, bushy fur. He looks intimidating, but he has a good disposition and is very gentle. He loves to be outdoors in the winter. I select the hikes I take him on carefully to ensure that I do not put him in danger. For example, we don't hike the Presidential Range or the Franconia Range, with many peaks above tree line, because of their usually icy conditions and harsh weather. But Nigel went along when I did the Carters and Moriah, the Tripyramids and Hancocks, Twins, Galehead and Garfield, and Tecumseh. The minute we head up the trail, he quickly disappears from view, then soon comes bounding back—to make sure I am still following. He'll see me and then be off again; this scenario will be repeated throughout the day. He will also explore the woods beside the trail, sniffing objects where some scent attracts him. I've taken him on midweek hikes where we never cross paths with another individual the entire day. These hikes went without a hitch, but the gremlin of unforeseen consequences would strike.

One early January I took him to Liberty and Flume via the Liberty Springs Trail. When we reached the summit, a small rocky outcropping, I saw that there were patches of ice covering the rocks. I got the leash from my pack and put Nigel on it, to provide stability as we crossed the rocks. He appeared uncomfortable, but I coaxed him across. Once we passed the summit and began our descent toward Flume, I removed the leash and he resumed his normal activity, bounding down the trail and exploring. We arrived on Flume, rested a few minutes, then began retracing back to Liberty. When we were just below the summit of Liberty, Nigel was a few feet behind me. I took off my pack and took out the leash, planning to secure him for the summit crossing. When Nigel saw the leash, he turned and ran back down the trail toward Flume, quickly disappearing from sight. I called his name multiple times, but he did not return. I waited, calling to him for what seemed like an hour, but probably was 5 minutes, but he still did not return.

CLIFF NOTE Dogs can be very leery of some things in the mountains. For example, they typically do not like trail ladders. We once watched a man carry a large English sheepdog up a 15-foot ladder at Avalanche Lake. One 10-month-old Lab did not like ledges more than 2 feet high and had to be helped over them. On another occasion, at Johns Brook Lodge, a man who was expected for dinner never appeared. We learned later that his dog had refused to move. Although it might have been the rare case of a dog too tired to continue, perhaps it had been spooked by something and was too heavy to carry. No one knows what spooked Nigel. The lesson for dog owners: know the trail and remember that climbing ladders or mountains can require hands as well as feet. If your dog is too heavy to carry, be sure it can climb up and down steep places.

I shouldered my pack and headed back toward Flume, looking for him and calling his name all the while. I descended to the col between the two peaks without sighting him. I began to think that he had gone into the woods to circumvent Liberty and was descending on his own, back to the truck. I climbed back to Liberty, still calling his name. On my descent to the trailhead, I kept calling out to him, every minute or so, but he did not reappear. He was not at the truck when I returned, so it was a worried drive home. No one in the family slept well that night.

The next morning, at first light, I was on the trail, returning to Liberty. With my adrenaline pumping hard, I made it to the top of the ridge in record time! As I ascended the final short pitch to the summit, I loudly called to Nigel. A second later, I saw a large, black, furry creature coming full speed toward me. He almost knocked me over as he jumped on me with joy. I was as happy to see him as he was to see me. I fed him doggy treats as he wagged his tail and licked my gloved hand. At some point, Nigel must have returned to the summit of Liberty—the last place we had been together—and waited for me.

At home, on the night Nigel was out, my thermometer registered a low of –10 degrees Fahrenheit. On the summit of Liberty, it would have been 10 to 15 degrees colder. But Nigel was in good spirits and showed no adverse effects from his ordeal. Possibly his wolf ancestry provided him with the ability to survive such conditions. Since that event, he has gone on other winter hikes with me, but I have not taken him beyond his comfort level.

ALAN VIA

The Ravens of Bondcliff

When the Northeast 111 included only 111 peaks (it now lists 115), Bondcliff had not yet been promoted to the required 4,000-foot level, or perhaps it appeared too close to Mount Bond to qualify as a separate peak. Still, looking at it on a map and viewing its crags from the Bonds, I knew I had to climb it. We stayed in the Crawford Notch Hostel on Friday evening, then hiked Galehead, the Twins, and the Bonds over the weekend.

On Sunday, I decided on a solo excursion to Bondcliff, and was amazed to discover that I would have this peak to myself on a gorgeous summer day. Passing the Bond-Bondcliff col, I noticed a flock of ravens having fun around Bondcliff's summit. Moving closer, I sat in silence, watching these graceful flyers.

The birds would execute their stunts in pairs, flying right next to each other, belly to back, like avian Blue Angels. They would take off in pairs, dive, roll, and glide in tandem. Each pair would perform avian acrobatics for a few minutes, then land. Almost immediately, another pair would take to the air in a bird version of "we can top that!" I counted thirteen pairs of performers in all, with the rest of the flock joining me in watching some of the most acrobatic flying I've ever seen—bird or human! While these ravens were definitely aware of my presence, it didn't seem to inhibit them; some of their dives and rolls passed within a few feet of me. This acrobatic show went on for the better part of an hour and the ravens seemed to come up with ever more creative tricks.

That experience on Bondcliff is a memory that remains with me twenty-five years later.

PART VI

Odysseys
In Pursuit of the Possible

"Through my experiences I hope to inspire others to realize that anything is possible if you put your heart into it," writes Scott Rimm-Hewitt, author of the first account. Other odysseys follow, all demonstrating the intrepid human spirit.

SCOTT "TUBA MAN" RIMM-HEWITT

Hiking the Appalachian Trail with a Tuba

My bass tuba, named Charisma, took up 30 pounds of my 70-pound load. To save weight I didn't bring a tent or underwear, and carried only half of my music book. I wouldn't hike any other way; there's something about combining the arts and nature that inspires me. My trail name was "Super Scott the Tuba Man."

Maine

I decided to ditch the tuba pack and slack pack around the 5.2-mile Gulf Hagas loop, known as the "Grand Canyon of the East." I took off at lightning speed and saw many beautiful falls along the way, then went skinny-dipping with biodegradable soap. A nice family offered me some fresh water, but I said that I'd pump my own from the freshest streams of Maine. I had just helped a lady cross the small river to the Hagas Trail, when a sixty-year-old man tried to do it himself and slipped right into the water. He seemed to twist his leg pretty bad so I quickly went to his aid. I started pulling at his arm, but he was heavy and pulled right back. He pulled so hard that I lost my footing and fell in. Another man came to help and he got pulled in as well! There we were, all wet and getting nothing accomplished. Eventually we were able to move the old guy in two shifts, lifting him under his armpits, with one of us on each side. He had apparently dislocated his knee but it popped right back in. He was on his way back to his car when he came over to thank me.

Now I had to hike up a mountain, with pack and tuba, in wet boots. I met "Zigzag" and we climbed the beginning of the mountain together, but I kept going when he stopped. I had my first real digger and slid down a small hill with my pack in back. But I was fine and kept going. Now came the tough part: big strides uphill. I burst up a big step, then paused for the next step, but the momentum carried my sleeping bag out of the bell of the tuba, and down the mountain it rolled. This happened at least ten times and was very frustrating. When it began to rain, I hurried to the lean-to, reaching it by 5:45. The Gulf Hagas Trail had only taken about 2 hours of hiking time and was definitely worth the side trip.

While hiking into Monson, Maine, I was told about Shaws: Keith Shaw, the owner of the hostel, offers an all-you-can-eat breakfast. Ed Garvey's *Appalachian Hiker (Book 3)* mentions a hiker who attempted to break the egg record at Shaw's all-you-can-eat extravaganza. He got up to eighteen when his stomach couldn't take one more egg; he had to have his stomach pumped. The guy was upset because he had hiked 2,000 miles and was about to finish the A.T., with just the 100 Mile Wilderness and Katahdin to tackle. I was just beginning the trail and figured that, if I got sick and had to end my hike, I wouldn't be as disappointed. My plan was to eat only eggs and drink juice. This way I could consume as many as possible and break the record.

That morning I hiked in from the trail on an empty stomach. Keith Shaw asked, "How many and how you like 'em?" I was so hungry that the first dozen went down quickly. Now, these eggs weren't your typical farm eggs; they were extra-jumbo-sized, cooked in sausage grease. After the first dozen I asked for six more, over easy. Keith said that the last guy that came in there and ate eighteen eggs left on a stretcher; I said that I was there to break his record! After eighteen eggs went down, I told Keith I could go for six more before I was done. One of the eggs had been double-yolked, and I was starting to slow down. By the time I finished the last egg, I was in no condition to hike that day. I ended up eating twenty-five, topping the record at Shaws by seven. But I will never do that again!

My sister, Brooke, wanted desperately to hike the entire A.T. but was having complications with blisters, along with knee and ankle problems. I was hiking through the Bigelows with her when a huge thunderstorm came upon us and we had to run for cover. She pushed on ahead since she wasn't lugging 70 pounds of gear (30 of which was my tuba). She had reached the lean-to, dumped her pack, and started back to help me when the first crack of lightning hit. She froze in her tracks then high-tailed it back to the shelter. She was scared for me, not only because I was exposed, out on the open trail, but on my back was a huge lightning rod!

My tuba, Charisma, is made of brass and served as a protective cover for whatever I decided to put inside it—including my sleeping bag. Once my gear had been packed inside the tuba bell, I would cover Charisma

Scott Rimm-Hewitt in Mahoosuc Notch, Maine.
Photo courtesy of Scott Rimm-Hewitt

with a garbage bag and pack cover, so that everything inside would stay absolutely dry in rain. But a garbage bag wouldn't protect against an electrical shock. When I heard that lightning had hit less than a quarter mile away, I seriously considered ditching the tuba pack and making a beeline for the shelter. But I crazily held true to my instrument. I kept hiking with Charisma, as fast as I could, and reached the shelter with no ill effects, other than a rapid heart rate.

The Mahoosuc Notch is said to be the toughest mile-plus on the entire 2,160-mile Appalachian Trail, an agglomerate of huge boulders that requires either squeezing through very small places or climbing over the boulders—often with treacherous drops between them. With Charisma on my back, it was a real challenge, but I was determined to make it happen, even taking off my pack once to slide the tuba through a rock tunnel. It took me just over an hour to make it through that 1.1-mile stretch. If I hadn't been through-hiking I would have spent more time exploring the notch and Upper Goose Pond. The Mahoosuc Notch was exciting, beautiful, cool and refreshing.

When I got to tree line on Sugarloaf Mountain, the wind was howling; I was getting soaked and very chilled. The higher up I hiked, the more exposed I was to the dreadful conditions. I was starting to become hypothermic. Someone told me of a ski lodge at the top of the mountain and I decided to seek shelter there. When I got there, I stripped down to the bare nub and got in my sleeping bag. All my clothes and gear were drenched, so I decided to start a fire to dry off my clothes. I set my boots close to the fire pit, not realizing—until I put them on the next morning—that the rubber soles would melt off. My boots were dry, but I had no traction to grip the rolling rocks of Saddleback slopes. As I worked my way up and down the slabs of rock, I could feel the lack of friction. I was slipping and sliding on every downhill. Finally I took one too many slips. The weight of my gear plus the tuba caused me to fall backwards—all I could do was put out my hands to break my fall. I cut my hand pretty bad and had to make it into Rangeley as quickly as possible to get bandaged up. The next day I switched to a new pair of Cresta hard boots, which lasted me the rest of my through-hike to Springer Mountain in Georgia.

New Hampshire

All hikers should take my advice when I say that, for sections you are unfamiliar with, the best thing is to remain on the trail. I learned that the hard way on the Wildcats in the White Mountains. I left Pinkham Notch on a path that I thought was the A.T. but turned out not to be. To save time, I decided to bushwhack over to the A.T., but found a ravine in between me and the trail. I started to climb upwards and reached a point where I was rock climbing with 70 pounds on my back. I had gone so far up in one direction that down was not an option. Toward the top I was grasping onto any little handhold and foothold I could find, in fear of losing my grip and allowing all that excess weight to carry me off the mountain. I was scraping my arms and legs with twigs and branches, but this was a fight for survival—I had to get to the top and reconnect with the trail. After 4.5 hours of exhaustingly slow climbing and crawling, I was luckily able to reach a safe point and find the trail.

Every hut is unique in the Whites. Run by the Appalachian Mountain Club, each hut has caretakers that feed the hikers and maintain the cabin. I was always a welcome sight at these huts because I brought music to large hiker audiences of twenty to fifty people, depending on the hut. At the Greenleaf Hut, one caretaker had a flute. We played Bach duets to wake the guests one morning. What a treat, running into another musician on the trail! At the Lakes of the Clouds Hut, fifty people were doing the Chicken Dance. Charisma and I play anything from "In the Mood" to "Amazing Grace" and on to Pink Floyd and Bob Marley tunes.

And Beyond

All through-hikers get one free beer in Kent, Connecticut. Hiking down the Housatonic River was so relaxing. When I got to the Bear Mountain Bridge, I connected with another hiker going into West Point for the weekend and we ended up hiking the rest of the A.T. together. It's good to have a hiking partner when you are out there for so long. He was there when I lost my footing and toppled headfirst off a cliff—I heard a crunch, did a somersault, and fell another 10 feet. I immediately thought I'd broken something or was paralyzed. I saw that I'd fallen 25 to 30 feet and that it should have killed me. My friend came to my aid but it was Charisma that saved my life, taking the blow from the boulder, halfway down, that would've hit my head. After seeing Charisma's badly crumpled bell, I feel sure that my head would have been crushed. I had stitches in my right leg, but hiked 26 miles the day after the operation, and Charisma still sounds good!

Curses, Excursus
Hut-to-Hut Musings

For Carla, Harrison, and Galen, the intrepid triumvirate
I think of all the wild way.

The most common universal experience of reality is love.
The prose man falls in love once or twice,
or according to some psychologists, thrice. If he keeps it up,
he is in danger of becoming a poet.
—*Karl Shapiro, "What Is Not Poetry"*

PART I Warming for the Chance to be Invisible—Lafayette Place
Campground to Lonesome Lake Hut via Lonesome Lake, Cascade Brook,
and Fishin' Jimmy Trails; 1.6 miles, 10:30–11:00 a.m.

For a largely lazy White Mountain lifer like me, the hardest part of beginning a monster hike at communal Lafayette Place is that there are picnic
tables everywhere, and half the time I want to sit down at one of them, eat
my woefully meager sandwich, listen idly for random birdsong, wait for
the cool touch of evening to find me and then get back in my car and drive
home. But I get myself started by pretending I'm both sturdy horse and willing rider, and, well—*giddyap, yeehaw* and soon the two of us are moving.

As the crafty crow flies, the hike I've set my sights on is a nearly northeast
line, a fairly straightforward declaratory sentence for the spirit that will
lead me over 52-plus miles of White Mountain terrain from Lonesome
Lake to Carter Notch and require only the most momentary of breathy
cessations at each of the eight structures that constitute the AMC's hut
system. If I go as I know I can, bearing the bare minimum of necessities
on my back and thinking more carbo-loading tortoise than simple-sugar
hare, I figure I can do it in 24 hours. Add in the variables—the sidewinding
curves and tortuous turnings, the unforgiving unevenness of the surfaces
I'll be striding on, the strenuous ups and the knee-mangling downs, nearly
12 hours of encumbering darkness, and a final east-wending descent into
the Madison Gulf leading directly to a journey-ending pull up and over

the gnarly Wildcats—and the goal becomes exponentially more difficult, a test-quest for both mind and body, psyche and soul. I've hundreds of substantial climbs behind me in every form of weather, and I know the Whites more intimately than any place on earth, but every new venture betides newnesses and sometimes near-calamities one cannot possibly predict or foresee. Given vicissitudes of both self and sky, then, the end envisioned is rarely the one that one comes to at the end of the trail.

Three things I'll half-confess to before starting out. First, though I am fifty years old, I have the lungs and quadriceps of a much younger man. And, it must be added, a foolish, romantically tilted heart. Entrepreneurial, I'm not; practical?—perhaps you're thinking of the guy next door. From as far back as I can remember I've loved Cervantes and Shakespeare, Keats and Lawrence and Woolf—minds alive with the beseeching, questing, ineluctable, utterly useless pulse of words. Second, I have been labeled (libeled?) by many—as *crazy, intense, extreme* (not always in this order). As my dear mother put it: "You'll go for miles and miles in one direction just to see if you can make it all the way back." Third, and perhaps most important for the story I'm about to tell, I have been unabashedly and incurably in love with New Hampshire's White Mountains since a moonless summer night forty-four years ago when my father, younger brother, and I got caught high on South Moat without a flashlight and with a virtual posse of rangers frantically in search of us from all four points of the compass. And it wasn't the lostness that hooked me: it was the walking. I fell head-over-heels in thrall with the idea that I could go this way then that, up, down, over and around with only the best sort of carelessness and astonishment as companions. Father, brother, and I made it to safety on our own power those many years ago, and the only immediate consequences to my five-year-old worldview were the literal sting of a few good branch-thwacks to the face and an inexpungible, life-changing sense of adventure on high.

I begin my quest at 10:30 a.m. on October 10, 2008, a relatively cool day promising cloudlessness, light winds, and a minimum of human encounters. The birch and beech leaves of the low-lying canopied hulks at the trailhead have begun to yellow; the candied, stiletto reds of the maples, which I'd gazed down upon from atop a snow-dusted Mount Lincoln on a glorious azure day only six days before, have been replaced by the dull ochers and browning hues that signal the final death of summer and the solemnity of inexorable fall. Dressed lightly in shorts and long-sleeved shirt, two ratty bandannas knotted to my pack straps for color and luck, I step, as the saying goes, to get stepping, and an adventure begins.

A quick half-hour later—I've fairly jogged up the Lonesome Lake Trail, getting the blood to flow—I find myself balanced on the quaint two-log span that crosses the outflow from Lonesome Lake and from which you can survey, staring northward like a llama, one of the cherubic, impossibly round Cannon Balls as well as several of the inviting rocky outcrops along the fittingly named Hi-Cannon Trail. The lounging lake before me is delicately rippled; the air is clean and light, perfectly autumnal. A few more steps and I'm turning, like Lot's wife, to take in the stark sky-slicing serration that is Franconia Ridge. I'm juiced every time by the view.

At all-but-empty Lonesome Lake Hut I sign the register, trying to strike a moderately poetic balance between modesty and brashness: *T. Muskat, all the way (he hopes) to Carter in a day.* What I don't put down is how the inmost ego feels: anxiously anticipatory, a teensy bit afraid. My stopping-point, after all, is 56 miles away. How can I possibly go that far? And, more inveigling, what on this particular day compels me? Wouldn't I be better off simply basking by the lake for a spell? I purchase a bright shield-shaped hut patch for Galen, my younger son, shyly thank the caretaker for her minute's hospitality, and reach for the handle of the hut's heavy door. Freedom, it occurs to me, is sometimes little more than forward motion—and, of course, the worldly possibilities any sort of movement brings.

PART II A Paradise of Unrestricted Seeing—Lonesome Lake Hut to Galehead Hut via Fishin' Jimmy, Cascade Brook, and Lonesome Lake Trails; Old Bridle Path; Greenleaf and Garfield Ridge Trails; 12.3 miles, 11:00 a.m.–3:45 p.m.

My Business is Circumference.
—*Emily Dickinson*

The views from Lafayette—my ocular reward for having survived once more the soul-skewering *agon* of Agony Ridge and the flinty skedaddle from Greenleaf Hut and boggy Eagle Lakes to the summit—are scintillating. Mount Lincoln is doing its usual proud jut-up to the south; to the west, Cannon's formidable cliffwork shimmers in midday's dusty light; bluish Lonesome Lake is perfectly discernible on its high flat plateau beneath the guardian Kinsman Ridge; to the slow southeast, the giant's burial mound that is Owl's Head stands out in the stark Pemigewasset Wilderness like a groan. Garfield, my next stop, shows off its steep southern flank like an etching.

Because the day has cooled considerably, I change into fleece leggings and a turtleneck, and in deference to rapidly numbing fingers slip on a pair of thin purple gloves. Atop my sweaty head goes a thin watch cap straight out of *The Last Detail*. Thus transformed—I must look half-medieval, half-Jack Nicholson—I wolf down a handful of greasy pepperoni slices, swig the last of my pink lemonade-with-O.J., a time-tested brew, cinch up my slightly lightened pack, and get on with my going. The glistening dial of my watch reflects the west-drawing sun: It's 1:15 p.m. and, suddenly, I am aware of the cloistering press of time.

Those who are new to the rocky up-and-down reality of the Garfield Ridge Trail (GRT) are inevitably shocked, in the aftermath, by its severity, seeming endlessness, and out-and-out primordial feel. It tests you, especially below timberline, and most unsparingly when you're tired. The final huffing climb up Garfield's west-shouldered steep can be a killer. But when you begin, as I often do, on the Lafayette side, your initial impression of the GRT is fairly benign: you jaunt off from Lafayette's northern flank, locomote up and over its cairn-pocked north peak, mountain-goat your way to the Skook junction and, particularly when the sky is bountifully clear, you muse: *this seems but a friendly cousin to the airy Crawford Path*. Never could a first impression be so deadeye wrong. For once you take that post-Skook dive into the dark, cavernous, mossy and, for the most part, under-visited wilderness that separates magnificent Lafayette from the remoter, more mysterious Garfield—butt-sliding your way down a few more steep drops and unruly slick-slabbed pitches before the first of the high spruces all but cordon you in—you feel overcome by a grim foreboding that this is no ordinary White Mountain footpath. Anguish, alienation, foreboding, dread—along the GRT, the whole existentialist package saps you like a succubus.

Climbing down into and then *out of* the dark haunt that shelters ghostly Garfield Pond from all but the most adventurous of White Mountain trampers, you come up against what I have called cursedly over the years (especially in deep-snow winters), *The Final Fang*. It isn't unusually steep or toothy, by any means—not like, say, that near-vertical section of the Carter-Moriah Trail as it struggles, from the Imp side, to North Carter's nondescript top—but given the energy required to get you to the base of Garfield's cone, the final pitch up the GRT can be, especially on a long hike, a body-shredding proposition. The ascent never fails to trigger in me a decades-old memory, which, as it arrives, hits with both head-clearing wallop and unbalancing comic effect: My brother and I (he's a gung-ho eight-and-a-half; I'm a world-weary ten) are struggling up the west side of

Garfield late on a torridly hot July day; my lapsed-Quaker father, as near as we can figure it, is about a half-mile behind us, enjoying, I imagine, the sonless solitude. The three of us are mulishly overburdened with gear—and this, remember, was in the day of the all-canvas tent and actual *tin cans* of overly salted food; my "Army-issue" sleeping bag alone weighed about 22 pounds. Our goal is to get to the Garfield Ridge campsite by nightfall. The only immediate problem is that my brother and I have drunk every last ounce of our water—we're equally and simultaneously stupid in this regard—and, crabby and cotton-mouthed, have decided our only recourse is to shed our packs and wait for Dear Old Dad.

So, sitting there grouselike on two small trailside rocks, too tired to do much more than pant and stare, we're happened upon by a happy-go-lucky twenty-something hippie who seems delightedly entranced by the fact—this was 1971; you do the hallucinatory math—that he was descending. This last bit of information is vital to the story, and bears repeating: this young, obviously still-up-in-the-soft-clouds fellow was going *down*. So he says to us, "How you guys doin'?" as though he were the happiest camper in the world. If memory serves, I think the sparest, muffled syllable escaped me. (My brother may have been dozing.) Cloud-man, barely stopping, says, "Well, take care, fellas," and goes off, half-flying, down the trail. About a half-hour later my father appears, two enormous fuzzy black-and-red canteens strapped to his chest bandolier-fashion (we called them "desert specials"). My brother and I blurt out: *Water! Can we have some water!* My father, cheery as a priest on Sunday, says: "I gave the last swallows to that long-haired fellow—such a nice guy!"

Atop Garfield I engage in what for me has become almost ritual: I slip out of my pack just below the slab on which the old fire lookout cabin foundation still stands, mountain-goat in a single bound the rocky bulwark so I can lean for a moment against the foundation's southernmost wall, then heave myself up and over into the perfect square of it, a winded hiker's open-box paradise. Part crow's nest, part unfinished cupola, this stubborn remnant of Garfield's past provides security (it's an amazing tuck-in in an angry winter gale) as well as sitting room, and chance for idle dreaming. Closing my eyes, my back against the cool concrete, I cast back and imagine a lonely smoke-sniffing counterpart cooped in the cabin circa 1944.

The 3.1 rollercoaster miles to Galehead Hut pass quickly, though I'm waylaid briefly at the junction with the Franconia Brook Trail by a bumbling porcupine, who minds me hardly at all and, like a diplomat negotiating a treaty, takes his prickly sweet time in crossing from one wooded zone to another before giving me space to continue. At the hut, where a guest lolls on the fixed porch bench, reading a paper, while another checks a map and a third sips from a small silvered cup, I sort of semaphore a group *hello,* tap the structure's leading step with my walking-pole, take a gander at unassuming Galehead Mountain (which wasn't on the 4,000-footer list when I first completed it in the early 1970s) and turn toward the Twinway. Again I feel the tug of time. It's nearly 4:00 p.m., I've come almost exactly 14 miles in little under 5 hours, and I've a long, long way to go. But I'm feeling reasonably spry, and—I knock on figurative wood—the usual monster-hike happenstance has yet to befall me.

PART III As the Burdened Body Diminishes, Unbridled Mind Uprears— Galehead Hut to Crawford's Depot via Twinway, Zealand Mountain Spur, and Zealand, A-Z, and Avalon Trails; 12.6 miles, 3:45–9:00 p.m.

> *The story is his adventure in search of a hidden truth, and it would*
> *be no adventure if it did not happen to a man fit for adventure.*
> —Raymond Chandler, *"The Simple Art of Murder"*

Walking in the Whites, and walking so *far,* I come to engage eventually in a syntax of mundane struggle and occasional surprise, passing time by spinning webs of thought and speculation, most of them frail and single-stranded, but a sturdy few surprisingly capable of capturing, and sometimes holding onto, the untamed vastness around me. As I clamber up the steep first section of the Twinway, I come again to the realization that, despite the usual human quotient of sorrows, I'm lucky to be alive. A white-throated sparrow is trilling trailside—the low first note followed by a piping sequence of four euphoric highs—and above me the arching sky has turned translucent, the blue of it water-color diaphanous and pale. A tenth of a mile or so from the summit of South Twin I turn and reconnect with one of the White's most spectacularly sudden views, the sharp point of Garfield rearing up, almost deliberately centered, between the edges of the downward-sloping trail. Nature's photo album has once again trumped anything I might put in mine.

From the summit of double-knobbed South Twin, looking south-south-east, the view on this languid afternoon is magnificent, and underscores for me the ineluctable, ineffable, endlessly alluring beauty of the Whites. Flowing away from me is the ravishingly green, gently undulating sea of forest I will walk through on my way to Guyot, Zealand, and beyond. The bulk of boreal Bond hulks in the center of this dreamscape, and in the middle distance mighty Carrigain is power and resplendence surcharged. But beyond the parade of names before me, those almost-personages with their storied pasts—Bemis, Nancy, Anderson, Lowell, Passaconaway, Whiteface, Tripyramid, Hitchcock, Osceola, Tecumseh, and bedeviling Vose Spur—what strikes me is how little we know of the mystery of these mountains, the reach and splendor and profundity inherent in their forms and silences that will always be beyond our grasp and striving.

I ease off South Twin like a rowboat slipping from its mooring, every knot of consciousness untied. On a gorgeous day like this one, this 2-mile segment of the Twinway seems a stroll through some enchanted allée; you're riding a topographical crest with occasional peek-outs to vista and sky, and the gentle ups and downs are lulling. But looks can be deceiving. On a late February afternoon two years before, in driving snow, I'd plunged off South Twin onto what I believed was this very same stretch—only to find myself, a feckless, zigzagging hour later, standing in my snowshoes in a tiny west-facing clearing jarringly northeast of the trail. (The realization that I had indeed lost my bearings was solidified on the spot by a stunning view of—Hale!) Perhaps the single most beguiling truth about the Whites is that, no matter what you think you know of them, you can never entirely pin them down. Every trail can turn chameleon at any time. Acknowledging this simple fact is as important for the sake of survival as anything you choose to carry in your pack.

Sunset—more graceful diminishment than stark black curtain strike—comes at 6:16 p.m. Though I've stopped for brief look-sees on globular Guyot and zaftig Zealand (no summit in the Whites boasts a more whimsical sign), I've been walking at a good clip since Twin and now, almost to Zeacliff, find myself standing surveyor-like atop a last little stony hump, marveling at spectral Mount Washington to the northeast as soft violet streaking ushers out day. Like a phrenologist, I fit my headlamp to the shape of my skull (odd how the smallest adjustments in the mountains are often the most vital) and flick it on, the particulate beam fanning out to illumine a nearby cluster of stunted trees. Minutes later, astride Zeacliff, I can discern in the blackened east the eerie penumbral shapes of nearby Willey, Field, and Tom, and the chalky murk of Whitewall just below. It's cool, windless; I close my eyes and listen. Nothing—no leaf or hidden creature—stirs. I am at the epicenter of absolute calm.

I arrive at Zealand Falls Hut at exactly 6:45, coterminous, it seems, with dew. The place is packed with guests who have finished dinner and, from the sound of it, are just beginning a raucous, post-prandial game. I pull out my camera and snap a through-the-looking-glass picture of the revelry inside. The sudden flash startles no one; I am invisible in the darkness, unnoticed, contentedly part and parcel of the ebb and flow of things. I cinch up and get a move on; the narrow slinking corridor of the A-Z Trail awaits me, a shivery evening pull up and over the Field-Tom col. Less than 2 hours later, practically running on the final friendly flat of the Avalon Trail, I realize I am almost halfway to my goal.

Per "the plan," my wife, Carla—who supports, and occasionally questions, my trail-tending wackiness—is waiting for me at the appointed hour (8:45) in a warm car at Crawford's Depot. She has brought dry clothes, including a critical fleece, and every ridiculously caloric item I scribbled on my gastronomic wish list the night before: Double Whopper with cheese; extra-large order of super-fatty fries; one elephantine orange, pre-peeled; a chunk of chocolate; cool milk; and, for the wash-down, a ludicrous, caffeine-laced combo of ice-cold Coke and a spine-straightening cup of hellishly hot joe. It's the quasi-culinary wagonload I figure will catapult me to the conclusion of my climb. But (and this comes as no surprise to commonsensical Carla) I find eating almost impossible; my day of aerobic exertion has—here's an official physiologic explanation—"plummeted my ghrelin levels, while saturating my system in peptide YY"; my body is basically feeding on itself, a depleted core. Moreover, the last two dark hours have proved psychically unnerving: along the wet lower section of the A-Z my jittery mind worked to convince me of the existence of a fanged, one-antlered moose rising from the bog with bad intentions, and every slightest sound from the fringes would leave me jumpy. The cumulative effect is debilitating: a vital rhythm has deserted me, and without it my inner storehouse of gumption and fortitude has been all but drained.

The convenience-store coffee, which I save for last, is biting and bitter; it feels almost toxic in my throat. I manage a few gut-wrenching swallows, then pour the vile bulk of it out the car window, dark flowing into dark. Mizpah, where I'm supposed to be headed, seems impossible light years away. "Can I do this?" I ask my wife, pathetically. "You don't *have* to, you know," she responds, cool as the proverbial cucumber. Then she offers up, as if to a six-year-old child: "You've come pretty far already, don't you think?" But the fumes of foolishness are all about me and, despite this perfectly logical, two-for-one deal of counsel-*cum*-perspective, the mountaineering maniac in me digs in. I get out of the car, bend to tighten my bootlaces, stand to face nightfall and re-shoulder my pack, then, doing my semi-level best to sound like John Wayne going off to battle while at the same time feeling *at* best like a morbid Woody Allen confiding his inmost fears to a shrink, give voice instead to pencil-necked E.T.: *Beeeeeee careful. Will. Can do this. Whew: dark, cold.*

My wife stays long enough to watch me cross deserted Route 302 to the old Crawford Path trailhead; as she pulls away, the car's headlights curving out to meet the road, I think: *Well, there goes sanctuary.* And I have to wonder—am I *sane?*

Forty-five feverish minutes later and about two-thirds of the way to Mizpah I'm done in, predictably, by the lethal one-two of junk food and dark. I'm lightheaded, woozy, wobbling like a top at whirl's end. I'm drenched in sweat; goose-pimpled by nervousness. I drop knees-first to the ground, like a penitent, and stretch out on my back—literally, right across the rock-strewn trail. A few stars flicker greetings above me; suddenly I see thousands through a latticework of trees. My tired being splits evenly in two, and a strange metaphysical dialogue ensues between my supine, barely breathing body and my stuporous, barely present mind. *Can we do this, brother?* says Body. *Who cares, partner?* says Mind.

In the midst of this internal soap opera—or rather, at a weird, hovering remove from it—I manage in a single moment of lucidity to remember my cell phone, which I have carried in the Whites with great reluctance in the past half-decade but which I must carry—I've made a promise—in deference to my wife. The "display" photo ripples to life, a clownish shot of our gimpy bull terrier. Miraculously, there's reception—three full bars. In the eerily artificial light of my headlamp, I thumb the "4" and then the bigger-buttoned "Send." I hear a familiar, friendly "Hi. What's up?" My wife, who works in human resources, is a glass-half-full kind of person, and has a way of sounding sunny in even the direst of circumstances. "I'm dying," I tell her, only slightly exaggerating. "No, you're *not* dying," she counters, ever the pragmatist. "I can't go on, though," I say, trying a different angle. "I'm broken." To this bit of bathos she responds with a typically practical question: "How far are you from Mizpah, anyway?" Wife and car were nearly home—about 50 long miles from where I was, so spousal rescue was out of the question. "About a mile, I'd guess," I say, hedging, even as I know she *knows* I know precisely where I am; "I think I'm just below the cutoff." "Can you get yourself to Mizpah?" she asks, in a perfectly even, impossible-to-override H.R. tone. Then she continues, delivering the last little drop of medicine: "Because if you can get yourself to Mizpah, to shelter, from there you can take better stock of yourself and see just how you feel. If you feel awful, you can sleep; if you start feeling better, maybe you'll feel like continuing." "Okay," I say, conceding. "I'll get myself to Mizpah."

PART IV Whistling (Sort of) at The Witching-hour—Crawford's Depot to Madison Hut via Crawford Path, Mizpah Cutoff, Webster Cliff Trail, Crawford Path, Eisenhower Loop Trail, Crawford Path, Mount Monroe Loop Trail, Crawford Path, Westside, and Gulfside Trails; 14.5 miles, 9:30 p.m.– 5:30 a.m.

> *To know the dark, go dark. Go without sight,*
>
> *and find that the dark, too, blooms and sings,*
> *and is traveled by dark feet and dark wings.*
> —*Wendell Berry*
>
> *I sing, as the Boy does by the Burying Ground—because I am afraid.*
> —*Emily Dickinson*

All my hiking life I've battled a fear of the deep-forest dark and, even now, making my slow unsteady way up the Crawford Path—a surfeit of supposed experience behind me, the little lighthouse beam of my headlamp emblazoning the familiar trail—I remain ridiculously scared. But my fear, I've found, is also alluring, as it draws me toward potent wonder and opens in me an attentiveness and acuity I have never known as a prisoner of crowded, dulling day. I crave, you might say, the uncertainty of darkness—the possibility, or probability, that something altogether unbidden and gloriously out of my control might befall me. Not injury or accident, by any means, but more *encounter*—of the Wordsworthian or Faulknerian kind, with something even imagination cannot canvas, or sharpest mind foretell. (I met an enormous bull moose once near midnight in deep-snow January on the North Twin Trail. He stood; I stood stock-still, prisoner to my fear but filled with purling wonder.) It's both perverse and paradoxical, this fear of mine, but walking through the Whites at night is for me a kind of letting-go, a relinquishing of cloying selfhood and the armored trappings I, like so many others, use to conceal and protect myself in the un-mountained world.

It's exactly 11:00 p.m. as I stagger down the final few feet of the Webster Cliff Trail and massive-roofed Mizpah Spring Hut comes dimly into view.

Five young men, talking quietly in a small circle in the grassy flat on the building's south side, barely register my arrival—if, in fact, they have seen me. Indeed, listless and waif-like as I now feel, I must appear as little more than a phantom, shuffling shape. My energy is completely gone, my forehead is beaded with fearful sweat, and my middle-aged lower limbs can barely do the perambulatory one-two. Worst of all, I feel as though I'm about to vomit. I get to the door, push my body against it, and it swings open—ah, how fatigue brings on mawkishness—like the entrance to a tomb.

The interior is completely dark, but as I know the place fairly well I grope my way dizzily to one of the dining benches and, slipping my pack from my back and letting it fall, stretch out horizontally on the hard wood, my sweat-soaked body shivering violently. My immediate goal is simply to keep nausea at bay. I want to eat something, but nothing I could keep down is close at hand, and the powder-based energy liquids I've brought with me are about as appealing at this point as poison. I close my eyes, bring my knees up toward my chest, and tuck my hands between my thighs, desperation recreating the fetal curl. I doze fitfully for several minutes, but the cold interior air seems intent on pillaging my bones. I swing myself into a sitting position on the bench, fumble for my pack, dig my parka out blind and throw it over my shoulders like a cloak. But even as I yearn for sleep a tireless inner voice is thrumming: *get up, get up, the journey's but half done, the trail outside is waiting.* It is mind, will, a weird mix of foolishness and fortitude, delusion and desire, perversity and pluck—and it rights me. I decide I can, and must, go on. Listless and broken as I feel, I strip down to the waist, change into a warm dry turtleneck, drink down half a quart of vile red juice, properly put on my parka, strap on and cinch up my pack, then head for the door. The air outside is bracing. I inhale, and look upward: the squid-ink sky is pocked with stars.

Fittingly, it's the witching hour. My start-up steps on the serpentine Webster Cliff Trail toward Pierce are halting, cripple-like; my feet ache, and a good half of me is choked with apprehension and fear. But if I can just get marching again a necessary rhythm—and forgetfulness—will find me, and vital strength and focus will return. And, I tell myself, if I can get past Pierce and onto the lovely near-unbroken continuum of the sky-kissed Crawford Path—where I will hike in starlight until sunrise and not be cordoned off by miles and miles of encroaching trailside trees—I'm fairly convinced my exhaustion will give way to exhilaration all along the shimmering sublunary way.

Alas, it is not to be. As I emerge from the final krummholzian corridor
atop Pierce—still enervated but looking forward to fiery firmament—I
am struck by something altogether unanticipated: fog. In fact, it's so thick
and sudden-covering it strikes me as almost unfair. I can't see past 50 or
so feet in any direction, and above me, where I had imagined a canopy
of blood-stirring stars, a bleak, low-slung, impenetrable ceiling fires back
my headlamp's puny ray. Equally egregious, a northwest wind is stirring
off Eisenhower, making for the worst elemental concoction a climber in
my condition can possibly head into. Fear, like a wave, threatens to break
over me. This will be a test of wills. (Note: Two weeks after I'd completed
my journey, I checked, with an almost residual wariness, the Mount Washington Observatory Web site for the summit report of my night of peril.
What I saw added a dimension to the spookiness: that eerie night, Mount
Washington and its high brethren were the only White Mountain peaks
enshrouded by freezing fog.)

I'm no stranger to adversity on high. Once, on a frigid late-February
evening long after darkness had fallen, I found myself on the west side of
Mount Washington's summit cone, clinging in gale-force wind to a lone
ice-coated cairn somewhere in the vicinity of the old corral at the north-
ernmost terminus of the Crawford Path. Conditions were bleak, to say the
least; visibility was a negative number; wind and fully blooming whiteout
were working to convince me I had better get down. And fear's big wave
was roiling. But I beat it back, digging out of my pack a 100-foot length of
thin twine I'd carried for years but never before had need of—but which
I knew I *could* use in the event I'd ever completely lost sight of an above-
tree-line trail. I made a loose lasso of one end, looped it over the tip-top of
the cairn I was anchored to, then vanished slowly southward, paying out
line. Soon I was in the vicinity of the next cairn, and once I *knew* it was
the next cairn I sent a little wrist flick up and through the twine, felt the
release, and pulled—then I recoiled my lifeline and tied into my next stony
friend. In this fashion I "twined" almost the entire Crawford Path—and
then the blow cleared and the Lakes of the Clouds shimmered into view.
Another time I got caught in September on the Mount Clinton Trail well
after dark, smack dab in the middle of the section where it seems one is
crossing and recrossing a small barely percolating tributary brook about
700 times. I just lost the trail—it happens to the best of us. I had a friend's
dog with me, a Brittany with a Bengal tiger's heart and, thankfully, because
he stayed relatively calm, the two of us, after an hour of frantic zigzagging

and backtracking, eventually got ourselves back on course. But the point is all about the fear: I knew it that night, and it was ready to come over me like a wash.

At the Eisenhower Loop junction I'm forced by stiffening wind into parka, balaclava, and my trusty pair of summit mitts (note to fellow crazies: I carry them everywhere). The small thermometer dangling from my left pack-strap registers about 32 degrees, and my exhalations, as if to confirm this chesty measure, are rimy puffs in my headlamp's hazy glow. I tilt myself toward gusty Eisenhower—of the hundred-or-so ascents of the former Pleasant Dome I've made in my lifetime, only a handful were halcyon—and begin the ages-old, tired-hiker practice of counting one's steps.

It's 1:15 a.m. Crouched like an infantryman on the lee side of the quasi-pyramidal (though plainly weather-blasted) cairn at the tip-top of Eisenhower, I look northward and laugh. Ike is so socked-in that, if I didn't know any better, I'd think I was on the *inside* of a mountain rather than on top of one. Mica flecks stitched in summit stone flicker in the wildness as I stand and spin for a circumambient gander. I resume my lurching-forward, rattling off attractions to come: Red Pond, Mount Eisenhower Trail junction, that *deep, canyon-like cut* as one begins the tug up Franklin. I'm actually *talking,* like some half-crazed guide. Several minutes after this fool's recitation—and this is to underscore just how gimpy and exhausted I was—I'm struck by the realization that, given the atmospherics, I'm not going to *see* these familiar landmarks even as I pass right by them. All I can do is walk nose-down into the wind and hope, if not for an out-and-out clearing, at the very least for a lessening of the foment.

Halfway to Monroe I manage to find underfoot one of the old iron ladder-supports some Victorian pounded into the rock in the service of smoother climbing, and the discovery makes me smile. I've stripped off my summit mitts and, squeezing one in each hand because I can, croak out of myself what must be one of the world's worst renditions of *On Top of Old Smokey,* the famous, slightly fatuous lover's ballad I first learned as a boy. By the time I've gone through it a dozen times, changing in my lunacy the final stanza to fit my current situation—

On top of Cold Franklin,
All covered with blow,
I lost my true gluh-uves,
For a-walkin' too slow . . .

—the always-off-kilter post to which the Monroe Loop junction sign is fastened blears into view. Relieved by this re-discovery (it's amazing how precious an encounter with the simplest trail sign can seem in the middle of a mind-bending trek), I drop to my knees, sling off my pack, and dig out an enormous chunk of slimy Muenster cheese.

As I work my way up and over the two rough jags of Mount Monroe—it remains and probably always will be my favorite of the high Whites, in part for its "duplicity"—I'm jolted to jumping by a frightened high-altitude junco which, having secreted itself in a small trailside crevice for the night, springs like a banshee straight up into my light beam. The gray and white feathers illumine grotesquely, and the small bird seems hawk-monstrous, so, playing my part perfectly, I scream like a terrified child. Two hundred quaking steps later, as I come within spitting distance of the southeast corner of Lakes of the Clouds Hut, shuttered for winter and, in the growing fog and gale, utterly inhospitable, my heart is still beating hard. Ahead of me—somewhere in the vicinity of the dark "up there"—is Mount Washington, but in the glowering fog all I can register is a few flat slabs of rock and my own very palpable frailty.

Odd as it may seem, I actually see more, and more microscopically, as I half-circle an utterly shrouded Mount Washington along the Westside Trail during the cold early start of the day. For one thing, all I can focus on is my footfall. Consequently, the rents and contours and pocks and divots and crevices in every single rock I step on stand out to me as if backlit supernaturally. Their geometries invigorate; the geologic is—new. Eerie rings of lichen appear suddenly on flanking boulders and, as I pass, recede into the darkness that has birthed them. A tiny summit spider scurries. A strange footprint fairly glows. The beauty of walking entirely alone in total fog on a freezing windy night in mid-October on the highest peak in the Northeastern United States is precisely the pith and passion of a well-fashioned poem: profound, timeless, challenging, buoyant—and undeniably true. It is also a kind of renunciation—of knowledge and knowing, of base camps and baser perceptions. I am one with wind and cold and stripped of every single motive and idea and impulse save a vague notion that my forward-going is good for me, in part because, amid all this tumult and beauty, survival is the furthest thing from my mind.

Once I hit the Gulfside Trail I know I am, as the saying goes, home free. I've decided to skirt the summits of Clay, Jefferson, and Adams—eliminating three laborious ups and downs—so that I'll reach Madison Hut on the relative flat, and relatively quickly. The wind, peaking from the northwest in gusts of roughly 40 mph, is beginning to rend the fog-shroud around me to tatters; in fact, as I look back over my shoulder, it is as though Washington is rearing up, trying to shake loose of its cold night's garb. Having passed the halfway mark somewhere during the difficult, leg-weary ascent of Pierce—triggering a subtle octane boost, I imagine, somewhere in the recesses of my subconscious—I am feeling stronger, particularly as I begin to see signs (a hint of blush, is all) of oncoming dawn.

As the Gulfside begins the back half of its easing curl around Clay, passing by the Jewell Trail junction, it descends gradually to a small spur loop on the left. "Spring," the sign reads. If you choose to follow the little sign's lead here—being either adventuresome or overly curious by nature or, because you're out of water, severely parched—you'll eventually arrive at a tiny, barely sputtering spring that goes by the Gaelic-sounding name of Greenough. Now, don't get me wrong: it's a fine little, perhaps even postcard-ready spring. In picturesque August it practically burbles amid spongy tufts of alpine grass. But finding it in the gloomy dark on a mid-October night—it isn't, whatever the guidebooks may lead one to believe, a hop, skip, and jump from the Gulfside—is no small feat. So picture me: pathologically afraid of the dark, in black tights and black turtle with a black watch cap on my crest, weenie-stepping my lanky 6-foot 1-inch way down a torturously narrow Hobbit-like corridor of rootwork and krummholz, one empty Nalgene bottle dangling from my left hand.

Twenty minutes later (it's now almost 4:00 a.m., to the second), after I've washed down a king's breakfast of sliced albacore, two tasteless granola bars, and a bag of peanut M&Ms with a hearty quaff of Greenough-infused iced tea (prudently laced with an iodine tablet for good health), I feel almost wholly restored, even as the various parts of me are silently lobbying the body for sleep. Stars have reappeared overhead and, before me, the ziggurat-like outline of monumental Adams looms. I snug everything I won't need in the bowels of my pack and, rearmed with plenty of water for the relatively milder miles I've left to travel, feel almost giddy with anticipation of trumpeting day. I sally past the north end of the Mount Clay Loop, scramble up and over the little rampart just past the Sphinx Col, and feel myself almost floating as the great Monticello Lawn plateaus out to greet me. Off to the right of me and down, down, hidden denizens of the Great Gulf begin their phantasmal waking.

A word or two about the so-called Dingmaul Rock, which you either recognize or don't care to recognize as you wind your way down the Gulfside Trail about two-tenths of a mile above Edmands Col. For one thing, it's oddly named. For another, it's not *that* spectacular—Quimby's Pillow, which one finds four-fifths up the way to Mount Moriah on the Carter-Moriah Trail, is much more of a trailside extravaganza. But the Dingmaul is a good flat prominence to have lunch on. In fact, my oldest son, Harrison, working for the AMC as a hutman at Lakes of the Clouds last summer, walked all the way from Lakes to this stony peculiarity just to enjoy an afternoon nap on its bed-like form. Now I don't "do" Dingmaul at all—I merely say its crazy name to myself every time I pass, and this long hike is no exception. It's my vaguely superstitious way, I suppose, of paying my toll to the Gulfside gods, in case they want to ding or maul me in some fashion, for the sport of it.

My titular tithing seems to do the trick, for in less than an hour I'm touching the night-chilled stone of Madison Hut and the sun, still 45 minutes or so from officially breeching, is sending up every manner of pulsing and tremor from the east. Feeling, you might say, my oats, I hop-skip the tenth of a mile or so of the Star Lake Trail to the Parapet, shattering the cool glass of the tear-like tarn with a perfectly parabolic pebble-toss along the way. From the Parapet the last little dogleg of my journey becomes telescopically clear: I can see deep into the Madison Gulf and over across Pinkham and the Peabody to the Wildcat-Carter ridge line in the near beyond. A long-lost Latin fragment wafts in on memory's wing: *Quod sit, esse velit, nihilque malit.*

Roughly, it means: *Who would be what he is, desiring nothing else.* Here on this legendary ledge on this perfect morning born of imperfect night, it suits me to a tee. I want nothing; all need has vanished; I am alone on this mountain, drinking in the loveliness around me and feeling the boon of an unbroken peace.

PART V Morning Comes Redemptive and Surcharged—Madison Gulf headwall to Carter Notch Hut via Star Lake, Parapet, and Madison Gulf Trails, Old Jackson Road, Lost Pond, Wildcat Ridge, and Nineteen-Mile Brook Trails; 13.0 miles, 5:30–10:45 a.m.

> *How do most people live without any thoughts?*
> —*Emily Dickinson to Thomas Wentworth Higginson*

No contour lines can quite do justice to the sudden and pointedly precipitous *down* that is the Madison Gulf headwall. As I begin the tricky descent, thinking *squirrel, cat, antelope*—creatures, namely, that are good on their feet—I am struck by how much consciousness climbing requires, every grueling step of the way. To put it in Madison Gulf headwall terms: if the mind isn't perfectly open to everything, sizzlingly aware, chances are good the body will fall. Some of the rocks I must negotiate are literal boulders; some, knowing only shade, are slickly resinous with moss and dew, demanding not only proper foot placement but crevice-clenching fingers and whatever roots are available for awkward grasping. Every manner of challenge presents itself—dicey plunge, sheer-face overhang, knee-shattering drop-off, sloping slab with one brittle handhold, maw-like recess leading to a bottomless dark—and parts of the trail I take, almost happily, right on the duff. (Sometimes the fanny's the only way to fly.) And the stream gurgling just beneath this wild-ride trail—appearing and disappearing like some slow-slithering subterranean snake—can be downright haunting. By the time I reach Mossy Slide at the foot of the headwall, mere tenths from where my vertiginous descent began, I feel as though I've been hiking, and trembling, for hours.

In the shade at the foot of Sylvan Cascade (which, this time of year, drapes over its sloped bolster of rock like a folded white fan), I stop for a bite to eat and to snap a picture—not that I'll ever forget a single particular of this Edenic spot. Half refuge, half dwelling-place, it represents for me, as so many hidden nooks in the White Mountains do, perseverance's reward—the cooling pause after fervid struggle, the taut mind's chance to unspool. But it's also simplest rest: I sit on a small round rock, stretch out my legs, and sing out quiet praise for the bounties of nothingness.

It is 8:00 a.m. as I ramble off the Old Jackson Road and into Pinkham Notch Base Camp, having broken stride only briefly on the swaybacked suspension bridge that swings one over the Peabody to take in the lovely xanthic leaves of a riverside mountain ash. My legs are stiffening, I've but dollops of energy at my disposal, and I know the final steep climb awaiting me up the Wildcat Ridge Trail to nondescript "E" is going to be a grind. Pinkham—the din is palpable—is beginning to thrum with activity, and I'm momentarily startled from my murkiness by a man about my age who offers up *Good morning* as he begins a hike on the wide and welcome thoroughfare toward Tuckerman Ravine. Discounting the evening crowd at Zealand and the circle of laughing men at midnight Mizpah, he is the first fellow perambulator I've seen in nearly 50 miles.

After unfolding my tattered trail map a final time, at the start of the Lost Pond Trail on the east side of Route 16—tracing with my finger the neatly demarcated, nearly 6-mile line separating me from the Carter Notch Hut—I'm approached by a large and boisterous Russian contingent (I recognize the language) consisting of two middle-aged men, two middle-aged women, three small girls, two boys of about thirteen, and an old white-haired woman who must, I assume, be the babushka. They're dressed as if for a company picnic. One of the men, in extremely halting, heavily inflected English, gestures at my map and asks: "How fere eez to dis Llost Pond?"

"Not far at all," I answer—though almost the moment I let loose with this encouragement, I realize his notion of a half-mile through the hardwoods may be light years removed from mine. So I show him on the map with thumb and forefinger precisely where we are and where just-ahead Lost Pond lies. "You go dis way, too?" he asks, plaintively, gesturing down the trail. "Yes," I say, shyly, refolding my map. Then he looks me up and down, like a man considering a museum piece that offers no immediate clues to its purpose or provenance, and says, with an almost fatherly concern: "You look *tie-eerd;* you should seet and rest."

About a mile into the Wildcat Ridge Trail, the Russian's sweet "tie-eerd" tattooed into consciousness, I realize after about a dozen creaking steps—scuffles, really—that my legs have turned taffy. My "up" gear is gone, kaput; the joints at hip, knee, and ankle are utterly cashiered. I look at the steep ahead of me, a slope I've practically skipped up dozens of times, and the quaintly alphabetic "E" is suddenly Everest. It's an exhaustion I've experienced before, and reflexively I reach for the time-tested antidote, a little mental mountaineering game I call *Fifty Paces.* It's a simple game, and versions of it have been "played" in all sorts of mountain ranges by all sorts of hikers in every manner of worn-out, dog-tired, broken-bodied state. You simply pick out a tree or rock or peculiar swell somewhere ahead of you on the trail that—this is the game's lone rule—you believe you can get to in exactly fifty paces. Then you start walking and counting. What happens after a while is the speculative measuring takes complete control of your brain, and you become obsessed with perfecting your stride-to-distance ratio and getting to that twisted tree to the left of the stump that looks like a crouching bobcat—is it a bobcat?—in exactly fifty measured paces, no cheating, and pretty soon you've come to where you thought you'd never come to when (when was it exactly?) you were so fatigued. I'm practically a game-show host as I emerge on the first of the humpy bare knobs the Wildcats are known for, and the barometric altimeter looped about my neck reads 3,700 feet. (Though hardly a GPS, this exquisitely old-fashioned instrument serves me faithfully as both telltale and talisman, and works wonders in combination with a compass, in a pinch.)

Once I'm atop "E"—and the evil Everest that had so impinged on me has all but evaporated from thought—I take to the swells and dips of Wildcat Ridge like a surfer, pausing at every proffered viewpoint for a westward glimpse at the jagged and jutting Presidents across the way. Mid-morning effulgence has turned Mount Washington green-tinctured blue, and from its spruce-mantled middle to its broad, deciduous base, yellowing beech and birch trees resemble a tattered army in full retreat of coming winter. Adams and Madison, farther to the right and boy-kings by comparison, are topped by fluffy diadems of slow-scudding cloud. I reach "A Peak" at symmetrical 10:10 a.m.—tea time, I think—and from the aerie-like lookout gaze out over Carter Notch toward burly Carter Dome. A thousand-plus falcon-diving feet below me, but seeming in the bright autumnal air almost neighborly near, the green-metal roofs of the Carter Hut buildings are bright with sun. The smaller of the two Carter lakes is half-shadowed by edging trees and, though I have looked down on it from this precious perch on numerous occasions, I notice for the first time, perhaps because I feel so happy and so free, how much it resembles a bow tie.

EPILOGUE Reflection and Recovery; Cool-down—Carter Notch Hut to Nineteen-Mile Brook Trail trailhead on Route 16 via Nineteen-Mile Brook Trail; 3.8 miles, 11:45 a.m.–1:30 p.m.

> *What was it he had seen? He couldn't tell now. It was as though he had seen it in another world, a world that once left could not be recalled. All that he knew about it was that it had been complete and dazzling.*
> —Henry Roth, Call It Sleep

Anton Chekhov, for whom truest freedom entailed both a freedom from violence and a freedom from lies, would have found in the White Mountains perfect refuge from the cant and caviling cantankerousness of the everyday world. Emily Dickinson, who gazed out almost every day of her life at the Holyoke Range from her homestead in Amherst, Massachusetts, would have admired in the Whites their stolidity—their silence and majesty in the face of, and despite, so much petty human noise. I cannot say with any surety what (or where) all my wild White Mountain climbing has brought me; I can't in any way say it has "taught" me much of anything. But what I discover in the Whites each time out is the worst or coarser parts of me are leeched away and lessened by the tramping as well as the travail, and that some better, more soundly human self emerges, whatever the wear and tear to the overall system. I couldn't tell you the mechanism by which this transformation is effected; I couldn't begin to suggest what bizarre inner and inward-driving transmogrification occurs. I can only vouchsafe for the beauty of the experience, and the occasional heart-stopping terror the Whites will drop smack in the middle of a dreamy hiker's for the most part meandering path. I'll admit, one has to be either stupidly daring or daringly stupid to embark on the kind of point-to-point hiking I do, but in my experience more often than not a view from on high is made all the sweeter by the perils and hazards that were part of the getting-there. As no less an orographic authority than Henry David Thoreau well knew, mountains—"among the unfinished parts of the globe"—in some way exist to test our mortal mettle, to "try their effect on our humanity," provided we are daring and perhaps insolent enough to climb them.

As to the more pedestrian details of my experience, at 10:45 a.m. on October 11, 2008, I reached the green-trimmed entryway of elfin Carter Notch Hut, nearly a full day after touching-off from the western edge of Lonesome Lake with little more than a sense that I'd be walking a good long ways. And at the teleologic end I was basically the selfsame guy. Sure, I was glad to be "done" with it; no doubt I felt a small stirring of accomplishment; and I'm sure I let out the usual end-of-hike exhalation—a tired body's way, I suppose, of saying sayonara to the martinet mind. But no celebratory impulse overcame me. I didn't whoop, clap, or ululate, though I'll freely admit I anticipated with some relish a piping-hot bath. Literally the first thing I did, though—after snapping a plainly nostalgic photograph of the Carter Hut sign—was to limp back to the littler Carter Lake, where I pulled off my boots and socks with abandon, plopped myself down on a reasonably flat shoreline stone, and stuck my tired feet in the drink. The relief was immediate; I was overcome with gratitude for simplest things. A few hours later, Carla—as planned—met me about a mile up the Nineteen-Mile Brook Trail, smiling broadly. "How was it?" she said—cutting to the chase in her usual sunny way. "Fine," I said, understating in a single word almost everything. And there in the midst of some of the most beautiful wilderness in the world, after a brief hug and the briefest of conjugal conversations, we turned and walked out together to the car.

POSTSCRIPT Reasons for Being and Not-Being—Lonesome Lake to Carter Notch, 52.3 miles; hiking time, 23 hours, 40 minutes, plus 2 hours, 28 minutes at huts, and an additional 1.25 hours at Carter Notch Hut.

We are unknown, we knowers, ourselves to ourselves.
—*Friedrich Nietzsche*

For a poet-dreamer-tramper like myself—who, over the course of the usual up-and-down lifetime, has 1) enjoyed some pretty over-the-top orographic experiences; 2) proved to more level-headed and not-so-peak-obsessed others, not so much unbearable as out-and-out bear-went-over-the-mountain; and 3) perhaps put at risk the *next* fifty years of his existence shambling thousands of miles in all four seasons in search of bliss, beauty, terror, and the calming, self-abnegating exhaustion brought on by a good long trudge—nothing beats New Hampshire's White Mountains for their steadfast munificence, their broad-based tolerance of the crazy-hiker cause.

I'm being both facetious and wishfully anthropocentric here, of course: the Whites in all their silence and solemnity couldn't give a hoot for my fidelity and, frankly, on more than one occasion seemed to want me killed. But the point is when we climb them we should pay more than the usual heed to both their mystery and their autonomy, because, whatever our most wishful thinking might concoct to the contrary, they exist apart from us, in a wildly separate realm. Inscrutable to the end—the more so, paradoxically, the more we insist we have them well in hand—they'll be hanging around among the clouds long after we're gone, more than kings in a kingdom all their own.

Finally, it should be noted, before anyone out there gets the wrong idea, that I don't "go long" for the challenge of it, or the exercise; that, though perhaps fleeter on my feet than some others, I'm not into speed records or tests of endurance or (would that the term had never been coined!) *peakbagging;* and that, when I get right down to it, I'm out there mostly meandering—working to strike up enchantments and, like the storybook bear, see what I can see. After all, the Whites are for me like a very good poem: hypnotic, transfixing, and somehow different each time through. So I'll keep walking them, I imagine, because I've never seen reason to stop. I'll see you atop Adams in the blow.

TEDDY "CAVE DOG" KEIZER

Descending into the Maelstrom

In this story, Teddy Keizer describes a 2003 attempt to break the record for hiking the Long Trail, which traverses the spine of Vermont's Green Mountains from Canada to Massachusetts, over thirty-five major peaks with countless small climbs. Known as Cave Dog, Keizer—with a support crew called The Dog Team—has set hiking records around the country. In September 2000, he climbed all fifty-five Colorado peaks over 14,000 feet in 10 days, 20 hours, and 26 minutes. In June 2004, he set a new Long Trail record of 4 days, 13 hours, 15 minutes.

The night was hot. It was humid. Everything was wet—the leaves, the blades of grass, the blackberries, the ground, our bodies, our feet, everything. The night was black and our headlamps lit up the suspended water vapor in the air, rendering them useless. We had to take our lights off and hold them at our knees so that we could see the ground. Even when it was not raining, the condensation was so intense that water rained down from every surface overhead.

Trails that I had traversed just a week ago were now utterly unrecognizable. Usually the trail is 2 feet wide and looks like a thin brown line through the woods. But hikers had been trying to walk around the mud, only to cause more mud on the edges, with those following skirting ever wider. Now there was a 30-foot swath of deep mud charging relentlessly ahead. Every step was an unknown venture into the depths of the muddy abyss. Sometimes a hidden rock would stop our falling feet. Other times, our legs would plunge in past our ankles or mid-calves or even over our knees. Mud would ooze into my shoes and squish between my blistered toes, sore from the deep crevasses formed by four days of soaking conditions. I looked up only to see a cratered landscape of water-filled postholes created by unfortunate souls like myself.

I was hiking with "Night Dog" (Ralph Ryndak) through this dismal darkness. Night Dog has an incredible spirit. He is one of those people who gives more of himself than even he knows that he has within him. He is kind, cheerful, and a friend of the highest order. He is a wonderful person to hike with under any circumstances. I was so very glad to have him with me through that night as I began my descent. Night Dog was charging ahead into this quagmire, pushing with everything he had. His heart is big and has a lot to give. My only mission was to follow his feet.

I was beginning to have difficulty with object recognition. I had been in that situation before, at the beginning of the last night of the Adirondacks challenge, in a lightning storm atop the Dix Range. That time, I was alone and feeling it. It took me extra time to see and recognize objects. I was unable to keep up a stiff enough pace, under those conditions, to keep warm in the storm's downpours and the night's cooling. The crewmember atop South Dix forgot extra clothing and a headlamp and the night wore on me slowly.

Now I was on the Long Trail, pushing for another adventure. But this time I had Night Dog. We were on a 22-mile hike over Bromley Mountain, up Spruce Peak, past Stratton Pond, finishing with an ascent and descent of the tallest peak in the region, Stratton Mountain, at 3,936 feet. I had hiked the Long Trail in training and enjoyed this section very much. It was peaceful, refreshing, and had a nice mix of greens and browns. There were tall peaks with nice views, serene ponds, and lush forests full of life: squirrels, birds, snakes, deer, butterflies, dragonflies. But my hike this night competed with reason and challenged the higher goals of our plan. For some unapparent reason, our group was working as extremely dedicated *individuals* instead of the well-oiled *team* I had become accustomed to. Communication seemed crosswise and crewmembers were reinventing the wheel at every turn. The inefficiencies had resulted in missed re-provisions in the backcountry.

Missed rendezvous have happened to us before: at the Collegiate Peaks in Colorado, Big Indian in the Catskills, and Balsam Gap in the South Beyond 6,000. Each time it happened the mistake was devastating, nearly cutting our record attempt short on the spot, but somehow, through guts and determination, we persevered and forgot. One situation came particularly close to jeopardizing our efforts. In the Pemigewasset Wilderness of the White Mountains, I was missed three times in the same day, all by the same person. I was dangerously dehydrated and low in calories, hiking in the heat of the day without water or food. I would have abandoned the effort, if not for the heroic, multiple 20-plus mile hikes by Yankee Dog, which rescued the entire White Mountain attempt. Unfortunately, a day that we had expected to be our biggest mileage day ended up being our shortest.

A missed re-provision has many consequences. Naturally enough, it dehydrates and depletes the system of calories. In such a state, the uphills are painfully draining; you feel light-headed; your blood becomes thick and sluggish, and it is extremely difficult to stay awake when sleep-deprived. It is also extremely devastating to morale. This sport is much more about the mental game than the physical game. When you feel completely depleted and that nothing is working correctly, it is ten times harder to push through the hard terrain and conditions. When one is hiking 60 miles a day, back to back, it's extremely difficult to keep up with fluid and caloric needs—to keep up and catch up at the same time. One missed rendezvous can take time to recover from completely, perhaps the rest of the challenge. Of course, it would be much simpler not to schedule re-provisions, to take a bit more weight instead and cover the distance without assistance. However, when you are trying to break records, you trim everything possible to push the limits. It is the nature of the game. It is not everyone's game. In fact, it is very few people's game. But it is my game.

During the Long Trail record challenge, I did not find support crew in the backcountry, where I was expecting them, at nine separate locations. Many times I had to hike an additional 5 or more miles without any food or water in very hot and humid conditions. In normal situations this would be terrible, but in a record attempt it is disastrous. Hiking up Clark, Mayo, and Bolton completely depleted of glycogen—my blood so thick that my heart was pounding double-time and double-strength—the muscles of my entire body were screaming with pain, their tissues eating each other for calories. That might have been enough for me to call it all off right there. But there was Alpine Summit Dog, running up the trail with his injured big toe, bailing me out near Harrington's View. Plunging ahead, on Duxbury Road, I pounded down as much pasta as my knotted digestive tract could take and sucked down Alpine Summit Dog's ice cream bars with delight. Not yet feeling recovered, I charged up the hardest section in the entire course, up and over Camel's Hump and Burnt Rock, the best I could in my depleted state.

At that point, I was voicing much more strongly that backcountry support needed to get it together—or forget it. I was not accustomed to being in this position, and it confounded me. If anything, my message seemed to be getting through *too* well. Now backcountry support were reaching their rendezvous locations hours before I could reasonably get there. The team member that missed me on Nebraska Notch was so distraught that he spent 14 hours atop Mount Ellen, to make sure there was no way I could outrun him. This was a touching display of remorse and commitment to the cause, but it also meant that crewmember was unable to help out in other areas for a long time.

Unfortunately, more difficulties had arisen as the attempt went on. Now I was with Night Dog, pushing the tempo to catch up to record pace. Going into the night, I was low on calories, hydration, and sleep. I had tried to sleep for 90 minutes on the first night, to no avail, but had succeeded with 90 minutes on the second night. I slept 60 minutes on the third and now, on the final night, there was no more time left for sleeping, only pushing. Night Dog pushed and I followed. But, by the time we reach the top of Spruce Peak, my object recognition had started to become delayed. In such terrible conditions of darkness and foul weather, recognizing rocks, mud, and blowdowns can be very difficult. Your mind lets your imagination fill in the gaps of its slow recognition, and the results can be scarily comical. In your peripheral vision, you see pickups, signs, tables, houses—whatever comes to mind. It is not until you look at them directly that you see them for what they are: trees, rocks, mud, roots. I have only been in this state a couple of times and I hated it. But I was willing to continue on in those previous situations, because I had been completely aware of place and time and able to make reasoned decisions. The delay in recognizing peripheral or fleeting objects had been annoying, but it had not affected my ability to see where I was going or stepping.

This night was different. The delayed object recognition was happening more often and to a greater degree. I also had temporary lapses in remembering why I was out there. I would start to think I was doing something else and slow down. Although Night Dog was there to keep me oriented, this was a hard night. We walked up streams that used to be trails. We traversed the depths of bogs that used to be forest floors. We waded through the thick foggy air that offered little visibility. Night Dog pushed and all I could see were his feet. He plunged forward with a conviction I have seldom seen before, his footsteps ever churning. Splash, splash, splash, plop, plop, plop, swish, swish, swish, splash, splash, splash; Night Dog kept going, relentlessly. Every step was a splattering adventure. We never could be sure to what depths our feet would plunge, or what hard surface would stop their descent.

In addition, I was barely able to stop the descent of my own condition. As we pushed on, our next re-provision should have been at Stratton Pond, just before our ascent of Stratton Mountain. We drank and ate everything before reaching the pond and were in desperate need of more supplies. Lo and behold, Stratton Pond proved to be yet one more miss. The torture was deep; it was so very deep. My blood sugar was so low that I could barely stand, and I was having more and more trouble remembering that I was in competition. But we would do what we had to do: scale Stratton Mountain without supplies. Little did I know then that this would mark the beginning of a very long and tedious downward spiral, churning my mind over and over into the oblivion of other worlds and consciousnesses, a slow, deep maelstrom. I assured Night Dog that Stratton was no big deal. I had hiked Stratton just a week ago. In training, I had practically flown up, enjoying a limited view atop the fire tower because of fog. It had seemed like nothing at the time, and nothing like some of the bigger peaks up north.

"No problem," I said. "We'll charge up and then it's all downhill to the next road-crossing support."

My god, the mountain grew before our very eyes. We fought for every step, yet our steps did not seem to be getting us any closer. We dug, we scrapped, we clawed our way forward with what was left of our wasted forms. Ages were created and ages died as we relentlessly and indefatigably pursued the stars above on a stairway into the sky. I counted every hundred vertical feet of our progress. One hundred feet never came so slowly. Each passing hundred feet felt like an incredible achievement. Our bellies ached for nutrients. Our mouths were parched for fluids. The night's darkness crawled through our beings.

We made the top just as the sun began to show signs of rising. We found a caretaker there, a real gentleman. He instantly recognized us as the fellows that were going for the Long Trail record. He offered us water. Trying not to look greedy, we drank it ravenously and got more. I sat down on a rock and began to realize that my world was taking a new form. Everything seemed surreal, somehow glossed over. Night Dog was ecstatic. We had done it. We had scaled Stratton despite the layers of obstacles before us. There was still time to beat the record. He told me to leave him and run like the wind. "Go for it," he said. "Do not stop until you have that record. We got through the much tougher night and all you have now is daylight!" How little did either of us realize the true nature of my deteriorating condition. But the lack of supplies could not be compensated for now, with so little time left. And Night Dog's enthusiasm was as infectious as always.

I ran. I bounded. I flew down that trail. I jumped off rocks. I felt the wind in my face. I was going to make it. I felt great. But it seemed to take much more time than was reasonable. As the minutes wore on, I began to realize that this was a foolhardy endeavor. With 40 miles to go and less than 14 hours left on the clock, and considering my deteriorated condition, it seemed unreasonable to hope for a record-breaking effort. When I reached Groove Dog at the Stratton-Arlington Road, I told him it was useless at this point. But he rose to the situation, responding enthusiastically that yes, I would have to keep up a stiff pace, but it was well within my abilities. He laid out his Groove Dog passion. There were only 2 miles to the next road crossing. So I decided that there was no need to decide now. I could do the next short section, then make up my mind before going into the 20-mile section over Glastenbury Mountain.

I descended far on this short trail, quickly beginning to hallucinate. I have never hallucinated before and I never want to again. Period. It was awful. I will never know what really happened on that trail. There were so many people, but I think at least two were actually real—two nice ladies who helped point me in the right direction of travel. Everything seemed real but it could not have been real. I made it about half a mile at first, before realizing that I was in a serious situation. The game was over. I was entering a different world, one which I wanted no part of. I sat down dejected, whipped, hungry, thirsty, exceedingly sleepy, but strangely not tired. My body seemed to have lots of energy but my mind was failing. I laid down, and slept.

I woke up disoriented. I knew where I was but had only a hunch as to which way to go. I floundered around a bit—and that's when the two nice ladies came by. I asked which way to go. They affirmed that my hunch was correct, then left. My immediate goal was to get out of the forest. The closest way would've been back from where I had come. Unfortunately no one would be there, as Groove Dog would have already driven to the other side of the trail. That was a mile and a half away, three times as far, but I knew that I would be taken care of there. Since I was still going in the direction of Massachusetts, I decided to run like I was still going for the record and soon felt that I was. I made it another mile before my descent began once more. I laid down and slept again.

When I woke up, I was completely out of touch with which way I had come and which way I should be going. I made my best guess and began to saunter down the trail. It took a long time but eventually I made it to the end, U.S. Forest Service Road 71. Night Dog and Burns Dog were there waiting and they were worried. It had taken 1 hour and 40 minutes to hike only 2 miles. Groove Dog had gone in one of the cars to try to figure out why I was taking so long and would soon return. I explained that it was no longer possible for me to break the record. Burns Dog jumped into action, explaining in his plain logic that I only needed to keep up a 3.149-mph pace. This might have been a tough pace to maintain over the whole course but, pushing for the finish, it was well within my limits. He was right and I could not deny it. I had lots of energy left. I felt that I could run the rest of the way, if I wanted. But I was also in a mental condition that I had never been in before and did not fully understand. Everything seemed real and I could not say for certain what was or wasn't true. I felt good, especially since I'd had a chance to get some more food and drink. The crew's logic seemed undeniable. I told them okay, I would continue—but only if someone went with me, because I was having difficulty determining what was real and unreal. You would not believe how many times I would later pray that I had left the Long Trail, right there on USFS Road 71.

Night Dog was beat from his valiant hike through the night. Groove Dog had to get home to work. Burns Dog had been one of two crewmembers to twist an ankle during the challenge. However, he volunteered to keep going anyway. The sacrifices that everyone on the team makes are deep. Burns Dog should have been on his back, with his swollen foot up. Yet, here he was taking one for the team. We set out at a good pace and maintained it for many miles. But it became clear that I could go faster—and there seemed no reason for me to be holding back when there was a record to catch. So, eventually, I ran out ahead.

On this section of the trail, up Glastenbury, began one of the strangest and most intense out-of-body experiences one can imagine. Everything began to seem like I was watching television. Everything was flat and unreal. My ability to feel my surroundings quickly became limited. There were no smells. Sounds seemed distant. Eventually I could only feel with my hands and my mouth. Then pain disappeared.

Hucksters were all about. At one point I was the best rock jumper in the world, astounding the masses with my inhuman ability to jump great distances, from one rock to the next. I also could run up hills with amazing speed and agility and, for some reason, I only wanted to go uphill. Soon I had gained the power to change the trail. Whenever the trail dipped downwards, if I concentrated just right, I could will it back up again. But each new power would soon bore me. I would sit down along the trail. Eventually Burns Dog would catch up with me again and immediately tell me to drink. But I no longer needed water, food, or even air. Not wanting to hurt his feelings, I would take the tiniest of sips. Amazingly, the fluids felt real. Nothing else seemed real, but that cold energy drink felt distinct on my lips. Soon we would move down the trail again. But as I was faster, I would lose him once more, only to enter new worlds and situations beyond explanation.

Burns Dog and I were yo-yoing. I would take off at lightning speed. Then he would find me sitting in the trail, apparently in deep thought, only to take off again. He said that Sugar Dog was up ahead, at the Caughnawaga Shelter. Getting to Sugar Dog became my new fascination. I tried to will her around each corner but she never came. I began to ache for her. Where was she? I needed Sugar Dog. It was taking forever and I could not understand why I could not conjure her up. Eventually we got her on the radio and, finally, there she was in person, at the appointed shelter. I could feel her with my hands. She was real. She asked what I wanted, like all the support crewmembers do when I arrived. She was astounded when I said that I did not need anything. She said I had to drink, so I drank. She said I had to eat, so I ate. Burns Dog fixed up my next fanny pack of food and fluids. But he could not figure out which pack was the new full one and which was the old spent one because they both looked the same. I lay down and was content. Sugar Dog said that I needed to get going. This struck me. In all of my challenges, no one has ever had to tell me that I needed to get going. So, Burns Dog and I got up and headed out again. My descent was now occurring at a faster rate.

Soon I no longer felt that this was reality but a bizarre dream and I did not like it. I was no longer living the dream. I was living in a dream. I spent a lot of time contemplating reality and dream. Could some of what I saw be real and some not? I decided that nothing was real and little mattered in this world. I could now hike with my eyes closed, but not for very far. Then I got bored with that game. I scraped a swatch of flesh from my calf on a passing rock. It did not hurt. In fact, I kept expecting to look down and find the dripping blood gone. I was sitting atop Glastenbury Mountain, pondering the farther reaches of the soul and mind, when Burns Dog caught up with me again. I wondered why it was that he kept catching up with me. Somehow everything seemed strangely real when he was around. Was he in fact real? I bet myself he was real, and decided that I would no longer hike out in front. I would make sure that he was always ahead and present. As we found our way down Glastenbury, I became less and less interested in the task at hand. I let Burns Dog figure out everything. But I would help him if necessary. When he was distraught that he could not find any blazes on the south side of Glastenbury, I conjured up an old blaze straight out of my mind. Time was slipping ever so slowly by.

Eventually we caught up with my brother, Rad Dog, at an overlook, with about 7 miles to go before hitting the next road crossing, Route 9. Rad Dog was pumped. "We are going to make it," he said. "There is just enough time. When you start sprinting for the finish, the record will fall." Off running he went and I followed. But the trail was becoming exceedingly tedious. I was beginning to wonder why it was that he wanted me to follow him. How could a dream be so deathly boring? On and on we went and I just could not understand why. Geologic time moved faster than this. *I am through,* I thought to myself. I searched for ways to wake myself up, to no avail. My descent took a precipitous turn now; I was nearing the center of the maelstrom. It began to rain and the skies pounded with thunder. The rain was like a vertical torrent, as if Zeus had dropped a hatch and let all the water out at once. I was drenched to the bone and shivering, even though it was quite hot out.

I was now entering new worlds beyond my comprehension. For some reason, the masses wanted me to descend this mountain, then ritualistically scale a mountain-sized, spiral temple and place a piton atop the apex. But I was done. I knew neither how far I had come nor how far I had to go. I had no idea how much time was left on the race clock. All I knew was that I was utterly finished with this ridiculousness. I would descend this mountain but that was it. In fact, I would rather have ended the dream right there, right then. I kept looking at my brother and thinking, *Why? Just stop!* With a mile to go, my pace slowed dramatically. My brother told jokes to try to inspire me to continue to push ahead, but I was done and it was obvious. He used Split Rock as a landmark to push toward. We would go a little ways then stop. It was tediously slow and I did not care. For the first time in my life, I just did not care. This existence was nothing but torture, and mind-numbingly tedious torture at that. Painfully, we pushed forward.

Because I was shivering, he radioed down to Sugar Dog to hike up with a fleece and raincoat. Sugar Dog was somewhere down there. She was all that I wanted. All would be well when Sugar Dog arrived. My brother started to sing, anything to cut the terrible situation. Rain continued to pound us and lightning continued to fall. Where was Sugar Dog? She'd said that she would be right up. Time had a different dimension now. It fluttered ever so slowly forward. I do not like to sing but could not resist joining my brother. We sang and we sang. It almost sounded beautiful, in some warped way. At every large object, I asked my brother a question, "Is this Split Rock?" No. No. No. Where was Sugar Dog? How could it take her so long? Is that Split Rock? No. Is that Split Rock? No. My brother was amazingly patient. How far is it to Split Rock? It should not be too far. I sat down and entered the center of the maelstrom, where the mind spins the fastest. I would not stand up again under my own power.

These challenges are about living the dream. They are about being free. They are about attempting something unique and exceptional. They are about pushing the limits of the human experience. They are about challenging the soul and rising to the heights of mountains. They are about inspiring others to live their dreams as you live yours. These challenges have been immensely rewarding. I have gotten the rare opportunity to intensely study one mountain range and forest after another. I have met amazing people that are active and taking on interesting projects. I have been introduced to numerous American subcultures across the land. I have spent enormous amounts of time in fabulously beautiful areas. I have experienced some of my highest and lowest moments during these challenges, memories that are mine to the end of my days. I love these challenges.

But now, I'd gone way beyond all of this. I was way over the edge and falling and hating every last bit of it. Life was now tenuous and I did not care about winning or losing, beauty or harmony. I did not even care about life or death. All I cared for was seeing Sugar Dog, my only beacon in the dark forest. She was all that I had left. I wished deep into the recesses of my being that I had called it off at USFS Road 71. It baffles me now how I could have been talked into proceeding again. It is utterly unfathomable, but I was in states that I had never been in before and could not understand. This is not what I am about, nor why I do these challenges. This was absolutely insane because I was going insane. It was not worth it, absolutely not worth it.

I have turned around shy of my goal many times. During my climbs of the Colorado 14,000-footers, I turned around thirty-five times because of lightning alone. During my month-long solo in Glacier National Park, under winter conditions, I turned around half a dozen times. Why I missed the boat home this time, I'll never know. In Colorado, we used to say, "Them there mountains ain't goin' nowheres." What I can say now is that I have been there and back. I know the signs and do not plan to go into the depths of that deep spiraling abyss ever again. I do not have a death wish. I am a lover of life in all its beautiful forms.

Sugar Dog found me just below Split Rock, sitting in the trail with Rad Dog trying to convince me to continue. She gave me a kiss. I could feel it. It felt so incredible, smooth and delightful. It had been such a long time since I could perceive any external stimuli with any certainty. I felt so relieved. With a helping hand, I immediately got up and announced that we needed to get off this mountain. I was now having difficulty using my limbs. With one of my arms around Rad Dog and another around Sugar Dog, we crept down the trail. As we made our way down I leaned more and more upon their shoulders. Sometimes they would have to move my legs for me because I could not seem to move them around all of the big rocks. The trail was not always three wide, so Sugar Dog sometimes fell back, but as long as we held hands I would continue. I could feel her hand, so warm and unblemished. It was my only portal into this world. The other worlds that I passed through were far, far away. It would take an eternity and a bit longer but slowly and surely we made it down. As we neared the bottom, Sugar Dog left to move the car closer to the trail. I went completely limp and closed my eyes. I was really done. Thor's hammer was pounding the cumulonimbus anvils with a vengeance. Everything was saturated from the persistent downpours. I asked for big strong Sea Dog to come up and carry me off this mountain. Rad Dog explained that Sea Dog did not come for this challenge. I asked for Good Dog and he appeared in a flash. As we approached the car, Sugar Dog was back. I opened up my eyes and was strangely happy.

I would spend the next couple hours babbling incoherently, in soft tones, while downing Ensures and pizza slices. The meat-lover's pizza was exquisitely scrumptious, better than the sweetest candy. I would go to bed at 11:30 p.m., sleep hard, and wake up at 4:30 a.m., completely normal and full of energy, ready to climb a mountain. I rolled over; Sugar Dog was awake. I looked deep into her eyes and announced with conviction, "I am back."

DONNA BRIGLEY

Never Underestimate the Power of Pudding

October 2000 Autumn trees shed their leaves. A crisp leafy rainbow crunches underfoot on a trail that runs all the way from Georgia to Maine. I climb the last steep pitch before Zeacliff, putting one foot in front of the other, knowing the rock staircase will soon end atop a flat ledge overlooking the Zealand Valley, where I can climb no higher. My nose runs, dripping down my upper lip. I lay a finger alongside one nostril and blow out through the other, landing clear snot on the ferns at the side of the trail.

As the Appalachian Mountain Club's section leader for the area, I know every step across the Pemigewasset region of New Hampshire's White Mountains. Hikers say the Pemi encompasses the most beautiful stretch of the entire 2,160-mile-long Appalachian Trail. From the Franconia Ridge to Crawford Notch, majestic craggy peaks form a jagged horizon where they meet today's cloudless blue sky. I breathe in deeply. The woody scent of spruce forest is as familiar as my best friend's home. The waters of the Lincoln and Franconia Brooks, my Tigris and Euphrates, fall below me to the west of this ridge.

People die here. They come to the wilderness unprepared, and freeze to death in every season of the year. Sometimes they have heart attacks, or get hit by blocks of Volkswagen-sized avalanching ice. More often, they get lost, lie down, and die of hypothermia. It is up to me, in part, to make sure these things do not happen. I patrol the trail, cutting down trees, rebuilding cairns, keeping the way clear, keeping hikers alive.

Sun-warmed wind rises from the valley and blows through my hair. With mud-caked legs above my gaiters, I stop halfway up the endless stairway of rock to take a long swig from my water bottle. I pause and turn around. My companion is one white blaze away, hiking uphill toward me. As I watch him, I am taken back in time. Although he has only been my hiking companion for one year, he has always been a part of my trip along this simple footpath, long before we ever hiked a single step together. Today, as we flow with the trail across the wild Pemi, I remember when a trail that runs all the way from Georgia to Maine was never supposed to be part of my story.

August 1993 Eight miles from a road, in the Pemigewasset Wilderness, I have not seen anyone all day. I follow a faint path leading off the main trail through a grove of birches. Sticks lash out against my dungarees. Twigs snap and dead leaves crackle as my sneakers carefully choose my way through the woods. After a few dozen steps, I discover that the forest opens into a small clearing. I ease my backpack to the ground. The price tag dangles from the backpack's webbing, daring me to return it to the store if I renege on my plans.

I unfurl the $29.99 tent I bought last night at Sears. I could have spent ten times that amount for a modern backpacking tent, but I did not want to splurge for something I might only use once. The smell of new plastic spreads through the air, overpowering the scent of pine and spruce. I'm not sure why I've always wanted to try backpacking, to spend the night alone in the woods, but I have always been fascinated by the idea of carrying everything I need on my back. Only one year into a loveless marriage, the thought of escaping to the woods fills my daydreams, although I have never slept in a tent before. Now, with my husband away on business, I have the opportunity to escape my everyday life, to try something I have long wanted to do. The directions for the tent are easy to follow. Once it is erected, I begin to inflate the yellow rectangular pool float that I plan to use as a mattress. I blow air into the rubbery valve.

Suddenly, a rustling of leaves interrupts the silent forest. A bear? I listen. A snake? Nothing. I begin to think that maybe it is not a good idea for someone who has never backpacked before to have come so far into the forest, alone. As I blow, the mattress begins to show some signs of inflation. I inhale the plastic air again. A man unexpectedly crashes through the branches, entering the clearing. For a moment, we stare at each other, startled. "What a beautiful day!" he proclaims.

I stop inflating the mattress and rise to my feet. "Oh," I say nervously, "I thought I heard something in the woods, but I haven't seen anyone all day."

The hiker, with a scruffy beard and long black hair pulled into a ponytail, surveys the clearing. He walks over confidently, and deposits his backpack on the ground. Smiling broadly, he says, "It's time for me to stop for the day and I can't find anyplace to camp around here that's not right smack in the middle of the trail."

Leaves rustle nearby. We both turn our heads toward the sound for a moment. The noise stops. The man dismisses the sound with a wave of his hand. "Probably a chipmunk," he suggests. Far more wary of camping alone than with this stranger, I blurt out, "You could always camp here! There's plenty of room for another tent."

"No, I really don't want to disturb you," the man says.

Thinking of the bears and snakes, I encourage him to stay, "No, really, please stay. This is my first time backpacking, and I'd really appreciate it if someone else was around."

"Well, if you really don't mind," he says tentatively. "But if you let me stay, I insist that you join me for dessert. Tonight we will be having chocolate pudding."

My talkative companion sets up his camp in a matter of minutes. He explains that the Appalachian Trail begins in Georgia, some 1,800 miles south of here. Over a tiny campfire, he tells me about the trail. He says that if I follow the white blazes south, it will take me to Springer Mountain in Georgia, north will take me to Katahdin, in Maine. New to the burden of a pack on my back, I never dreamed that such a trail existed. As the August sky fills with stars, I listen to his stories about the Appalachian Trail while we eat the chocolate pudding.

The man tells me stories about what he calls "trail magic," when whatever thing you desperately need seemingly appears from nowhere. He tells me about "trail angels," locals who leave picnic coolers filled with soda and goodies near road crossings. He tells about the camaraderie of through-hikers, about there always being room for one more in the shelter on a rainy night. He tells me about townspeople who take you home with them and take care of you because they want to be a part of your trip. I listen wide-eyed. The man does not believe that his trip is extraordinary. He simply flows along with the trail, an unemployed engineer with a degree from Harvard.

"Anyone can do it," he says. "It's the most fun you'll ever have."

"But I really don't know enough about backpacking to stay out for that long," I explain, reminding him that this is the first time that I have ever spent the night in the woods.

"You should probably take a class about backpacking or wilderness survival," the man suggests. "That would give you a good start. I mean, you obviously wanted to try backpacking badly enough that you came all the way out here. But, look at you—you're wearing jeans and sneakers. You have a cheapo tent and a pool-float for a mattress. You have the desire to go backpacking; you just need a little help getting started with the right equipment." His voice is soft and kind. I agree that my situation could be greatly improved by following his advice.

After dinner, the man pulls a can of beer from the top pocket of his backpack. "I almost forgot! I picked this up back at the road crossing earlier today." He pops the top open and pours half the beer into his Nalgene bottle, then hands the can to me.

"Cheers," he says, as our drinking vessels collide.

After nightfall, the man points out the many constellations that he can identify. A slow-moving satellite creeps through the summer sky. We fall asleep in our tents and in the morning go our separate ways. I call after him as he makes his way out of the clearing under his neatly repacked load.

"Hey, I didn't get your name," I say.

"Jay," he tells me, before disappearing through the woods.

"Good luck," I say, "and have a nice life."

January 1994 Derek Tinkham died yesterday. He froze to death in −45 degrees Fahrenheit, on the slopes of Mount Jefferson. The engine in my car barely turns over as I leave the house for the wilderness medicine class that I am taking in order to become better prepared for a backpacking emergency. That guy Jay would be impressed to know I got an "A" on my last quiz. Our instructor, Bill Aughton, arrives late to our classroom in Pinkham Notch. Although today's class is supposed to deal with lightning, Aughton cannot get his mind off the two University of New Hampshire students who disregarded the signs of hypothermia. As a member of Mountain Rescue Service, a group of highly trained and experienced mountaineers who volunteer search and rescue aid to the New Hampshire Fish and Game Department, Aughton was one of the first people to reach Tinkham's body, only a few hours before class.

"And when we got to him, Donna, he was frozen as solid as this desk," says Aughton, slamming the palm of his hand down in front of me.

August 1994 Cresting the summit of Mount Clay, I see that Elroy and Stretch, the two college students I met in Vermont, have gotten a good half-mile ahead of me. The three of us have been doing 15-mile days since Hanover and I get the feeling that this high mileage through the Whites is not a good idea for my out-of-shape body. Above tree line, we follow the cairns that mark the way. Our vague plan is to get to Osgood Tentsite or any of the Randolph Mountain Club cabins north of the Presidentials if the weather turns bad. The air feels heavy, humid, and thick. Something is wrong with my right ankle. It does not feel right. I wish I had taken Stretch's advice to take some ibuprofen when we stopped for lunch, back on Mount Washington.

Thunderheads have been building all afternoon in the western sky, and now they begin to sound off, with crackling thunder close by on the western ridge. I have to watch where I step on the pointed rocks, following the line of cairns. Pain shoots up my leg from my ankle. I step gently and have slowed my pace considerably. I cannot imagine catching up to the guys. Off in the distance, I can barely make them out as they slip into the col between Jefferson and Adams.

Clouds begin to sweep across the ridge, obstructing my view. At the junction with Caps Ridge Trail, the sign says 3.8 miles straight ahead on the Appalachian Trail to Madison Hut. But Caps Ridge Trail turns sharp left, leading in 2 miles to a parking lot. I turn around to see how far I am from Mount Washington. I need to decide whether to head back uphill to the security of the summit buildings, bail out down Caps Ridge Trail, or continue to Madison Hut. The alien summit buildings are barely noticeable through the clouds. When I turn back toward Caps Ridge Trail, I can no longer see the trail sign. Waves of horizontal wind drive translucent icy chips of hail across the mountain landscape. I am enveloped by a black cloud. The air is electric. Hail leaves red marks on my bare legs. This is not the time to be above tree line! I drop my pack to put on my raingear. The guys must have made it below tree line or to one of the RMC cabins by now. They are probably wondering where I am.

I try to continue to the next cairn, but cannot see a thing in front of me. Thunder explodes. Lightning flashes. The clouds lift for an instant, and in the distance I can almost make out the figure of a man standing next to a gray cairn. The clouds wash over me, spitting hail. Lightning strikes the ground nearby and my hair stands on end. I make my way over to the cairn, trying to remain upright against the wind that threatens to dash me against the rocks. The man is a ghost, transparent against the swirling clouds, hiking downhill; the next cairn comes into view through the whirl-wind of cloudy mist. I know I am going to be hit by lightning if I do not get below tree line immediately. The scene of would-be rescuers searching my corpse for identification flashes through my mind. I don't want to die. I follow the hazy apparition of the man down the Caps Ridge Trail, where

I soon reach the safety of the parking lot. An hour after a quick hitchhike, the emergency room doctor tells me that I have torn a tendon in my ankle. I do not know what became of the man whose shadow I followed down the mountain. I never saw another person on the trail. I like to think the apparition was Jay, looking out for me.

May 1995 Tonight, Lone Star and I are camped at Abingdon Gap in southwestern Virginia. Lone Star, aka Jack Updyke, is a fifty-year-old former U.S. Marine and podiatrist from Houston, Texas. He and I met on the approach trail that leads from Amicalola Falls to the top of Springer Mountain, the southern terminus of the Appalachian Trail. When we arrived at the summit marker and the first white blaze of the official trail, we followed the tradition of the through-hikers that came before us. We licked the sign, spit over our shoulder, and picked up a small rock to carry to Katahdin. We agreed that we would camp together that night. Now, we have known each other for nearly two months.

Jack and I have pitched our tents in a grove of giant rhododendrons. The shrubs are so enormous that our tents fit easily beneath the branches. Tomorrow, we will cross a road near a convenience store, so we have compiled a list of wants and needs to purchase when we get there. Because I am pregnant, I need to stay extra hydrated. I plan to replenish my supply of powdered Gatorade, which has run out. We both look forward to ice cream, and Jack needs razor blades. Jack shaves his head bald, so people will not think of him as balding. Before he sold his podiatry practice and started hiking the Appalachian Trail, he got a tattoo of a panther on his left shoulder. He wears a diamond stud in his left earlobe. Jack is having a midlife crisis.

Apparently my husband is also having a midlife crisis. Last month, he volunteered to work 800 miles from home for the next six months. Although I am five months pregnant, I am not bothered by the separation. His absence is a refreshing change in our troubled marriage. I was grateful that my midwife gave me the thumbs-up to spend my maternity leave backpacking. I am in the best physical shape of my life.

I try to sleep, but the weather has been brutally hot in the south. My right arm is badly sunburned from walking north day after day with the sun's strongest rays radiating from the east. Funny, I can always tell a south-bounder on the trail by their sunburned left arm. The baby moves around, trying to find a comfortable place, probably wondering why we have stopped moving.

I ran out of water on the trail today and, when I arrived where the spring was supposed to be, it was dry. Whenever I am faced with challenges, from dry springs to hailstorms, I always look to the sky, shake my fist, and shout at the imaginary companion who first told me about this trail, "Damn you, Jay, what am I supposed to do now?" This never fails to amuse my non-imaginary fellow hikers. I will give that guy a piece of my mind if I ever get the chance.

Jack calls out from the dark of his tent, "Darlin' are you still working on our shopping list for town tomorrow?"

"Yes, Jack. What do you need?"

"Well, I seem to have lost my earring somewhere on the trail."

"O.K.," I answer from my tent. "We'll make sure to get you a long dangling one this time, so it won't get lost so easily."

July 1997 I shuffle through paperwork in the stuffy attic at the Joy Street headquarters of the Appalachian Mountain Club. My two-year-old son, Ethan, plays nearby with an old snowshoe. As a member of the Trails Steering Committee, responsible for the protection of 1,400 miles of trail in the northeastern United States, I sort through the stuff of Environmental Impact Statements and National Forest Management Plans.

"So, how did you get involved with the AMC?" another volunteer absentmindedly asks. As always, I tell the story of an August night when I ate pudding and learned about the Appalachian Trail from a hiker named Jay.

May 1998 Patricia Turner leads a group of ten hikers on a 16-mile backpacking trip across the Pemi, overnighting at Guyot Campsite, just off the Appalachian Trail. Ethan is with my ex-husband this weekend. Although I am also an AMC Trip Leader, I have joined Patricia on this linear hike in order to get a ride back to my car after inspecting a good chunk of my Pemi trail section for winter damage. Only a few patches of snow remain on the ground and the blackflies have already started to spawn in the warm air. I throw my mosquito netting over my head before I set up my tiny one-man bivy on the empty caretaker's platform. When I am finished, I grab a water bottle and head down to the spring. On the way, I stop to chat with Patricia and the members of her group.

An hour later, when I arrive back at my tent platform, I discover that a lone hiker has set up a tent next to mine. He sits in the moraine beside the platform, wearing sneakers with his gaiters.

"Nice hat!" he says, pointing to my mosquito netting.

"Nice sneakers," I reply, rolling my eyes. I can't believe that some newbie hiked all the way up here in white New Balances.

"Hey, I'm just hiking in the sneakers because I'm breaking in new hiking boots. I only wore them halfway up here," he says. He takes his custom-made Limmers out of his pack. I am wearing the same style of boots. Handmade for my feet only, the boots took four years to arrive.

"Well, make yourself at home," I say, there's plenty of room since the caretaker doesn't start until next weekend."

"You know," says the man, as he unpacks gear, "I thought that little bivy would belong to a guy. You usually don't run into women who camp in anything that small."

We laugh. "What's your name?" I ask routinely. Over the thousands of miles I have hiked, I've often stopped a familiar-looking hiker to strike up a conversation, mostly curious to know if his name was Jay.

The hiker barely looks up from what he is doing. "Jay," he replies.

Never knowing what I would do if this moment materialized, I stumble the two steps to where he is sitting, hug him and stupidly say, "I've been waiting my whole life to run into you again!"

At last, my stories could be told to the man who sent me on my way when he made pudding on an August night and I was first alone in the woods. Jay did not remember me at all, although I was able to recount his stories from that distant night as if I were a lifelong friend. After all these years, I could finally tell him what I had accomplished in respect to the trail since he first told me about it. We ate chocolate pudding, again. I told my stories of trail magic, stories about dry springs and hailstorms, stories of all the people I've met. Indeed, my trail experience was just as he had said it would be. We stayed up until dawn, sitting on the edge of the wooden platform, our feet dangling into space above the Pemigewasset, not far from where we first met.

October 2000 Last year, through the wonder of e-mail, Jay described a trip he was planning to Guyot and invited me to go along. By the time we reached the first white blaze of that Saturday morning, we had learned a lot about each other. Strange coincidences began to surface, ranging from us each having a "Got Milk" sticker on our respective rearview mirrors, to the fact that my son, Ethan, and Jay share the same birth date. We camped for the second time in the place where we first met and he invited me for pudding.

I stand on the rocky treadway now, watching his too-familiar face. My mind wanders. I wonder if I knew him in another lifetime, if such a thing is possible. It might explain some of the synchronicities, if he had taught me something important in a previous life as well. I think perhaps I am a tiny clump of sugar, modified food starch, and preservatives, being ever so slowly tossed in a great cosmic pudding bowl over infinite time. I collide with the dry clumps of others, granules breaking off and blending, until milk is added and we are stirred. With each turn of the mix, a lifetime passes. The same clumps rarely intersect twice, but sometimes they do, if there is an important reason for them to blend on their way to smooth oblivion. Maybe Jay and I have collided again, in this lifetime, so I could learn about the Appalachian Trail. The lessons I have learned on this simple footpath have certainly made me a more enlightened, or well-blended, steward of the trails. Or maybe I'm just a bit dehydrated.

Last night, under the same stars that were there on the night I first learned about the Appalachian Trail, the pudding was butterscotch. Today, I walk the trail with my partner. He stops next to me on the endless stairway of rock and mysteriously asks if I think I belong to a different period in time. Somehow, it does not surprise me that he can read my thoughts. The cosmic spatula must have scraped the edge of the bowl. He thinks I should have lived over a century ago. I think I would have had fun chopping down krummholz to put in a trail, when this very spot was a true wilderness and the Appalachian Trail was not yet a dream. If I did live in that time, perhaps we were here together, as we are on this day, when I have no choice but to believe in the power of pudding and the lessons learned on a trail that runs all the way from Georgia to Maine.

MARY ELLEN BAROSS

Going Long with Fat Packs

When Mats asked me to join him on his 2009 White Mountain Direttissima, I thought, *You've got to be kidding. Me, hiking 25 miles a day for ten days with an enormously heavy pack?* I hike a lot but never entertained the thought of torturing myself with such an epic adventure. Yes, I can do long miles and carry a heavy pack, but could I do both? My pack would get lighter as the days went by, but I was not sure I could make the first day. Would I still be smiling? Would I enjoy testing myself as I have never done before? Would I prove my friends wrong, the ones who would think I was crazy? The only way to answer these questions would be to give it a go.

Mats had successfully completed the Direttissima in 2007, so he gave me advice on how to prepare. "Go for a long hike with a fat pack," he said. "Your body needs to get used to carrying a lot of weight. It's always good to train." I agreed, knowing I would never set out on my own with a fat pack just for training. In July I successfully completed the 272-mile Long Trail in nineteen days. I've been told that if you can complete it in less than twenty days you are a very strong hiker, so this boosted my confidence. My pack weighed 35 pounds and I averaged about 14 miles per day. I did not take days off, but resupplied my food bag four times. The Direttissima is 245 miles in ten days over the most difficult terrain in New Hampshire, and unsupported—you must carry all the food for the entire trip. Mats assured me that the first three days are the hardest, as the body adjusts; the rest of the trip would be all mental. Three days to get over the hump? I could do that! Little did I know how big the hump was going to be.

I organized my food and loaded my pack, which weighed a whopping 53 pounds. Weeks prior to this I had hurt my back and, after wearing the pack around the house, I found myself in a great deal of pain. I could barely go up the stairs! The floodgates opened and the tears were unstoppable. After all this preparation and finally becoming excited about the trip, I was distraught to think that I would not physically be able to do it. Mats suggested that I see his trainer for some sessions on resistance stretching.

To my surprise, after only two sessions I was able to bend and touch my toes again, relatively pain-free!

On the Long Trail I had used a pair of Asolos that had ripped out two days before I finished. For this hike, I thought I could wear either old boots or my new trail runners—but then I panicked about my feet. In 2007 I'd had surgery on my right big toe; the doctor removed several bone fragments and bone spurs. Although there was much damage and hardly any cartilage left, he saved the joint. Since then, the keys to keeping my foot happy have been to keep the toe from bending too much and to make sure there's enough room for my toes to spread out. I had been buying men's Asolo boots because of the wider toe box, but the store was out of my size. I ended up with women's boots, the cut slightly narrower. But everything would be fine, I hoped, if I wore a thinner pair of socks.

August 13 We were on our way up the Mount Cabot Trail at 6:15. Adrenaline, excitement. Was I the first woman to give this a try? Hiking with my fat pack resulted in a much slower pace than normal and I worried about not being able to keep up. But Mats's pack weighed 70 pounds and I was thankful that something slowed him down too. Our destination was the Jefferson Campground on Route 2, which was 24 miles away. It was a beautiful day and the miles slipped away to the summit of Cabot, the Terraces, and then the Weeks. As much as I love views and outlooks, there is something to be said about remote, wooded trail. This was my first time hiking the Kilkenny Ridge from Cabot to Waumbek, and it was most wonderful. I even enjoyed the brief rain shower on one of the Terraces. My legs were a wee bit tired coming down Waumbek, but surprisingly I still felt really good overall. Even the road walk to the campground was enjoyable. Sleep came fast after a hearty freeze-dried dinner. Mats had advised that it was a good idea to have a treat each day, perhaps chocolate for dessert, so I added truffles. Heavenly!

August 14 After a good sleep I was ready to take on Day 2, an easy day just shy of 20 miles, continuing on Route 2 for 5 more miles. At the spring a gentleman filling water jugs informed us that we were in for a heat wave, not good news. I had backpacked once in extreme heat and suffered from heat exhaustion; I made a point to drink extra. At the trailhead I turned my ankle—an old sprain has weakened my right ankle and the slightest misstep will cause it to roll. This happens frequently enough that I knew it would be fine after getting through the initial pain and mumbling of four-letter words. Mats suggested that I be more careful where I place my feet. We started up the never-ending Castle Ravine Trail. The lower section is relatively flat and it was nice to be in the shade, with bountiful water, which kept the pack weight down.

Mats was ahead of me as we picked our way up the headwall, over boulders, toward Edmands Col. I was tired and hot by then and had to fight back tears of frustration. It was nearly two o'clock and we hadn't even made the first summit. All I kept thinking about was how far we still had to go, even though I knew it was important not to concentrate on each day's destination or it can be overwhelming. Reaching Edmands Col we took a long, well-needed break. I collected my thoughts—just focus on the next task and the rest will follow—reminding myself that all I had to think about was climbing Jefferson. We left our packs and it was joyous not to have that weight slowing me down; above tree line it was absolutely gorgeous viewing! Back at the col I had renewed energy and started first toward Thunderstorm Junction while Mats lingered. Knowing I would be ahead was all the motivation I needed and my spirits lifted even more. Sometimes a mental boost like this can go a long way. I thoroughly enjoyed a five-minute break at the junction, waiting for Mats. We did a packless, quick up-and-back to Adams, then went on to Madison Hut. After refilling water bottles and taking a Clif Shot, we climbed Madison, the last peak of the day and all downhill from there. We summited at 6:00 p.m. but it took nearly four more hours to get to Barnes Field—we were traveling just slightly over a mile per hour going down. It was an exhausting descent, all I could do to keep moving. Never had I felt so depleted in all my years of hiking. We walked to the Dolly Copp campsite by headlamp and the second night was a blur. Mats handed me a dish of ice cream that a friend had brought, to cheer me up, but I wanted to do the hike unsupported and left the dish near my pack. In my delirium, I forgot all about it; later, I took some stuff out of my pack and put it right in the ice cream.

August 15 The hardest day, according to Mats. If we made it through Day 3, the rest of the trip would be less difficult. The packs were getting lighter and the legs getting stronger. If I told myself this often enough, maybe I could convince myself he was right. I thought I'd already had my food woes with the ice-cream incident, but I found my Day 3 food bag to be a mess of melted chocolate. The hot sun had caused all the truffles to melt. Grumpily,

I wiped off the chocolate and would have thrown away the remains—but Mats ate them! We had a 3-mile road walk to the Stony Brook trailhead on Route 16; road walks are hardest on my feet and I was in extreme pain. After the first bridge crossing, I had to tend to my feet. Mats was very patient as we taped things up; I also loosened the laces, which helped. I was good briefly but then the pain was back and so were the tears. I seriously considered ending the hike, but after adjusting my boots to reduce pressure points, I found the discomfort tolerable and we continued. I got a little ahead of Mats and had a nice long break on a shady cool rock at the Carter-Moriah Trail junction. But it was extremely hot on the open ledges to Moriah and the blazing sun tapped all my energy. On the descent I slowed considerably, feeling dizzy and sick to my stomach. I had felt this miserable only once before on a backpacking trip, when I suffered from heat illness. Once again streams of tears rolled down my cheeks. Worse, we ran into friends and they witnessed my absolute low point. Although they were very supportive, I couldn't help feeling like a failure. I should've had more water, eaten more, trained more with the fat pack, and not waited till the last minute to get new boots. Everything had caught up with me— the lack of sleep and calories, too much weight, too many miles, and not enough recovery time. Mats suggested we camp at the Imp Shelter. I fell asleep within minutes; it was just what I needed. We had a hearty dinner and Mats was kind enough to share his chocolate for dessert. I made a point of drinking plenty of water and loading up on calories. Sleep came quickly and I was ever so grateful for cutting the day short.

August 16 It is amazing how well the body responds when you treat it nicely! I woke the next day feeling strong, vibrant, and excited about continuing. I enjoyed breakfast and a Clif Shot, and drank over a liter of water before heading out; Mats was still packing. The Wildcat-Carter-Moriah Range has always been a favorite of mine, offering a variety of terrain from bog bridges and green mossy patches, to steep climbs and ledges with sweeping views of the Presidentials and the Wild River. Today I made a point to eat and hydrate continually throughout the day. Mats caught up with me at the North Carter Trail junction and we hiked together for the rest of the day. After breaks, I'd get a little head start but he always caught up within 10 minutes. At the beginning of the hike, my food bag had weighed in at just over 30 pounds. After three days of food consumption, my pack still seemed heavy, but my legs were starting to feel very strong.

We made the steep descent to Carter Notch and took a long break at the hut. Snacking throughout the day is important and I was excited when Mats pulled out a can of sardines—how delicious they would be! Digging in was delayed, though, because Mats sliced his tongue pretty badly while licking the oil off the lid. It bled profusely and I worried about how deep the gash actually was. Thankfully the bleeding stopped after a few minutes and we were finally able to enjoy the treat!

I had another Clif Shot, giving me energy for the steep climb to Wild-cat A. We took a brief summit break and then bumped along the ridge to Wildcat D. While resting on the summit, a rabbi and his children arrived. They wanted advice on the trail going down. Mats was very direct; he told them they did not have the proper shoes, clothing, or gear, and that it would be best for them to go down as they had come up, via the gondola. I'd only descended from Wildcat D via the ski trails (though I'd climbed *up* to Wildcat D via the hiking trail), so this would be my first trail descent. A mouthful of four-letter words is the best way to describe this steep, rocky, rooty trail. It did a number on my knees and feet. Going down, I tried to concentrate on how wonderful it would be climbing out of the notch up to Glen Boulder. Crossing the river near the bottom I fell in. Mats reminded me to be careful where I step, but I was too busy laughing and splashing around to pay much attention. Surprisingly, a wave of renewed energy rippled through me—maybe cooling off in the water was just what I needed!

When we began the final climb, I was amazed at how strong my legs felt, this late in the day. I was feeling so happy inside for not quitting. I felt that I'd conquered not only my physical limitations but also my mental state. It's always good to push yourself to the next level, otherwise how will you truly know your potential? My spirits were high and not much could wipe the smile from my face. We camped at a nice spot just above Glen Boulder and it was a beautiful starlit night.

August 17 I've always been an early riser and the morning started with a beautiful sunrise over the Wildcats—could one ask for a better way to start the day? After breakfast the task was to tend to our feet. I had developed several pressure points, the worst being near my pinkie toe, and taping my toes alleviated the pain. Mats's feet were a different story; he had several blisters and it took twenty minutes to get his feet taped. It was another hot, humid day and we each had 1 liter of water to make it to Isolation and then

Mary Ellen BaRoss and Mats Roing on the Crawford Path, Southern Presidential Range.
Photo courtesy of Mats Roing

up to Washington. The effects of dehydration set in quickly as we climbed to the summit of Washington. I was feeling sick to my stomach and very weak, but knew we'd have our fill of water shortly. In the building we each drank 2 liters of water, and the color soon came back into Mats's face. We hiked the Southern Presidentials, one of the most beautiful sections of trail in the entire White Mountains, and the weather was spectacular! We filled our water bottles at Lakes of the Clouds Hut and Mizpah Spring Hut, so we benefited from lighter packs. On Jackson's summit we encountered a through-hiker who was enjoying a cold beer; how nice that must have tasted! It is only 2.5 miles from Jackson to Highland Center, but this trail rivals the Wildcat Ridge Trail in its nastiness. This is my least favorite trail in the entire White Mountains; it has many roots and is steep, rocky, and wet—a nightmare for someone who has a tendency to fall, which I did on several occasions. Mats again reminded me of how important it is to carefully place each foot. The pounding did a number on my feet and they were in a great deal of pain upon reaching Highland Center. We got bunks at the Shapleigh bunkhouse and I laid awake for what seemed like most of the night. Sleep had not been an issue before; usually I would be asleep within minutes. But that night my throbbing and aching feet kept me awake. Four tablets of "vitamin I" couldn't take the edge off. I kept my feet elevated but that didn't make much difference. Thoughts of quitting entered my mind, but I decided to see how they felt in the morning.

August 18 Mats was getting ready when I shuffled into the common area, my feet tingling and the pain in my pinkie-toe area unbearable. My toes resembled mini sausages; cramming them into my boots would have only made matters worse. I cried again as I told Mats I wouldn't be going on. I enjoyed a hearty breakfast, going back three times to refill my plate, then a friend brought me to my car. Mats was doing a big day on the Willey Range to Carrigain and then out Sawyer Pond Road, planning to camp by the river on the Olivarian Brook Trail. I had a good chance of meeting him at that trailhead and made a cozy bed in the back of my truck, in case I spent the night there. After an hour, I made out a faint light coming my way. Mats! I gathered my gear, put on my trail runners, and together we hiked another mile to set up camp at a nice spot on the river.

August 19 Mats continued to Passaconaway, Whiteface, and the Tripyramids, while I hiked the Osceolas with a light pack and trail runners. I headed down the Livermore Trail to wait at the first intersection for him; within five minutes he arrived. He still needed Tecumseh and planned to climb the trail near the ski area while I approached from Tripoli Road. That trail is open and occasionally hard to follow. The day was almost over. I had a 3-mile approach plus a 10-minute drive, while Mats had just over 2.5 miles to the summit. I don't mind hiking alone in the dark but it wouldn't be my first choice. To my surprise I summited in daylight, thrilled to make such good time even with sore feet. Twenty minutes later Mats arrived and we made the long and painfully slow descent back, where we set up camp.

August 20 Mats would be climbing over the Osceolas and I planned to meet him at the Greeley Ponds Trailhead. I loaded my pack with two days of food, waited for him, then taped up his feet, which were getting worse. The blisters were big and liquid-filled and his toes were pruned beyond recognition, but his spirits were still high and overall he was doing quite well. I think his spirits were lifted even more when I told him I'd be joining him again. After a short walk up the Kanc, we started on the Hancock Notch Trail and dropped our packs shortly after the intersection with the

Cedar Brook Trail; Mats carried the lid of his big pack. I was starting to feel like my old self again. Just a little way up the Bondcliff Trail, we found a nice spot to set up camp.

August 21 We woke to foggy and misty weather. Mats had planned a big day—the Bonds, the Twinway over Zealand to Zealand Hut, up Hale with a descent on the old fire warden's trail, then up over the Twins and down to Galehead Hut. I joined him on the Bonds then headed to South Twin and down to Galehead Hut. I arrived at the hut at 2:00 p.m. and explained to the croo that we just needed a space on the floor for the night and would not be eating food; the hut master said we could stay for $10.00 each. Huts are nice if you need shelter or water and they also get current weather forecasts—today they were predicting tropical downpours from the remains of a hurricane! The winds picked up, the sky darkened, flashes of lightning and thunder began, and torrents of rain started. A huge waterfall of water came off the roof. Mats was out in this violent storm and I prayed that he was down low while it passed. At 6:00 p.m., those of us not paying for dinner waited outside while the croo and guests ate their meal. Around seven Mats arrived, soaked but with a big smile. He did the quick up to Galehead, then we paid our $10.00, had dinner, and set up camp underneath a dining room table.

August 22 After breakfast and feet taping, we headed toward Garfield, then had a gentle downhill to Thirteen Falls. We'd been warned of a decaying moose carcass on the Owl's Head slide, but no one mentioned the stench! As we started up, we encountered a bad smell—tolerable at first—but it only got worse and soon I was gagging. I plugged my nose and tried holding my breath, but it did no good. I started to *taste* the smell, which made me gag even more! My eyes and mouth were watering and I thought I would vomit. I went as fast as I could and when we finally passed the remains, I was astonished at how little of the moose was left. How could it still be giving off such a horrid smell? I had expected to find rotting flesh and maggots, but all we saw was hair and part of the rib cage. I was amazed at how quickly the smell dissipated a few steps upwind and was relieved to take a full breath. Mats was ahead and suddenly started yelling and flailing his arms. The biggest, meatiest spider ever was hanging off Mats arm! Thank goodness the spider found him and not me! It took a few swats to finally break its web, then the scary spider dropped to the ground.

We parted at the Osseo Trail. While Mats went over Franconia Ridge, I planned to head out to Lincoln Woods, hitchhike to my car, then grab a campsite at Lafayette Campground. I threw out my thumb with my best look of despair and finally a car stopped—it was my friend Arm! Setting up the tent in the rain was quite a challenge. At 7:30 p.m. Mats would be just reaching Flume, making good time, and I had no doubts he would be done by midnight. Later I was awakened by a torrential downpour—the water seeped through the tent walls and quickly everything was damp or wet. Thankfully it wasn't a thunderstorm, with Mats on the open ridge. It was well past midnight. *He'll be down any time now,* I thought. One o'clock rolled by, then two o'clock. I began to worry—*maybe he's slipped and hurt himself!* Finally, at 2:45 a.m., I saw a faint light closing in, ever so slowly. By the way he was walking, I knew Mats must be in a great deal of pain. I thought for sure he would let me drive him to the campsite but he was still determined to keep going.

August 23 Mats had just four more peaks to successfully complete the Direttissima, but when he awoke I could hear defeat in his voice. His feet were a terrible mess. It had become a matter of what was best for the body. Should you continue and risk injury? Or was it better to toss in the towel, knowing you'd done the best you could? Instead of packing up and putting on hiking shoes, we slept in, then met friends in Woodstock for a hearty breakfast. As Mats had often said to me, *If you can keep the feet happy, your legs will take you where you want to go.*

The White Mountain 4,000-Footers Direttissima

The "Four Thousand Footers Direttissima"—that's what Henry T. Folsom, aka The Good Reverend, called this project in his December 1971 *Appalachia* article. His idea was to "start at one end of the New Hampshire Four Thousand Footers and walk all the way to the other end in the fewest possible miles while passing over each of the forty-six summits." (Bondcliff and Galehead were not yet on the official list.) Each summit would be reached by foot only; the hiker would walk between the mountains as well as over them; and no bushwhacking would be allowed. Henry completed the project over nineteen days between June and September of 1971. He started on Cabot and finished on Moosilauke, sleeping five nights along the route. After finishing a few sections, it was sometimes several weeks before he returned to the trail. His route covered 245 miles.

When I studied the map, intrigued by the possibility of doing forty-eight peaks in a continuous backpacking trip, I came up with almost exactly the same itinerary as Henry—it's a natural line to follow. My route covered 235 miles, doing Lincoln Slide to get to Owl's Head and the old fire warden's trail to Hale. Because the Kilkenny Ridge Trail didn't exist in 1971, Henry had to walk roads between the Cabot and Waumbeck trailheads. (He often had to decline offers for a ride; when I did it, not a single car stopped—how times have changed!)

Unlike Henry, I planned to stay on route the whole time and bring everything with me from the start, except water. No pre-placed stashes of pickled herring for me . . . remember, I was raised in Sweden. I thought late August to early September would be ideal, with blackflies and mosquitoes gone, and hot muggy days less common; the shorter daylight hours were a favorable tradeoff. Here's a list of the gear I decided on: Big Agnes Seedhouse SL2 tent, about 4 pounds with the footprint; North Face Propel 40-degree synthetic bag, 1 pound; Therm-a-rest ProLite 3 sleeping pad, ¾ length, plus a Z Lite sitting pad; Osprey Atmos 50 backpack, plus a small,

300-cubic-inch race pack for use when leaving the big pack and tagging a peak; one pair of medium-weight Gore-Tex hiking boots, with a pair of running shoes for relief on easy sections; cereals mixed with powdered milk; Clif Shots, Lärabars, sardines, and other snack food; two-serving portions of freeze-dried food for dinners, with chocolate, often, for dessert; Jetboil with two small gas containers; Black Diamond Spot headlamp, plus a Petzl e-Lite as back-up.

AUGUST 31, 2007 Moosilauke, Kinsmans, and Cannon, 25.1 miles, 10,040 vertical feet.

My friend Cory drove me to Beaver Brook trailhead and we were off at 4:47 a.m., in fog, up the mile of steep slippery rocks and finally to foggy views from Moosilauke, where I did the ten push-ups I intended to do on each summit. Down a bit after nine o'clock, I tended to my feet, hoisted my backpack, "Fat Bertha," and stumbled toward the Kinsman Ridge Trail. After 100 feet I took a break, realizing that this was going to be a long day, now solo. After PUDs—Pointless Ups and Downs—in periodic light drizzle, I reached the Mount Wolf intersection three hours later, switched socks, applied more Sportslick on my feet, and refilled the bladder with good water by the shelter. Off toward the Kinsmans, 2,000 vertical feet higher. Harrington Pond showed up after a seeming eternity. Everything was soggy and slow going on very slick rocks, and occasional leg cramps forced me to take it slowly to avoid triggering more. After 4:00 p.m. I did my push-ups in zero visibility on South Kinsman and, an hour later, left North Kinsman toward the Cannon Balls. The sun peeked through occasionally and I stopped for foot maintenance and Clif Shots. Steep down after the second Cannon Ball—one left. More uphill and to my disappointment I realized there was a fourth one! Trekking poles were extended for the last downhill toward the Lonesome Lake Trail junction, and down farther before the steep blocky uphill section began—*the last uphill for the day.* Finally coming up to Hi-Cannon cutoff, I dumped my pack and did the last push-ups on Cannon at 7:20 p.m. Below the steep section I heard a big rock fall in the dark and was glad I wasn't close by. Doctor D was at Lafayette Campground with a beer at 9:20—what's better than a cold beer after a long hike? Jen Gross showed up and we had a good time by the fire.

SEPTEMBER 1 Franconia Ridge to base of Owl's Head, 15.5 miles, total: 40.6 miles; 6,550 vertical feet, total: 16,590 feet.

Trying to cram everything into the 50-liter pack, we started late, with later consequences. Jen and Cory were ahead of me on the Falling Waters Trail and Cory guarded our belongings while Jen and I headed for Liberty and Flume. Tough to keep up with her sometimes . . . in good condition she is (Yoda voice). We re-saddled and headed for Lincoln, where push-ups were done in company of a female lacrosse team. At the Lincoln Slide cutoff we left the big mama packs and ran up Lafayette for ten push-ups. Owl's Head and Garfield weren't going to be easy. Cory found a good way to the north prong of the slide; we finally crossed Lincoln Brook and onto the trail. At the end of a long hiking day, everything seems to take an eternity—we went all the way to the Owl's Head cutoff where we set up camp at 6:30 p.m. We were not psyched to come down that slide in the dark—one slide a day was enough! I took a very refreshing bath in Lincoln Brook. We ate in the dark; no mosquitoes! I got cramps during dinner, though, and my cell phone had been left on overnight, searching for service, so I was now dependent on the portable charger running on a single AA.

SEPTEMBER 2 Owl's Head, Garfield, Galehead, South and North Twin, 18 miles, total: 58.6 miles; 8,050 vertical feet, total: 24,640 feet.

After Owl's Head we headed to Thirteen Falls. I met a barefoot hiker who told me that he does wear shoes in winter. *Would it be possible to do the Direttissima barefoot?* It didn't strike me as too appealing. There is lots of uphill to Garfield, although I was surprised how flat the first part is. The summit resembled a Japanese subway station in rush hour! Galehead Hut had few people and I took a long break before taking off to Galehead Mountain. It was a beautiful evening, sun over both Twins. I went down the North Twin Trail and found a lovely camping spot just south of the old fire warden's trail cutoff.

SEPTEMBER 3

I was on top of sunny Hale Mountain at 8:00 a.m. and, by 1:00 p.m., I was over the crest to the Bonds, delayed because of plentiful lingonberry patches. I took a long break on spectacular Bondcliff, enjoying completion of the Pemi summits. Then I began the long trek to the Hancocks and missed Doctor D by just ten minutes at the Hancock cutoff! I fantasized about filet mignon with béarnaise sauce on a bed of wild rice.

I went up the Hancocks clockwise next morning; it was nice to go light. I dropped the camera, which exhibited a funny, inconsistent behavior the rest of the trip, the self-timer and shutter working only occasionally. On South Hancock the wind increased dramatically and push-ups went fast. I reached the Kancamagus Highway about 11:00 a.m. and cruised 0.7 miles to the Osceola trailhead. I switched shoes and had the best can of sardines ever, soaked in lovely olive oil that went down like silk. I decided to go light up Osceola so I didn't top off my hydration pack in the creek, which would have later consequences. After the flat section to the cutoff, the *looong* uphill started—it seemed like it took a couple of years to reach 3,000 feet. The sun was getting stronger as I finally reached the open slide a few hundred feet below the ridge—a very welcome sight—although there was still some uphill before reaching the first summit. I avoided the chimney, reached Mount Osceola's summit and headed down the other way. My water was gone. This trail likes to treat you with many tilted ledges, good ankle training. The sun was strong and there was no water. *How would those beers have tasted if I'd made it to the Hancocks on time?* I headed to Vista Campground on the hard pavement, very tired, my throat dry as dirt. *Maybe the campground will appear after the next turn, or the next . . . no . . . not yet.* Then a Jeep with a hottie at the steering wheel passed me and stopped! "Hey, you're going in the wrong direction," the hottie said, walking toward me. "There's a beautiful trailhead the other way to Tecumseh." It was Cath Goodwin—great to finally meet this White Mountain legend! She offered me one of those R.W. Knudsen's Recharge drinks—exactly what I needed. It was a long time before I saw the campground sign, then a long road in. But I was the only one there! *Woo-hoo!* The attendant warned that eighty college kids would soon arrive, but it's good they're out in the woods—they could be doing worse things.

SEPTEMBER 5 Tripyramids, Whiteface, Passaconaway, 18.6 miles, total: 126.9 miles; 6,750 vertical feet, total: 48,190 feet.

Cold and dewy this morning; the first miles of the Livermore Trail were flat enough for a Lamborghini to drive on without getting scratched. This changed dramatically after turning right on the North Slide Trail. Henry Folsom said that the Passaconaway-Pyramids loop was the hardest day of the summer for him—no wonder, he went *down* the North Slide! Though my pack was a bit lighter, it wasn't a cakewalk to ascend the steep slide; the Scaur Ridge Trail would have been faster. I took a break on North Tripyramid, celebrating the halfway mark. Down South Tripyramid, I kept looking for the Kate Sleeper cutoff and saw a funny-looking double-arrow in yellow, painted on a ledge. I continued down and down and down, in the scorching sun. Eventually the trail flattened out, but I didn't feel good about going west. I pulled out the map—**$%k!* I had missed the cutoff, 1,000 vertical feet up, at the top of the slide! Back up in the relentless sun, I came again to the funny-looking arrow: the Kate Sleeper cutoff! That trail was nice and gently rolling. I ran out of water before I got to Whiteface, so I did my push-ups, then was eager to get to Passaconaway and down the other side to find some. At the Dicey's Mill cutoff I took a left up the hill and . . . lo and behold! The little creek before the last cutoff had water! It must have been fresh spring water. I drank a number of cups, enough to get me up and over the pass. It still seemed to take an eternity to get to the top. I had to go below 2,000 feet before finding any drinkable water on the cutoff trail and indulged immensely. I then entered the Oliverian Brook Trail and continued toward Crawford Notch at 1,400 feet: the lowest altitude so far and no mosquitoes!

SEPTEMBER 6 Sawyer Pond to Mount Carrigain to Ethan Pond Campsite, 23.6 miles, total: 150.5 miles; 5,950 vertical feet; total 54,140 feet.

I got going with running shoes and crossed over the Kancamagus again, psyched that I was going to be north of it for the rest of the trip. On the map it looked like a road could be a shortcut to the Signal Ridge Trail, but the bridge over the Sawyer River was gone and there were deep trenches every eighth of a mile across the road. At 1:40 p.m. I reached the false summit and enjoyed some lingonberries before a 20-minute hike to the tower. I checked the well a quarter-mile from the summit and it was empty. Doing push-ups on top, I was thinking about how the moonlight dance party would have turned out, if we'd had one. The tower itself looked sturdy, but maybe not for a live concert with a Swedish Viking metal band. Desolation Trail has steep parts but was very pleasant. At Stillwater Junction I took the Shoal Pond Trail and crossed the creek five times, meeting a large group of youngsters at a crossing before reaching Shoal Pond and the Ethan Pond Trail. *Should I go over to Willey, Field, and Tom tonight or tomorrow?* I was pretty tired and the Ethan Pond campsite had one platform left. A hike to the pond to resupply water, then a shower with my MSR DromLite. The site has a designated dining area where I cooked my dinner with a dozen high school kids. A pot-smoking young couple, doing the A.T. since mid-March, occupied the shelter. Tomorrow I'd be on the Pressies! Exciting!

SEPTEMBER 7 Willey, Field, Tom, Jackson, Pierce, Ike, Monroe, Washington, 23.0 miles, total: 173.5 miles; 9,800 vertical feet, total: 63,940 feet.

Going downhill on the Ethan Pond Trail before taking a left toward Willey, there was a *looong* uphill. On to Mount Field and push-ups celebrating number 30. On Mount Tom, I met the first hikers of the day. Down to Crawford Notch: it was hot and I started toward Jackson around noon. It was good to drink water out of a clean bladder at Mizpah Spring Hut. I met the pot-smoking young couple again—they were pretty stoned. She slept on a rock ledge in the scorching sun while he talked with me, slowly, about many things. I refilled my bladder, took care of my feet, and moved up toward Pierce. Mount Washington looked far away and the sun was hot. At 3:45 I stood on top of Eisenhower; I stood on Monroe after 5:00. Down to the crowded hut, close to dinnertime, to refill. Took the Tuckerman Crossover to Davis Path, leaving the pack to go light up Mount Washington—oh so light, without the big pack! Windy . . . sun not as warm now. By 6:22 I was doing pushups at 6,288 feet. By 6:40 I was on the Davis Path toward Isolation, and took care of my feet just below timberline. My eyes wanted to sleep, as did the rest of me. At 4,300 feet I came across a rock with a camping spot behind it. Perfect—and happy to be horizontal. It was surprisingly warm and the sky was clear, so I didn't set up the fly. I gazed at the stars for seven seconds before passing out.

SEPTEMBER 8 Isolation, Wildcats, Carters, and Moriah, 25.0 miles, total: 198.5 miles; 9,750 vertical feet, total: 73,690 feet.

Strong winds woke me at 2:00 a.m. I was well protected, in thick woods behind a rock, but it was noisy. I considered taking a leisurely night stroll to Isolation, breaking camp, then heading back to the Glen Boulder trail.

Not much water left, but if I hiked slowly it might work. I sat on Isolation looking at the stars at 3:50 a.m. *The most effortless Isolation attempt ever.* By 6:30 I was at Glen Boulder, happy to get off to the leeside—it was very windy! At the first creek crossing I refilled water and met the father and daughter who were carrying the flag for Isolation for Flags on the 48.[20] I went a few hundred vertical feet up Route 16 before a breakfast break, aired out my feet, and started up the Wildcats—the trail seemed to go on forever. It was very foggy; I thought I was on top of Wildcat A and did push-ups, but it was Wildcat B. At Wildcat A I saw the flag on top of the summit. I did ten more push-ups before descending 1,100 feet to the hut, then changed to light shoes before going up Carter Dome. At 2:20 I was on top, where I took a break before heading down to Zeta Pass and up to South Carter. I was getting more tired but kept moving toward Middle Carter; it looked far away. I wanted to be heading down Stony Brook before dark. Moriah was still a few miles away and I had to go up and down North Carter first. Up wasn't bad . . . but down was more of a challenge on slippery rocks. After an eternity, I made it to the Imp campsite cutoff; tempting, but I was determined to get to Moriah. At the Stony Brook cutoff, heading toward Moriah felt a little better without the pack. I saw dark clouds forming when I could see the Pressies . . . *Shit! I forgot to cover my pack!* I started to run up—didn't want to be caught in a thunderstorm. I flew over the ledges: some quick pushups, a photo, then down at lightning speed. One minute from the pack, the heavy rain started; the round-trip had taken 52 minutes. With the headlamp I headed down Stony Brook, slow going on slick mossy rocks . . . tiredness and thirst set in. I found a decent camp spot by the first creek crossing with water, drank a bunch, and was close to falling asleep while eating. My sleeping bag wasn't wet!

SEPTEMBER 9 Madison, Adams, and Jefferson, 20.3 miles, total: 218.8 miles; 7,350 vertical feet, total: 81,040 feet.

I shook off dew before packing—for the last couple of days, everything had actually fit inside the pack—and filled up the bladder. After 3 miles on asphalt before hitting the Dolly Copp cutoff, I thought I had enough water to Madison Hut. I'd never been on the Daniel Webster Trail, a little over 4,000 vertical feet to the summit of Mount Madison. After 20 minutes it started raining. At 3,000 feet, the *slurp-ti-slurp* sound from the bladder meant it was close to empty. I was sweating with raingear on, but it prevents hypothermia; I found water running down a ledge and drank a few cups. It's always exciting to be on a trail you haven't been on before! It had lots of good ripe lingonberries. It became windier; I finally gained the ridge at 4,800 feet and saw the summit sign at 2:02 p.m. It took 20 minutes to re-sock my feet and I headed toward Thunderstorm Junction. A hiker told me that my friend Hamtero had turned back after Adams when he didn't see me. It was no fun to hang out up there in fog and rain. I was at least 3 hours behind schedule.

I left my pack at Thunderstorm Junction and did the round-trip to Adams for push-ups and photos. The diminished Bertha was heavier now, soggy with rain. I had to be very careful stepping on slick rocks, as usual. I met five hikers with ripped-to-pieces PVC rain gear on. They were not happy when I told them how far it was to Madison Hut; it was their first time on the Pressies. At Edmands Col I left the pack and made the round-trip to Jefferson in 45 minutes, elated to hike the last peak of the day. I studied the map to ensure that I took the correct trail down Castle Ravine. I hoped to catch my friend, but my pace slowed on the steep boulder section, where I exercised extreme caution on slick, unstable rocks. I eyed the next cairn for my short-term goal; for every cairn I reached, it seemed five more showed up. I wanted to descend the steep alpine section before dark. Then the rain stopped, the fog disappeared, and I could see the beautiful valley! Trees appeared, and bushes; dirt actually showed up on the trail for traction; boulders became larger and at times tricky, and I slid down some on my butt. I was in the woods! Although it was just 7:00 p.m., I had to resort to my headlamp. I came to the Bowman trailhead at 9:20 p.m.—no car with Hamtero. He'd arrived at the Israel Ridge trailhead at 5:00, smart enough to avoid Castle Ravine; experienced he is (Yoda voice).

I hiked west on Route 2, soaked, feet hurting, as semi trucks stirred up a foggy mist. A bed and breakfast sign! I wouldn't eat there, but it would be a dry place. A surprised and very gentle man welcomed me; I apologized for stinking and being dirty; he just smiled. I put towels on the carpet to prevent soiling it. He went back to the living room where he sat in a sofa and cuddled with his partner. I had never seen my feet so wrinkled! I fired up the Jetboil in the bathroom, to prevent the bedroom fire alarm from going off. The bed had sixteen pillows, a bit of overkill. Rain hammered the metal roof and I was glad to be there drying things. It felt weird to be in a bed! Tomorrow evening I wouldn't have to set up camp either . . . unreal.

Mats Roing on Mount Cabot, his forty-eighth peak of the Direttissima.
Photo by Mats Roing

SEPTEMBER 10 Waumbek and Cabot, 25.9 miles, total: 244.7 miles;
7,800 vertical feet, total: 88,840 feet; trailhead-to-trailhead time: 10 days,
14 hours, and 2 minutes.

At 5:00 a.m. the rain was still pounding. At 6:11 a.m. I left with raingear
on; it stopped raining as soon as I walked outside. After much road walk,
I turned right, uphill toward Waumbeck, and soon I was on Starr King,
hydrated and snacking to make sure I had the energy to power through
Kilkenny Ridge. I did the dip before Waumbeck and now just Cabot remained, but it was a long approach with six 3,500-foot-plus peaks along the
way. South Weeks was 2.5 miles away, but this trail was good. Lots of low
vegetation kept my legs and feet soaked, making for super-wrinkled feet
every time I aired them out. South Weeks and Middle Weeks weren't bad.
I took another foot-care break—my boots were so wet. North Weeks was a
long haul and dropping 1,200 feet down to the York Pond Junction seemed
to take forever, but I've done 6.2 miles since Waumbeck! *Yee-haaa!* I took
a 20-minute break before continuing 900 feet up Terrace Mountain. One
step at a time—there are three Terrace summits. The sun peeked through

and I saw Cabot—the last one! But it seemed very far. The final downhill to Bunnell Notch and then I started up Cabot, excited but a little tired now. It was still foggy but no rain. I hit 4,000 feet, and soon the Forest Service cabin appeared.

Halfway to the summit a moose sat on the trail. He continued up the trail then waited for me . . . continued a little more . . . waited. He passed the summit slightly ahead of me. He skipped the push-ups, though. At 4:54 p.m. I felt a bit nostalgic to reach number 48. I drank water in the creek with the sign "last good water." It was after 6:00 and I saw a hiker with a dog; when he learned that I had just done the 48 in one hike, he invited me for frosty tall ones and dinner. His wife cooked up a storm while I sat with a cold Corona in a glass—suddenly I was in heaven. Pan is a doctor at Lancaster Hospital and his wife used to be his nurse; he's from the Netherlands, she's from Wales, and I'm Swedish. Here were three Europeans sitting by Mount Cabot trailhead in northern New Hampshire! Their dog and cat took a liking to me, I presume because of my interesting smells. After dinner Pan's wife offered me delicious homemade ice cream. Fernanda met me for the trip back to Boston. The weirdest thing was getting used to traveling faster than 2 mph; I was a bit scared in the car at first—40 mph seemed like lightning speed!

DIANE DUGGENTO SAWYER

Enjoying a Frozen World

Tom Sawyer, always a fellow with restless feet, is never happy unless he has a list on which he is working; Tom was the first and perhaps only person to have completed all the 3,000-footers in New England in winter. I go along for exercise, camaraderie, because I don't want Tom to go alone, and to experience nature up close—at times too close! Many times we'd have a snowy, icy ride to a destination and once, in Maine, we just missed hitting a moose on a dark road! Our routine was to leave each Friday after work. During Christmas vacation we would prepare our Mountain Smith sleds for a weeklong camping trip. After arriving at an icy logging road, chains would be put on the van, then an hour would be spent chopping and shoveling a space well off the road in which to park it. Wearing headlamps, we would sled to the base of a group of remote mountains and set up base camp. We would check each other frequently for frostbite on cheeks and noses, use face masks or, if the wind was really ferocious, stay in the tent. Later, we might move our tent to shorten the trips we needed to make each day.

These treks were our transition from the hectic, mind-spinning work world and the tranquil, frozen, timeless world we were entering. Here our minds and souls would rest and heal from the bruising of the week's work and worries. Here we would return to the past, to the lives led by our ancestors, the simple struggle for survival that focuses one's attention on the meaning and value of life. The weather tended to gloomy days and beautifully stormy winter skies, with temperatures during late December ranging from the single digits to –15 degrees Fahrenheit, then growing colder as the winter wore on. Lots of moose, deer, snowshoe hare, otters, and grouse—along with the occasional fisher cat, bobcat, or lynx—roamed in these remote, deserted areas, shy of people. Camping out at 20 or 30 degrees below zero, getting mired in spruce traps, snowshoeing 20 or more miles per day, in the dead of winter, led us to some unforgettable experiences.

For example, we made it a point to travel by moonlight after dark; even a half moon's glow provided more than enough light to find our way off a mountain. If conditions were very overcast, or if we were stumbling or

Get a dogsled! *Photo by David White*

slowing down too much, we might use artificial light—but we resorted to this reluctantly and rarely. At first, I was nervous in the dark; I couldn't relax and enjoy what it had to offer. It took many trips before I learned that the darkness is not a scary time, but one filled with wonders not known or explored by many. Today I'm comfortable hiking at night, when we often talk about things that seem to come up after dark, things that frighten us or leave us confused—why things work out the way they do, or the sadness we feel about things in our lives we can't control.

Of course, it's not always easy to hike in winter. I developed ocular rosacea after my eye tissue may have frozen. How does one get frozen eyeballs? Try hiking for 10 hours at –40 degrees, in howling wind and blowing snow, with ice collecting on your face. I have completed the Northeast 111 peaks in winter, 80 percent of the New England 3,000-footers in winter, and Vermont's Long Trail in winter, but now, in cold and wind, I am susceptible to blurred vision and even temporary loss of vision, so I'm careful to use goggles when out in adverse conditions. Back problems have made me think I'd be unable to carry a heavy pack again, but by using a large fanny pack—which can hold an amazing amount—I can still carry a small load.

On one trip to Maine's Colburn Gore area, near the Canadian border, the weather forecast predicted record cold. After climbing some peaks,

Tom was tired and wanted to stay where we were, 10 or 12 miles in the wilderness on a dirt road, but I urged him to drive out and park near a store. This was one of those times when we'd hiked in and out on the same day, sometimes doing up to 25 miles to get back to our van to sleep. It was indeed –50 degrees in the morning and the van wouldn't start; we were towed to the nearest garage about 70 miles south. The electrical wires in the van had fractured because of the cold. Three more tows got the van to the dealer, who had to install all new wires. It was the only time we've had a vehicle problem.

Even at –50 degrees, winter camping was always toasty for us, with our King Tut sleeping bags good to –40 degrees and a North Face V24 tent. Now we use a combination of a very light Mountain Hardwear down bag and a bulky Moonstone synthetic bag; this allows us to do almost any type of camping.

When cooking inside a tent, it is very important to vent it well; otherwise everything becomes damp or even wet. We open the two vent holes in the tent ceiling when cooking and leave the front door open as well. We cook things that don't need added water, like bagels with cheese and ham, to start the meal. I prepare a prepackaged, fully cooked meal at home so we can warm it with a minimum amount of water. Hot dogs and beans need no water. We have favorite things to eat that help keep our spirits and energy up on the rough hikes, like brownies and hot chocolate with a shot of coffee brandy.

When we need to boil a lot of water we put the stove outside the tent. Water is heated to fill bottles for our sleeping bags; we wash in heated water in the tent vestibule, which soothes the tired body and lets us relax and get warm quickly, like a shower would. We aren't cold when we wash, though maybe cool; we do it after we've eaten, when the tent is always a lot warmer than the outside air. If we cooked in the tent vestibule, the temperature inside might get into the fifties! We change into clean long johns and crawl into the bag—it always feels good with hot water bottles in there. I use one at my feet and one near my stomach.

Overnight, each person generates at least 200 milliliters of moisture just by breathing; this becomes frost on the cold tent walls. When you get out of your sleeping bags, however, warm air escapes and melts the frozen moisture, which then drips on you, your bag, and your gear. I use a microfiber towel to wipe it off; if we have a lot of moisture on the tent, inside or out, we always spread the tent out and shake it vigorously to get off as much frost or water as possible; this keeps its weight to a minimum.

I've even used one or two Bounty or Viva paper towels to dry the tent; they hold a lot of moisture and will withstand wringing out; less expensive paper towels don't hold up at all. While this won't completely dry the tent, it sure helps a lot.

Tom always warned me to put my boots in my sleeping bag, but boots would make the bottom of the bag very cold. Shuddering, I'd place them in the bag, keeping legs curled up to avoid contact! Then I just couldn't do it anymore; I put them in a large stuff sack, wrap that in my poly-filled coat, then put that at the foot of the tent. My boots will be cold but not frozen, and my feet usually warm them up quickly, even before we start to hike. Once I left them out in the vestibule and they were frozen solid by morning! I had a horrid time getting them on. That was a lesson quickly learned! I had to just force my feet into the boots, with lots of kicking and cursing. Tom's boots were in a stuff sack in the bottom of his bag—his feet can get cold in 90-degree temperatures, so he probably would have had frostbite in boots like mine. It usually takes 30 minutes of hiking uphill to warm his feet adequately.

Stopping to sit and eat during a hike is difficult in the frigid atmosphere.

CLIFF NOTE No matter how carefully one moves through snow-covered spruces, it is impossible to avoid sudden drops into spruce traps—some so deep that people drop completely out of sight. What makes it truly frightening is that you never know how far down you will sink. The snow can be 10 feet deep—or more—in windswept areas or after blizzards. It is exhausting to get out of a spruce trap and help is often needed to extract oneself. "A sudden terrifying collapse into seemingly bottomless snow on Gray Peak got me in over my head, and I'm 6 feet tall!" a woman wrote. "Had I been alone, I don't know if I could have escaped that last spruce trap—I could not reach my snowshoes. My 'geezer gang' wanted to enforce the 70-pound rule: they'd come back for me when I was down to 70 pounds and could be carried out!"

Taking off gloves is done only for seconds and it takes many minutes to re-warm hands; doing the simplest things without taking gloves off is a struggle. Dealing with tent poles is the most challenging job—gloves just slide around on the metal poles and frost-nip is always possible. Tom has the job of staking the tent by burying sticks tied to the ends of the tent poles. Another challenging task is getting water before total darkness; we typically break the ice on a nearby brook, then bury the water so that it won't freeze. The banks of brooks are usually steep and slippery and we are wearing snowshoes. Once, when Tom was looking for water upstream, I heard a horrible moaning. *Oh no,* I thought, *Tom has fallen in!* But when I shouted, he answered. We listened to the mournful sound of a lonely moose in the settling dusk; the next morning, we found moose tracks nearby.

There were some truly bizarre moments. On a bushwhack to Santanoni Peak, with our friend Pat and her husband, we encountered a dense spot just north of the Panther-Santanoni col. Pat and I were behind the men, catching up on news and enjoying the warm sunshine, when she disappeared into a horrendous spruce trap. Pat is 5 feet tall and was now well below the level of the snow, suspended on numerous spruce branches below. She is a real scrapper, a tough and resilient hiker and rock climber, and this was the first time I'd seen her exasperated and frustrated. She was cursing at the guys, whose tracks she'd been following—they were heavier and had stepped there, yet had managed to float over this hazardous spot. I watched her struggle, calling unsuccessfully to the men. I circled, trying to find some way to get close enough to help, without falling in too. I thought I'd found a place where I could offer a hand but, when I reached across, the snow caved in around me. In seconds, I was eyeball to eyeball with Pat. She was none too happy that I'd reburied her snowshoes and was now standing on them, making it even more difficult to move. We both worked for a long time, trying to free ourselves. Each time one of us tried to kick a step into the side of the hole, hoping to work our way up, we would discover yet another spruce trap.

Finally, the guys came back, wondering why we were so long in coming. They roared with laughter when they spotted us far down in a great hole. There wasn't much they could do, they informed us, as the entire area was a minefield of spruce traps. So they watched. Pat finally made her way out but I feared I never would! This was an exhausting, exasperating, and discouraging bushwhack phenomenon. It was nearly an hour after I'd seen Pat disappear into that god-awful spruce trap before I got out, with a hand from Tom. The giant crater that had been created by our struggle was 30 feet across and 7-plus feet deep! We wondered what the next party would think when they found this spot.

My advice is: learn to rely on yourself, and no one else, for help. I've grown in many ways because of my experiences—one is my ability to find my way in the woods with a compass. Relying on cell phones and other locating devices, or your companions, can give you a false sense of security. The mountain will be there for a long time, but you might not, if you go unprepared and are too anxious to get to a summit.

PART VII

Lost, Unprepared, Leader Lapses, and Bushwhacked

Two-thirds of these stories feature veteran hikers who make one of the most elementary errors—not bringing a flashlight— and half of those tales occur in winter when days are short. This simple lapse could be deadly. Other stories deal with inadequate gear, unexpected conditions, and groups separating on a hike; many illustrate what I call the "pitcher plant" phenomenon. Hikers are enticed by their goals like flies to a pitcher plant and— either through innocence or optimism—venture into situations from which it can be difficult to escape.

MARTA BOLTON QUILLIAM

Bivouac at Twenty Below

From the beginning, everything was going wrong that day. After getting up late we lost a precious hour trying to thaw the frozen car doors. That morning I kept going into our daughters' bedroom to kiss them and to tell them that I loved them. I packed an extra sandwich, put more clothes in my pack, and wore more than usual. Did I have some kind of premonition? Thick fog slowed down our drive to the trailhead. After stepping out into what felt like 50-mph wind, I wanted to get back in the car. Sparse trail markers on the unbroken West River Trail caused us to lose our way. Breaking trail in knee-deep snow up the Wedge Brook Trail, it took 5.5 hours to reach the col between the Wolf Jaws.

But the last, steep 500-foot ascent wasn't bad and, standing on Lower Wolf Jaw's summit, John said, "Since we've already gained all this ascent, why not go for Upper Wolf Jaw and Armstrong? It's only a mile and a half!" The going got tougher on Upper Wolf Jaw, and the snow deeper. Eventually, we reached the vertical cliff up Armstrong, where a large ladder is bolted to the lower half of the cliff and a metal cable hangs halfway down to a ledge, to help climbers maneuver to the top. It was all buried in deep snow.

I was frustrated. "I can't get a secure foothold," I said.

John scaled the cliff and lowered a rope. Once above the cliff we kept losing the trail, snowshoeing off in different directions, trying to locate markers obscured on snowy trees.

"We've got to bushwhack straight to the summit," John asserted, "and stop wasting time searching for markers."

"It's my turn to break trail," I offered, and made my way around him.

John kept us on course with map and compass but, when we reached the edge of a drop-off, I yelled, "I don't want to die!" in sudden panic. Four long hours after leaving Lower Wolf Jaw, hiking sometimes in waist-deep snow through windswept areas, we reached the Armstrong summit—it was four o'clock.

"Now we're home free," John grinned. "It'll be fairly easy sailing, down-hill."

It was February 29 and daylight lasted a lot longer than it had two months ago. *We'll at least get down to Lake Road before dark,* I thought. We lost the trail again at the col between Armstrong and Gothics, but soon found a clearing where we could begin a bushwhack.

"This is fine! That narrow trail up and down ladders on the cliff face scares me," I shivered. "It always seems that one misstep and you'll fall a long way down—what would it be like in winter?"

After much time bushwhacking steeply down the mountain, I asked, "Do you know where we are?"

"We're on a Beaver Meadow Falls tributary," John replied, "and every stream leads to a bigger body of water. We're heading for the lakes." Just

CLIFF NOTE One of the ten essentials for any pack, in any season, is a flashlight or headlamp—one for each person. Because its peaks are close to each other, the Great Range often tempts hikers to go beyond their limits. The area is uniquely rugged, exposed, and even treacherous in places (see "Fall from Saddleback Cliff").

In addition to its value in route-finding and fire-starting, a map can be put to at least one more use in the woods, shared by "Ditt" Dittmar, long-time Forty-Sixer Treasurer. After climbing Mount Colvin and Blake Peak, Ditt had dropped down to Lower Ausable Lake, planning to bushwhack back along the shore, but he found only steep mountainsides surrounding the lake. Ditt climbed up and down ledges, slabbing on nearly vertical terrain, until it became too dark to continue. Realizing that he would have to bivouac overnight, without proper gear or adequate clothes, he unfolded his map and put it between his body and his shirt to insulate himself. He said that it helped.

then one of John's snowshoes went through the ice on the stream we were following and got firmly lodged; hammering the ice released it only after what seemed like a long time.

Now it was dusk and we knew we weren't going to make it out. *Don't be afraid of the woods.* I could hear Grace[21] saying these words to me and it helped, but the temperature was plummeting. John immediately started gathering firewood. He tried to start a fire while I began searching for a blown-over tree stump, a large boulder, or a thick clump of trees to protect us—the temperature was forecast to be –20 degrees overnight!

"I can't get it started!" John yelled. "We're just going to freeze to death!"

"Bull!" I tossed my map over to him. "We won't need *that* if we freeze to death, will we!"

The map worked. We huddled together and I put my feet practically into the fire. We were well dug into the snow, under a clump of spruce trees, somewhat protected from the wind. Snow falling on my face woke me up but, because looking at it scared me, I kept my eyes closed.

At daybreak we set off and found the trail just 10 minutes later—we had been so close! We saw a search and rescue party organizing in Keene Valley and knew it was us they were going to search for; we stopped and told them we were out of the woods. They told us that a ranger and local caretaker had searched the lakes for 2 hours, after my sister had notified the Plattsburgh state police, at 10:00 p.m., that we hadn't come back.

Addendum

Newspaper accounts reported a temperature of –20 degrees Fahrenheit, with a wind-chill of –30 to –40 on the open Ausable Lakes, where state forest ranger Fred LaRow and Ronald Hall, a local caretaker, searched on snowmobiles from 11:30 p.m. to 1:00 a.m. LaRow, who headed the search team, said that the couple did not have a flashlight and that was the reason they had to stop. LaRow stressed that a flashlight or headlamp is essential in any season, as are sleeping bags and space blankets. A state police helicopter was on standby, waiting for heavy snow to abate. The couple drove by at 7:45 a.m., as six rangers and volunteers were organizing a search party in Keene Valley. LaRow cautioned them that he had carried a body out of that section of the High Peaks Wilderness before. Marta and John were summer 46ers, but they'd climbed only nine high peaks in winter before adding these three. They learned much about safety in the mountains on this excursion.

DOT MYER

Whiteout and Bivouac on Algonquin Peak

Ralph, Joan, and I had a chance to use survival techniques when we got disoriented on the open summit of 5,114-foot Algonquin Peak in early March. We had backpacked up to the Wright Peak junction at 4,000 feet, where we set up camp. The next day we climbed Algonquin with our daypacks and, in a whiteout, lost the trail on the descent. We tried to follow a compass course that we hoped would intercept the trail, but by 5:30 p.m. realized we would have to spend the night out without sleeping bags or other equipment.

My first thought had been to walk as far as possible, but that would have been foolish. Instead we followed a small brook until we found open water and decided to bivouac there. By sheer coincidence we found the remains of a shelter; it had a slight roof built of boughs, but was not a complete snow cave. We dug the snow out, put boughs on the snow, and added our snowshoes to the roof. Our fire never got going very well, even though Joan worked at it until nearly eleven o'clock. We ate bread and fruit and shivered through the night, sleeping only occasionally. We had a small space blanket that kept the snow from melting under us, but otherwise it didn't do much good. Fortunately it was not a very cold night, reminding me of a trip to Baxter State Park, when we found an igloo someone had built, near the Chimney Pond bunkhouse, and decided to sleep in it. It wasn't too cold to sleep in an igloo—it was too warm! The roof melted and dripped as if it were raining inside; I finally had to give up and sleep in the bunkhouse. The temperatures were so warm that we climbed Katahdin in shirt sleeves; one person hiked in long underwear. Two people had been killed in an avalanche just two days before we arrived. We hesitated when we saw the avalanche site, thinking about what had happened. It could have been us!

As the hours passed during this bivouac on the slope of Algonquin, I also remembered one of my most dangerous adventures on the Great Range, which occurred exactly a year earlier, on March 9, with Ralph, Jack, and Carlene. Mount Haystack was icy and some spots were very difficult, especially going up and descending Little Haystack. We had to chop steps in the ice in places on the descent. After Little Haystack, the four of us went on to climb Basin Mountain. We met a woman coming down from Basin alone, wearing crampons; we did not have crampons then, although we acquired them later for the White Mountain peaks. After difficulty finding the trail down the other side, we were descending very well when I suddenly lost my footing and experienced one of the worst falls of my life. I tried to slide toward a small tree but missed it and went sliding down a long steep snowfield at full speed, headfirst, on my stomach. It happened too fast to really think. I only remember seeing a big tree and thinking, *Should I slide into the tree or continue all the way down the slope?* Either choice could have been fatal. Fortunately the others

Dot was climbing in the years before good crampons were readily available and people often made their own. It is hard to imagine climbing the Great Range without *any* crampons! Even with crampons, the short 0.92-mile section of trail between Basin and Saddleback summits is treacherous, with very steep and exposed areas (see "Fall from Saddleback Cliff"). Dave and I saw a man lose his footing on Basin and slide 100 feet down the mountain, very similar to Dot's experience; he fortunately was unhurt.

were down ahead of me. Carlene, who is not particularly religious, said she prayed. Ralph caught me and saved me.

After our chilly night on Algonquin, we started walking at first light—it was much warmer than sleeping! Other than being tired and hungry, we felt fine and followed a compass course for 2 hours until we came upon snowshoe tracks; shortly after, we came to the trail just a few yards from the junction of the Van Hoevenberg and Algonquin Peak Trails. We had paralleled the trail all the way down! We then had to climb 1,750 feet back up for 3.4 miles, to retrieve our tent and equipment near the Wright junction. The really bad thing was that Ralph is a diabetic. Although he had insulin with him (to keep it warm), the needles to administer it were in his backpack up in our tent! Fortunately, we got back there in time for him to give himself a shot.

Most Difficult of the Winter 111

Seven of us did all three Bond Mountains, 21 miles in 18 hours, in January 1984. We started our trek at 6:00 a.m., snowshoeing along the Wilderness Trail and then following the Franconia Trail north until we reached the Hellgate Brook crossing. Our leader had selected this approach to West Bond Mountain, not an easy route. Trail-breaking through deep, crusty snow was strenuous, with the lead hikers breaking through frequently. I had shared this duty much of the day with just two other companions, because we were the lightest in weight and broke through the crust less often.

After 6 hours of hiking, we began the steep ascent to West Bond through dense scrub, underbrush, and trees. We reached the summit at 3:30 p.m. with the sun already getting low in the sky, and realized that we were less than halfway through our ordeal! There was no time to relax and enjoy the magnificent views of Lafayette and Bondcliff—and no turning back. We scurried ahead, as fast as one can on snowshoes, through deep snow and dense pines, in search of the trail to Bond. Alas, no brave soul had been over the trail recently. What we'd hoped would be a "piece of cake" was another mile-plus of strenuous snowshoeing. It was 5:00 p.m. when we reached Bond's summit—with breathtaking views of Bondcliff and West Bond before the setting sun. Oh, how the snow sparkled in purple, pink, and blue crystals!

We were tired but had no time to rest and enjoy this fully. With many hours and miles of snowshoeing ahead of us, delay was unwise. The sun set as we crossed Bondcliff. We were very relieved to find the trail below this peak broken out, which would make it easier to follow in the darkness. That was when we discovered that neither our leader nor his wife had headlamps! Fortunately, the rest of us did.

About 9:00 p.m., 15 hours after we started, I stumbled and fell headfirst into a snowdrift. I did not have the energy to push myself up and out. I was ready to lie there and go to sleep, so very tired and just worn out. My husband Phil pulled me out with the help of others and said I must keep

On the rocks, Bondcliff summit.
Photo by David White

going! The miles of snowshoeing down the Bondcliff and Wilderness Trails with headlamps seemed endless. I managed by concentrating on counting my steps up to 100, then starting over again. We struggled out to our cars by ones and twos between 11:15 and midnight! I consider this my most difficult hike of the Winter 111.

It was 10 degrees. Would our diesel engine start? More than once the car had failed to start in the bitterly cold temperatures of Northeast trailheads. Thankfully, it started this time. We hadn't been able to make overnight reservations because all the motels were filled with skiers or snowmobilers. We had left home at 3:00 a.m. with Phil driving; I always drove home. Trying to keep myself awake for the journey home, I began thinking about our other adventures. Once, an impending rain and sleet storm at Baxter State Park had required a change in plans involving a couple of 15-mile moves by snowmobile. I stood on the rear runners during one trip and Phil stopped about halfway to ask how I was doing. I stepped off the runners and said "Fine." He took off noisily, leaving me standing there. I was stunned, but the next half hour was unforgettable! I was in a silent, winter wonderland surrounded by massive, snow-covered evergreens, when a herd of moose appeared. I counted more than twenty—bulls, cows, and calves. They moved across the road in absolute silence. They were *huge*. I stood in amazement, with no camera. Too soon, I heard the snowmobile returning. Later Phil collected our friends and their gear and, taking a curve too quickly, spilled both of them off!

Our extreme day in the Bonds made me think about our first winter backpack, a year and a half after Phil and I met, a hike 7 miles over Avalanche Pass to a Lake Colden lean-to in the heart of the Adirondack High Peaks. My jacket thermometer read –14 degrees as we strapped on our snowshoes for the 900-foot climb. Evergreens were blanketed with half a foot of snow—it was a winter fairyland—and we walked across frozen Avalanche Lake surrounded by frosty high peaks. We quickly set up our tent and changed into dry clothes. I started heating enough water for dinner, plus two extra quarts apiece for the night—one canteen for each boot. The warm canteen keeps the boot from freezing, while the boot insulates the water, leaving it thawed for breakfast. The next morning, it was –27 degrees! While filling the stove with fuel, wearing only thin polypro gloves, I spilled some on my hand; this would have repercussions. We reached the

CLIFF NOTE In addition to not having headlamps, the hike leaders for this extensive hike made another mistake. A group's pace should be set by the slowest hiker and the group must stay together; what if someone had been unable to continue and needed help? Consider, too, that slower hikers might have done the lion's share of trail-breaking earlier in the day. About this group's separation on that long walk out, Bond Range expert Roy Schweiker commented: "I hope that at least one responsible person was waiting. I remember an Owl's Head trip with fifteen people straggling out; I waited with one person who was completely exhausted and when we finally got to the parking lot, only one man was left. The others had all gone home—quite different from times when the first people would come back for company, maybe even bringing hot drinks!"

summit canister on 4,363-foot Mount Marshall by late morning, signed in, and ate quickly. When my gloves were off, I noticed white skin on several fingers and a lack of feeling—frostnip! Likely the spilled fuel on my fingers caused it.[22] In spite of much exertion breaking camp and packing out, I became so thoroughly chilled when night fell that I stopped to put on my warmest sweater, but perspiration had frozen my jacket zipper and the sweater wasn't large enough to go over it . . .

My thoughts were interrupted, 15 miles from home, when a police car in Jaffrey, New Hampshire, stopped me. Apparently, I had taken a considerable time to make the left turn at Route 202. Phil woke up and told the officer he would take over. We returned 24 hours after leaving home.

AARON SCHOENBERG

Well, Hale Fellow Not Met

We started up the Hale Brook Trail from Zealand Road at 2:40 p.m., later than I'd hoped. Alex and Chris are somewhat faster hikers than I, but this was the first time we'd hiked with Karl, a youngster of twenty! I dillydallied behind, slowing them down, and when I arrived at Mount Hale at 4:30, the others were ready to head down to claim bunks at the Zealand Springs Hut. I decided to rest briefly and hike down the 2.7-mile Lend-a-Hand Trail at my comfortable pace, easily making it to the hut by six o'clock dinner.

Then it dawned on me—*I'd forgotten to pack my sneakers, my footwear for five evenings at the huts!* This was our first day of a multi-day Appalachian Trail trip. *Should I hike back down the mountain, drive to the Zealand trailhead and walk up the 2.8 miles to the hut, or continue without my sneakers?* I had snacks and lunches packed, so if I missed dinner I wouldn't go hungry, but being without comfortable footwear in the evenings would be a literal pain. *Okay, I would arrive an hour late.* I took off down to my car. On the trail up to the Zealand Falls Hut, I saw beaver swimming in the Zealand River. I managed to complete the 2.8-mile trail in a fast 1 hour, 7 minutes, even with taking a few moments to catch my breath, take a few pictures, and look around. When I arrived at the hut at 7:07, I learned that Chris had already left to look for me.

Because dinner had come and gone without my arrival, Chris was sure that I must be hurt. He'd taken off, without a flashlight, back up the Lend-a-Hand Trail to look for me. It would get dark around 8:45; would he be able to summit Mount Hale and get back before dark? We yelled, to no avail. Chris had already climbed the two Hancock high peaks today, a distance of 9.8 miles, then hiked over Mount Hale, for a cumulative 14.8 miles and over 5,000 feet in elevation gain. Because he feared I was hurt near the summit, he would climb all the way to the top of Mount Hale again, and wind up hiking 20.4 miles with a total elevation gain of approximately 6,400 feet!

Now it was dark. We checked Chris's pack and saw that his flashlight was still in it, so he was truly unprepared for night hiking. He'd also left without extra clothes for the night air. We informed the hut crew at Zealand of the situation. After 9:00 p.m. a search and rescue party was assembled. In the event Chris decided to do a loop over Hale, descending the way I had gone, one fellow went down the Zealand Trail with a walkie-talkie while other crew members went up Hale on the Lend-a-Hand Trail. There was a full moon, thankfully, which would assist somewhat in his descent and the search. As it turned out, Chris had floundered off the trail on his descent, in a deep wooded section, about half a mile from the hut. He saw the crew's flashlights and was guided back.

This story provides a lesson both about staying together, and about not going off half-cocked looking for someone. I was the butt of jokes—and understandable wrath from Chris, who was exhausted after a day like that. To top it off, Chris and I had to listen to the hut crew chastise us for our actions. But, being true friends, we understood why and how these events had happened, and I dearly appreciated the concern my fellow hiker and friend had for me, to undertake such a mission.

Addendum: Chris Connolly's Side of the Story

On our first day of hiking the Appalachian Trail, Aaron miscalculated the start time. It would have been okay with daypacks, but not with backpacks, as you surely feel the difference! After we topped Hale, Aaron didn't arrive until less than 90 minutes remained before our 6:00 p.m. Zealand Springs Hut dinnertime, so he sent us ahead while he, exhausted, rested (ah, yes, Aaron was *the* laggard on this trip). I arrived for dinner at the hut at 6:05 and expected Aaron by 6:30 at the latest, since he's gawky-fast on the downhill. With no Aaron by 6:45, we were worried that he'd fallen on slippery downhill rock. So *shtupid me* (as we Irish say), who had already put in 15 miles that day, left at 6:50 to retrace up the Lend-a-Hand Trail to search for our, ahem, "Leader." (And was a dim-enough bulb not to remember my flashlight!) I kept calling *Aaron, Aaron* till my voice got hoarse, but not a peep.

"Leader" arrived at the hut 15 minutes after I'd gone up, and wailed *Chris, Chris* in a forlorn effort to call me, well out of earshot. At first I was worried that he was unconscious somewhere, but by 8:15 I was approaching Hale's summit and praying something worse hadn't happened. Nary soul nor body was on the summit, so I frantically scurried back down, trying to cover the 2.7 miles before dark set in—but dark did set in, and I found my stumbling way by an almost full and blessedly bright moon. I knew I was less than a quarter-mile mile from the hut, because I heard the stream that flows near it. The moon disappeared behind the mountain at 9:45 and I backtracked to find a thread of lost trail. Then a light from below! I said *How do you do* to the hut crew, who'd left 10 minutes earlier, to search for the searcher. They were relieved to find me so close to the hut and I thanked the moon. I told "Leader" that I expected a full report of our Mad Mountain Adventure in his official trip report, along with certain profuse if not abject apologies. The crazy thing is—I had a wonderful time!

ANNE NORTON AND STEVE BOHEIM

A Chocorua Curse?

A group of us would annually celebrate New Year's by spending a few days in Meredith, New Hampshire, on Lake Winnipesaukee. One activity was the annual New Year's Hike, where we'd bare-boot a peak in the Whites, such as Willard, Sandwich, South Carter, Pierce/Clinton, or the trailless Nubble close to North Twin—no ropes, no crampons, minimal exposure to cliffs and ledges. Mount Chocorua was not one you'd include in the above group, given its spectacular, cliffy profile.[23]

One legend about the peak describes white settlers arriving on Indian land. Some of the settlers are killed, and so they hunt down the local chief. Cornered on Chocorua's summit, the chief refuses to surrender. As he jumps to his death, the chief curses all white men.

On December 31, it was ultramarathoner Zach who suggested climbing Chocorua, raving about the views he'd experienced on various trips. *Hmmm,* we thought. Almost none of us had climbed this peak before and there was no threat of foul weather or big wind, although it was much colder than it had been on the previous day. We planned a loop route: up Middle Sister Trail and on to Chocorua, then back down via Middle Sister or the Piper Trail, conditions permitting. We would have two cars, one at each trailhead on Route 16. The group had varying levels of experience; many of us had hiked together before, but there was also friend-of-a-friend Cathy, a new hiker. We all had hiking boots, gaiters, wool socks, sweaters, hats, and appropriate gloves; in addition, we had a space blanket, first-aid kit, the 1973 edition of the AMC *White Mountain Guide,* and appropriate food and water. But we didn't have flashlights, Microspikes, or crampons, and most of us wore cotton jeans. You'll see that this climb became two very different stories, and we still argue details about what actually happened. Perhaps there's something to the curse of Chocorua, after all!

We started just after dawn on a splendid day. There was snow on the ground but bare patches everywhere, and the trail was mostly broken by footprints. The snow deepened as we climbed but was never a problem; once up high, we found that the recent warm weather had melted all the snow off the rocks and ledges. We had sure footing and seemed well on our way. But Anne was moving pretty slowly—odd since she had easily done Mount Clinton two days before—and Matt was also moving unusually slowly.

Still, all was well until we got to the peak of Third Sister. That was when Cathy, our new hiker, started to get upset. The viewing was great, partly because the ledges made it look like you could take one step and drop off the edge of the world. Zach tried to reassure her by standing next to the drop-off and demonstrating that it was quite safe, but this foolhardy act (to her) only made matters worse. Discussion began. It was clear that she was not going to be able to complete the hike, as we had a long ridge with many such ledges ahead of us. What should we do? Should we all go back down, or split the party? We firmly believed, however, that whenever you split your party, you are tempting fate.

Anne said she was feeling very tired and vaguely unwell, and would go back with Cathy. Matt also was not feeling well and would go back too. Finally, Zach said that he had been to the summit before and would go down also. It seemed safe to split the group this way, since Anne was a nurse, a savvy hiker with a moderate amount of experience, and Zach was feeling fine. The other five hikers, led by Steve, would go on to Chocorua and descend via the Piper Trail. But Zach did not want to go down the

Mount Chocorua.
Photo by Steve Boheim

same way we'd come up—because that was "no fun"—and Cathy wanted to get off the ridge as quickly as possible. Maps and guidebooks came out; it was decided that the group going down would take the Carter Ledge Trail, then turn on the Nickerson Ledge Trail, which connects lower down to the Piper Trail, ending up at the same trailhead as the summit group. It sounded like a good plan. Anne's group of four waved goodbye and started down.

Steve's Tale

We five successfully climbed Chocorua, getting fabulous views, and hiked out via the Piper Trail, though it took a lot longer than we expected, with care required on steep and icy sections. It was almost dark when we got out, but the group of four wasn't at the trailhead. We'd expected that they would've easily gotten out ahead of us. We waited. Where could they be? Maybe they'd already come out and, since we had taken so long, had walked up the road to get their car at the other trailhead. Some of us drove up the road, seeing no walkers along the way, and arrived at dark at the Middle Sister trailhead, finding their car still there. So we drove back to the Piper trailhead, checking how many flashlights we have in the car, thinking that we'd have to look for them somewhere on their exit route. By now it was cold, we were tired, and it wasn't clear how long we'd have to be in the woods in the dark. It was not a great plan, so we dithered, waiting. The other group didn't show up. It was getting late. Before raising the alarm with rescue authorities, we went back to the original trailhead to see if they had come out on a different trail, the Carter Ledge Trail. But their car was now gone! And with no obvious exit footprints from the trailhead! Had the car been stolen? They *wouldn't* have left without making sure we were okay—Anne wouldn't have allowed it! Maybe we drove past them? We had no idea what to do, leading to a lot more dithering . . .

Let's leave the reader hanging here and go back to Anne's group. Remember our good exit plan? In retrospect, our maps had clearly shown steeper bits on the exit trails—steeper than we'd encountered so far—and those trail names ending with the word "ledge" seemed to confirm interesting times. But we paid no attention to those details, and we also assumed that snow conditions on the way down would mirror what we had seen on the way up.

Anne's Tale

We'd decided to take the Carter Ledge Trail, then turn on the Nickerson Ledge Trail and take it to the Piper Trail, ending up at the same trailhead as Steve's summit group. Almost immediately after the groups separated, Cathy began moving at a virtual crawl as we were still on the precipitous ledges. After we got below tree level, she moved a little faster, but the trail was steep here, covered with ice and snow, and no one else had been on the trail since the last snowfall. We were not making good time. Then I heard Cathy shouting for me to come back, as Matt was stuck! *Stuck where?* I thought. I hiked back up the trail and saw him halfway down a small cliff about 6 or 7 feet high. He refused to move, sure he was going to fall. I was able to talk him into *slowly* getting down. More time lost.

Now I was watching for the turn onto the Nickerson Ledge trail. Zach had come this way before and assured me that he would see it, but we learned that he had only hiked this trail when it had no snow cover. We kept descending at a turtle's pace, one factor being that Matt continued to have coordination trouble on the descent, although he didn't appear to be hypothermic. No trail junction. I asked Zach if we might have missed the turnoff.

"No, we'll reach it soon." More slow slogging downward through slippery snow. "We must have missed the junction," I exclaimed, but Zach didn't think so, and down we kept going. Finally I confronted him—"We *have* missed the turnoff because it is closer to the summit than this."

"I guess so, but it's no big deal," he replied. "We'll end up near the start of the Middle Sister Trail." Now I was really starting to worry: we'd get out to a different trailhead than the summit group would. The snow got deeper as we went lower and we needed to break through it, slowing us down again. It was 3:00 p.m. and it gets dark quickly in the mountains on December 31! I didn't know how far we had to go and asked Zach if he knew; he wasn't sure but said we had plenty of time—he guessed that we still had "four or five hours or so" of daylight left. Now I knew that we were in trouble! I'd been depending on him to get us safely out because he felt fine, but he did not realize we had less than 90 minutes of light left! Less able hikers were behind us and we had little food and water left. I thought about our situation. We were wearing jeans and had no form of shelter if we didn't get back to the cars. I'd read about people dying in the

White Mountains—the terrain is not as high as in other regions, but our peaks are at least as rugged and dangerous. I told Zach that I was afraid we wouldn't make it to the trailhead before it was pitch dark; we still needed to lose considerable altitude.

"The last part of the trail is an old logging road," he said, "and we can walk out even if it is dark."

"Without flashlights?" I asked.

"Sure, not a problem," he said. At that point, I thought, *We could die today, should a mishap occur.* The adrenaline helped my fatigue. I knew if I didn't do something, this could be our last hike. I told Zach that we were moving too slowly; we needed to pick up the pace. I would lead but he needed to come last and hurry Cathy and Matt along. What was wrong with this picture? The 5-foot 2-inch woman, not feeling well, was going to break trail, with the 6-foot-something man in the rear. But I wanted to live and I felt I owed it to Cathy and Matt to get us out safely. I have never been so tired but I kept pushing myself with every bit of effort I had. As the sun set behind the mountain it got darker and darker. We had descended most of the way, but I had no idea how far it was to get out and the summit group wouldn't know where we were. The trailhead would have no signs of hikers as the last snowfall had covered the trail. How I wished we'd gone down the way we'd come up! I pushed myself past what I thought I could do and, just before we lost the last light, we reached the road. But there was no car and no parking lot. In those days, the Carter Ledge Trail and the Middle Sisters Trail did not have a common access point from Route 16. I was done—I could hardly take another step. Zach said he would get the car and drive it to the trailhead. I slumped down by the side of the road.

Zach came back with the car in less than a half hour. We got in and he started to drive to Meredith, where we were staying the night. I said we needed to find the other group—we couldn't leave until we knew everyone was safe. He said he had talked to Steve and they'd agreed to meet back in

Meredith. I knew that wasn't right. Steve would never leave until he knew we were all safely out. I figured they had gotten out before us but could not know where we were. I failed to persuade Zach to stop, and would have been too exhausted to do anything, even if I had been successful, so we headed back to Meredith.

Later that year I was diagnosed with asthma, which is sensitive to cold air; this explained why I had felt bad that day. Also later that year, we discovered that Matt was an alcoholic and might have been attempting to hike Chocorua under the influence.

Back to Steve's Tale

It was dark. We had no idea where Anne's group was, not even their likely location, and their car was inexplicably missing. Maybe they really had left without us? We found a pay phone and called the place where we were staying in Meredith, a 40-minute drive away—and yes, they had just got there!

When we returned to Meredith, there was a lot of yelling, with a fair amount of "You said blah," "No I didn't," "I tried to stop him!" and "What were you thinking?" mixed in with "No big deal, we all got back okay, didn't we?" In hindsight, we learned many lessons about ourselves and about hiking that day. We had neither the skills nor the gear for that peak at that season—and were lucky to survive the curse of Chocorua!

STEVE BOHEIM

Democracy in Action

While plotting the approach for my final New England 4,000-footer, Mount Abraham, I thought I would also bag Middle Abraham, one of New England's 100 highest peaks. The Abraham mountain mass consists of eight peaks on a 4.5-mile ridge northwest of Kingfield, Maine, ranging in elevation from 3,400 feet to over 4,000 feet, with Mount Abraham accessible by road-then-trail from the east. The Mount Abraham Side Trail from the Appalachian Trail did not yet exist; west of this ridge was an abandoned railroad and some logging roads, but there was nothing out there for a long way.

We planned to climb trailless Middle Abraham first, starting the bushwhack from the fire warden's trail, then crossing the rocky exposed ridge to the above-tree-line Mount Abraham, and then descending via the fire warden's trail, a nice loop. This despite the AMC *Maine Mountain Guide* opinion: "Although the trailless ridge south of the tower has been traversed and is potentially one of New England's better ridge traverses, that route is not advisable since the distances are deceptive and the scrub is dense between peaks." The *Guide* also had admonitions about the poorly maintained, hard-to-follow fire warden's trail, with a dangerous crossing of Rapid Stream, which we'd have to do both first thing in the morning and at the end of the day.

Three souls came along with me: John and a married couple. They all had hiking experience, but none had trailless experience. We made the crossing of Rapid Stream soon after first light—the bridge was washed out so crossing was tricky, but doable. We then hiked along the old fire warden's trail until we hit Norton Brook, where we began the bushwhack. The brook became a gully with 6-foot walls and, though a pretty ascent, it was slow going through thick growth. Above the brook, trees were close together and there was tall, persistent brush; I encountered plenty of brush-in-the-face but, being tallest, I avoided what was a lot more in-your-face for the others. I had an internal-frame daypack and could dodge and weave, moving pretty freely through the trees and making good time. But John had an external-frame pack, just wide enough to catch on every tree he attempted to pass—so it was take a few steps, slam to a stop, then twist around the tree, over and over for an hour or more.

The smiles on the three souls—now victims—were long gone; they'd had quite enough trailless, thank you, it was noon and when were we getting to the top? As we finally neared the top of the ridge, there was the question of which bump was the right one; we had no clue, so started on the southernmost one. But the balsam and spruce on the summit ridge was stunted and very, very dense, as the *Guide* had said—crawl-on-your-belly dense, because it was way too sharp to climb over or through, and nobody had eye protection. John and I wore shorts and were bleeding from "cedar inoculations" in a gazillion spots, and the stunted tree branches flogged our raw skin, reminding us of the definition of *cripplebrush*. Needless to say, progress was slow and painful. Then we discovered that the southernmost peak was not the summit. There was cursing—new blue words were created just for this summit. When the next bump—with even thicker cripplebrush—wasn't the summit either, there was even more enthusiastic and creative cursing. We finally broke out onto the rocky ridge, and found the Middle Abraham summit at a spectacular erratic with great views, including north to Mount Abraham.

But it was three o'clock and the col between Middle Abraham and Abraham also was dense with cripplebrush. If we could just get beyond that point, things looked like they stayed rocky and should go quickly, but there was a big shoulder to deal with before finally getting onto Abraham proper. I figured we still could bag Abraham, but it would be past dark by the time we got to the old fire warden's cabin on the exiting trail and, since we didn't have flashlights, we'd have to spend the night there. Because we didn't know the weather report, in terms of temperature or rain, this plan was not greeted with any enthusiasm.

Our next choice was to retrace east and hope that a different route down would be a little better but, given the generally thick terrain on these mountains, it was unlikely we'd get out in time. Nobody wanted to face the thick stuff again, as our legs were raw and bleeding, or spend a night out in the woods on some steep slope. The final option was to go out to the west—unknown territory—but 800 feet below us was an obvious logging road turnaround, completely clear of blowdown. As leader, I voted for Abraham and the old cabin. The couple wanted to descend to the logging road, no longer trusting my ability to estimate time or distance. But we didn't know where the logging road went; it could've been 20 miles to civilization and was certainly many more miles farther from our vehicles. The peak route was better, I said. John made up two more swear words, but considered trying for Abraham with me . . . maybe. "Phooey!" the couple said. We couldn't break up the party, so I relented and we all descended hundreds of feet to the logging road turnaround—I'd been voted off the mountain!

We couldn't see where we were placing our feet through the thickest brush on the steep and often rocky descent; luckily there were no mishaps, and at four o'clock we were on the logging road. We still had miles to go— but to where? We were headed west, away from our starting point, with the main mountain ridge between us and the car.

"Look," I said, "there's a slide accessible from down here that will take us right up to Mount Abraham, avoiding all the cripplebrush on the ridge—it's only a 1500-foot climb, no blowdown, and we'll be on the summit! We'll still have to deal with getting to the warden's cabin, but at least we'll be on the correct side of the mountain."

"We're going *west*," the others said. In hindsight, I can only imagine what would've happened if they'd said yes. If somebody had sustained an injury en route to the summit, or on the descent off Abraham, then we'd have been out all night, possibly above tree line, with no preparation for an overnight on the mountain.

So we continued down, following our noses, with only a topo map to half-show us what was there. Today's aerial photos and Google Earth insights certainly would have helped! We found a lot of old logging road intersections—grassy, rutted, and eroding—and chose a route that took us west and down. We found a railroad bed and took it next. We walked and walked and walked, retreating into nowhere, with Abraham mak- ing mountain-ish raspberry noises at us. About an hour before dusk, we finally came out on a dirt road, with a house in the distance. We were still miles from anywhere, but at least we were out. The first house was dark and there was no traffic on the road. A mile later, the second house had a light. We were in East Madrid or thereabouts. The map hinted that it was about 8 miles from Middle Abraham to this point. We were done in. The house owner let one of the married victims call their bed and breakfast in Kingfield. After listening to our plight, the proprietor miraculously drove around the mountain—about 40 miles one way—and we were saved! The proprietor had this to say upon his arrival: "Cudn't ye jest foller yer sun?"

CLIFF NOTE This is an admirable case of a group staying together, in spite of numerous temptations to separate. But why no flashlights on a major bushwhack?

He charged the married couple a double sawbuck for his trouble; they never hiked with me again. John is still picking cedar pieces out of various orifices.

Well, I thought, at least we bagged one of New England's Hundred Highest. And John and I did successfully climb Abraham later that year, narrowly escaping a lightning storm. (The guidebook's warning says "Caution: The mountain's openness makes sudden electrical storms unusually dangerous. Watch your weather!") But Middle Abraham wasn't done with us yet. In 1999, the list of New England's Hundred Highest Peaks was adjusted to reflect newly accurate GPS measurements. After that adjustment, Middle Abraham was—wait for it—unceremoniously expelled from the Hundred Highest. So all of the above had been for naught, and there was weeping, and gnashing of teeth, and rending of ripstop nylon.

MARC HOWES

Don't Shoot!

The day was November 3, 2007, the first day of deer hunting season in Vermont. You might think this would be a poor time to go gallivanting in the woods of Vermont, and you'd be right. I was with my friends Kyle and Melissa. Our goal was to summit two 3,000-foot peaks along the primary ridge in Vermont, a ridge that starts in Massachusetts and extends into Quebec. (The names of these peaks will not be revealed to protect the identities of the people we encountered.) We left one car on a dirt road at the north end of the ridge, to make the hike into a traverse, choosing our destination based on an estimate of where an old trail, which once traversed the ridge, used to come out. This road was a real Vermont backcountry road, in stark contrast to what you might expect to see along Route 100 or in Stowe. It was poor, and podunk. Not a Prius or New Jersey plate to be seen.

The temperatures were cold—winter comes early in the hills of Vermont. We began our journey on the south side of the ridge. The first 3,000-foot peak provided nice views to the south. The old trail used to continue north from here, skirting around the northern summit then heading down to the backcountry road. Sadly, the trail remnants were not to be found, so our bushwhack commenced immediately. The woods were moderately open and our progress was good at first. We were in a spruce and fir forest, which was not unexpected; we were above the "spruce line," a not-so-imaginary line of elevation where spruce and fir tend to grow. The vegetation thickened as we approached the col between the two peaks. At this point our trek had become more like a New Hampshire bushwhack, which by and large are more difficult than Vermont's.

We could hear distant gunshots from time to time, like popcorn popping, a common occurrence at this time of year. None of us were alarmed—it's all part of being in Vermont in the fall. The distant gunshots probably came from different sources, and were more likely to be kids shooting cans with a .22 in a gravel pit than hunters. Hiking in Vermont during deer season always carries some level of risk, but bushwhacking multiplies that risk factor by several orders of magnitude. It is necessary to wear blaze orange to alert hunters that you are not a target, and I was wearing plenty of newly purchased blaze orange that day. But since hunters tend to stay near roads, you feel a sense of relative safety by hiking along the tops of ridges. After all, it's much easier to haul out a kill when you're 0.25 mile from the road rather than 3 miles.

There is, however, a "gotcha" to the general sense of safety on roadless ridges, and that's the dreaded ATV trail. An ATV trail extends a hunter's range, opening up otherwise inaccessible land. Unluckily for us, the dreaded ATV path was exactly what we found in the col between the two peaks. But luck appeared to be on our side: this particular path seemed to have fallen into disuse, and I didn't think much of it. We had heard no gunshots nearby, only distant fire from the valley.

From here the woods became more like the typical Vermont hardwood forest that bushwhackers love. Forward progress was easy and views were aplenty due to the shed foliage. The woods gave an almost eerie feeling, as all the high-elevation hardwoods were stunted and gnarled. The cold temperatures and gray skies added to the curious, almost spooky effect. We reached the steep summit cone, a mix of spruce and fir, surrounded by open hardwoods; only the top 30 feet of the peak had conifers. We signed into the jar quickly, took a bearing to the car, and didn't linger, anxious to get moving again because of the frigid temperatures. We proceeded into a small bowl-shaped area, stopped to change our layers, then heard the first of what would become several very loud gunshots.

This first gunshot was not like the other, distant ones. This one was tremendously loud, echoing off the side of the ridge. Worst of all, it had come from the direction in which we were heading. It was evident from the acoustics that the source was still quite a ways off, perhaps somewhere near the road. Kyle commented that it must be a high-powered sort of deer rifle. We proceeded down the side of the ridge, periodically hearing more loud gunshots. We might hear several over a 10-minute span; at other times, we wouldn't hear any for over half an hour. They became louder and louder as we got closer to the car.

As we descended we intersected the old trail and tried to follow it, but that quickly became impractical. We then fell off into a drainage where we found some very large maple trees that had been girdled and killed, an old forest management technique. The walls of the drainage steepened and narrowed, giving us plenty of trouble in terms of footing. Our minds weren't on gunshots anymore. We slabbed along the sides of the drainage walls, emerged near the base of the steep-walled section, then came upon an old logging road and ATV trail. We were near the road! We were walking briskly when we heard it. *Bang!* Another tremendously loud gun shot, this time very close. Too close for comfort. It was that high-powered deer rifle again, and it couldn't have been more than an eighth of a mile away, maybe closer.

I clanked my metal hiking poles together, to alert anyone nearby that we were in the area. Kyle advised me not to do that—as the noise could sound like antlers. We began talking at a higher than normal volume, trying to make our presence known. Soon another shot rang out. *Bang!* We stopped and reflexively crouched. Our hearts beat faster and adrenaline kicked in—we had been walking straight toward the gunshots! Kyle and Melissa came closer to me since I was wearing the most obvious orange. At that point, we just wanted to get the hell out of the woods and onto the perceived safety of the dirt road.

Before we knew it, we were bearing down on a house. *Good,* I thought, *the road is near.* We could see but not hear people milling around on the elevated back porch of the house when another gunshot rang out, the loudest and closest of them all. Kyle hit the ground immediately but, for some reason, Melissa and I did not. Maybe it was the shock of the blast, or maybe we thought we were dead. Not 200 feet from us was an old white wooden door, propped up and riddled with big bullet holes. We were about 30 degrees off from being directly down range of that door. Imagine a house with a flat, medium-sized back lawn, surrounded by forest. At one edge of the lawn is an embankment. About 20 vertical feet above the embankment, and 200 feet behind it, is a logging road. Now walk 100 feet up said road toward the house. That's where we were standing when they fired at the door.

"Don't shoot us!" I yelled. We saw armed persons on the porch shuffle about in a way which suggested that they acknowledged our presence. No verbal contact was made. We scurried down the logging road and onto the dirt road, expecting to be intercepted by the backyard marksmen, but no interaction occurred. After walking for a minute down the dirt road, we heard another shot ring out; they had resumed shooting, as if nothing had happened. After a few more minutes we were at the car. None of us have returned to that area since.

DONNA W. DEARBORN

A Well-Guarded Fort— Escape Not Guaranteed

Arctic air swirling with snow flurries blasted us as we loaded the car in the early morning darkness. Brrr. While I optimistically concluded it was a temporary, localized snow squall, Rhonda donned another warm layer. Winter had started to take hold in this remote region of northern Maine. Snow glistening on the high peaks in the waning hours of the previous day had caught our attention. I needed to pounce on this one last window of opportunity in order to attain peak number 99 this year, before storms deposited even more snow. Mount Katahdin and Traveler Mountain were already closed to hikers because of severe winter conditions. How deep was it and how much ice would we encounter? Did we have enough daylight to complete this off-trail mission? The night before, we had turned the clocks back, signaling the end of daylight saving time, and were suddenly robbed of a precious hour of late afternoon light, one that we could not recoup, due to the six o'clock gate-opening, miles from the trailhead.

I had called Rhonda the day before. "Are you interested in an adventure to Baxter?" I asked, knowing it was a long shot. "I'm ready to climb number 99 on my list of New England's 100 highest peaks, bushwhacking to Fort Mountain from North Brother. It looks like a decent weather window for a couple days this weekend. It's a 7-hour drive and then a full day of hiking . . ." How exciting when she said "yes!"

The clear skies forecast for this second day of November filled us with optimism and determination. We motored through Millinocket, then the 18 miles to Baxter State Park, and were at the Togue Pond Gate before six o'clock, the only hikers anxious to enter. An ambitious task loomed: not only to hike 4.5 trail miles to the top of 4,143-foot North Brother, but to continue in trailless forest for another mile to Fort Mountain, then return before darkness. The AMC *Maine Mountain Guide* says: "Keep in mind that this route comes at the end of a very tiring climb to North Brother." We needed every minute of daylight in order to attain our goal.

At 6:00 a.m., no one appeared to open the gate. Hmmm. Where was the ranger? We watched the clock: 6:01 a.m. Did someone give us the wrong gate-opening time? At 6:02—did somebody oversleep? At 6:03—this is not good! Finally, at 6:04: hallelujah—truck lights and a young ranger rushing to open the lock. We proceeded toward the Marston Trailhead and pretended not to notice clouds obscuring the high peaks, including the summits of Katahdin, The Brothers, Mount Coe, and Mount O-J-I. As we drove the last 14 winding miles, the atmosphere was quiet—a sharp contrast to the previous day, when we'd talked nonstop for 7 hours, driving from Vermont. We were each in the last stage of our own inner preparation for the impending journey—going outward bound. That old sailing expression felt apropos—the moment when a ship commits to the open seas with all its unknowns, hazards, and adventures.

What is the allure? What entices us into the unknown on this day, to explore one of Baxter's wildest corners? What draws me time and again to immerse myself in the natural world for a day or a week or more? Is it the tingling anticipation and thrill of what might be around the next bend? Can it be the rawness, face to face with the elements, that reaches the depths of my soul and makes me feel alive? It is not merely the dramatic, sweeping views from a mountaintop or the soothing musical notes of the white-throated sparrow or the fragrant whiff of a balsam fir. Not triumphing over nature, not conquering mountains, but rather co-existing, hand-in-hand, part of the environment of trees, rocks, and sky. It is more the feeling of wholeness and rightness, of being in synchrony with the universe, a sense that all is well with the world. It is feeling deep peacefulness and rare quietude from breathing in and soaking up, from observing, listening, and respecting. It is the miraculous simplicity of the lessons revealed when we dare venture beyond our secure confines. My hiking partner shared my curiosity and also welcomed the challenge; like me, she was ready for a grand adventure. We were thrilled to step outside our regular lives, leave comfort behind, and face what the day might bring.

Just before seven o'clock, Rhonda and I started up the Marston Trail, wearing insulated winter boots with gaiters, quick-dry base layers, light-weight fleece tops, windbreakers, warm hats, and mittens. The 20-degree air inspired us to stride briskly along. Respecting the fine line between feeling just right and not too warm, we soon stopped to layer down and avoid becoming sweaty. We stuffed more into our loaded packs, already bursting with warm layers, hot tea, lunch, plenty of high-energy snacks, headlamps, first-aid kit, satellite phone, space blanket, sleeping bag, chemical hand-warmers, and more.

A distinctive two-paw print suggested that a solitary fisher preceded us up the trail. No wonder the crafty fisher was traveling this route—abundant snowshoe-hare tracks crisscrossed our path, especially where the vegetation was thick. So far the rabbits had avoided becoming a meal for this loping predator. A moose on its way to the high country also took advantage of the open trail. We kept a lookout, hoping to get a glimpse. Easily recognizable Doubletop Mountain revealed itself at our first real viewing spot. The clouds had lifted off the higher peaks—just what we wanted and counted on. The weather forecast held true. We hiked steadily in the frigid, frosty air, stopping only for short breaks to drink, snack, and pee.

Snow covered the ground from the start, but there were only a couple of inches at the junction of the Coe Trail to South Brother, 3.7 miles from the trailhead. Having gained 3,000 feet of elevation in 2 hours and 40 minutes, we were right on schedule, with North Brother a mere 0.8 miles away. Our elation was short-lived, however, for this was a tricky and difficult stretch—covered in ice and near vertical. We desperately needed traction, so we secured the Velcro straps of our Stabilicers around our boots—with seventeen steel cleats studding the bottom, these devices gripped tenaciously as we ascended through deeply eroded gullies and up steep rock pitches. I hadn't remembered how steep that section was, although I had been there in August two years prior, under dry and clear conditions. We took our time on the ice and eventually broke out of the trees.

Our attention was quickly drawn to the grand, broad massif of Katahdin, attired in full winter garb, which dominated the landscape 5 miles to the southeast. The glassy, precipitous Knife Edge snaked its way to 5,268-foot-high Baxter Peak, renowned as the northern terminus of the Appalachian Trail; no through-hikers would be finishing their 2,160-mile trek from Georgia today. We had this high, alpine world all to ourselves and were so mesmerized by the sparkling, wintry scene above tree line that, at first, we didn't notice the wind. Hoods up, zippers cinched tight, heads down into the strong headwind, we carefully climbed to the North Brother summit sign, coated artistically in feathery rime ice. We didn't touch this delicate ice sculpture, not wanting to disturb it.

"There it is." I pointed northeast to the long ridge that was our destination—3,861-foot Fort Mountain. It had taken 4 hours to reach the summit of North Brother, under clear skies, so our target seemed within reach. Because no trail connects the summits of North Brother and Fort, we were prepared to bushwhack, finding our own way. Some people might imagine hikers bushwhacking with machete, loppers, and saws—clearing a path through thick woods by chopping down bushes and cutting branches—but that couldn't be further from the truth. The leave-no-trace ethic strongly encourages us to navigate trailless wilderness with as little impact as possible, even avoiding the use of flagging tape to mark a route.

"It doesn't look too bad," we agreed. Still, there was no time to spare. Dropping steeply off the summit of North Brother, we followed ice-coated cairns down to tree line. Fresh snow blanketed the scene and we searched for remnants of herd paths through densely packed, ice-coated spruce and fir trees, hoping to find a reasonable way through. One opening petered out quickly; another came to a dead-end in a thick wall of branches and blowdowns intertwined over boulders. There would be no easy way—we were in for one rugged bushwhack! With the snow cover, it was impossible even to see where previous bushwhackers might have gone. The route was a completely blank slate, as if no one had ever been there before. Aviation buffs have previously traveled through these woods, in search of wreckage from a military C-54 plane that crashed in June 1944, while on a routine mail and cargo flight between Washington, D.C., and New England. It hooked a wing as it flew in thick clouds near the top of Fort Mountain, killing all seven crewmembers. The plane sits almost intact, 100 feet off the summit ridge.

Looking from North Brother, we could have no clue just how thick, unyielding, and frozen the stunted spruce trees would be. With a compass bearing of 71 degrees and our eyes on the high point in the distance, we stepped off into terra incognita—vast unknown territory—and were swallowed up by the forest. How small we felt, two little specks in a vast wilderness. We searched for the path of least resistance, initially moving with some measure of finesse, going around or over or under each barrier. Rays of sunshine dancing off a patch of open snow seduced us to a tiny opening—only to reveal another wall of spruce, another dead-end. *There, to the left, now to the right. That looks like an easier way.* On this convoluted zigzag path, we made slow progress. Thinking we were never going to make it at that rate, I bashed straight through along the compass bearing like an unbridled, furious bull. Sometimes glimpsing our destination, I pushed and shoved and ducked; Rhonda was close behind. The snow-laden spruce trees were no longer pretty; they were our nemesis, shedding piles of snow down our necks and inside our jackets, no matter how tight the zippers were cinched. The edges of my sleeping pad quickly shredded—no match for sharp, protruding branches.

"This is *nasty!*" I finally uttered, releasing some of my mounting frustration. It was extremely nasty—as in unpleasant, disagreeable, trying, and potentially hazardous. "Nasty" became our favorite word of the day and uttering it seemed to help. I pushed the pace, crashing faster through the impossibly thick wall of spruce, in hopes of ending our misery sooner. I kept my sunglasses on to protect my eyes and, even then, closed my eyes as branches painfully snapped against my face. Turning sideways I maneuvered between two scraggly trees, caromed off the next one, then sideswiped a snow-covered clump of firs.

"Donna, where are you?" came a plea from Rhonda. "Wait!"

"I'm here," I quickly answered back, sensing trepidation in her voice. "I see you and branches moving." I was 10 feet away and she'd panicked when she couldn't see me—that's how thick it was. We absolutely needed to stay close together in this mass of trees. Suddenly Fort, which had looked so close from the open summit of North Brother, seemed a world away. A Herculean effort would be needed to reach our goal. Should we turn back before it got any worse?

"Rhonda, what do you think?" I asked, wondering how my friend was doing in her first-ever bushwhack experience. I hadn't imagined it would be this tough. If she said she'd had enough, we would turn around.

"We're still okay time-wise, and the weather's good—let's keep going," Rhonda answered. *Would any other person have answered that way?* I wondered. We didn't have the luxury of time to discuss it, so we pushed on. After descending to the saddle between North Brother and Fort, the terrain leveled but that didn't mean travel was any easier; in fact, it was more brutal. We reached a boulder field that lay camouflaged in the spruce. A seemingly impenetrable barrier of 8- to 10-foot-high rock giants blocked our way, impossible to climb over. Usually a positive thinker with an optimistic outlook, I tried to quell the onslaught of negative thoughts, and then I let them all run wild—

there's no way we're going to make it,
one obstacle after another,
this is painfully slow,
what kind of a friend am I,
it's taking us so long to get through the saddle—we're not even on the flank
of Fort,
this is ridiculous,
poor Rhonda—what must she be thinking?
we're exhausted already,
this is so nasty,
this is insane!
we have to turn around—and do this all over again . . .

It felt good to let it all out and be done with it. *Whew.* Two large breaths and it was gone. I refocused to plot our next move, concentrating on one step at a time to accomplish our goal. *Yes, we can do it.* We squeezed through narrow passageways between the boulders until we reached a dead-end. We had to go far out of our way to circle around this roadblock, and the effort took another huge toll; we were drained. It was close to turn-around time and I felt responsible for making wise decisions that would result in our safe return.

"Rhonda, how are you doing?" I knew she had to be tired, even exhausted.

"I'm okay," she replied.

"What do you think?" I asked. We had agreed to total honesty and more than ever I wanted that now.

"Well, this is what we came here to do . . ." Rhonda answered. *Wow. What is this woman made of?* I knew Rhonda was strong and determined; now I saw she was way beyond that. When we'd met three years prior on Mount Ascutney's Weathersfield Trail, I liked her right away. I intended to call her again, but didn't. Luckily she called me three years after we met to see if I wanted to hike in the White Mountains. We reunited for a breathtaking and rugged hike up Mount Adams. Though we didn't have a long history, I knew Rhonda was fun, adventurous, honest, positive, caring, loyal, capable, and uncomplaining—and she loved the outdoors. We respected and trusted one another, and were good teammates for this expedition.

Martin Luther King's words rang true: "The ultimate measure of a man is not where he stands in moments of comfort and convenience, but where he stands in times of challenge and controversy." In our time of challenge and hardship, Rhonda displayed some deep, inexplicable quality. A word my Finnish husband Wally taught me, *sisu,* was the word that could explain what I witnessed in my friend. Wally proudly emblazons this strongest word in the Finnish language on his truck's license plate, a word that cannot be fully translated. Characterizing the Finnish people for the last 10,000 years, it is thought to have developed from their harsh winters and forty-two wars with Russia, none of which they won. *Sisu* is a "special strength and stubborn determination to continue and overcome in the moment of adversity. It is a combination of stamina, courage, and obstinacy held in reserve for hard times, an extraordinary endurance, an inner fire." That's what I observed in my friend: *sisu.* Surely she must have some Finnish blood.

Since Rhonda was still game, I was more than willing to give one last big effort to reach the summit of Fort. How luxurious it was when we hit a patch of woods where the spruces were spaced 2 feet apart instead of inches. Making better time was crucial. But our good fortune was fleeting—soon we were wallowing in thick underbrush again and it was our projected summit time. "Five hundred feet more," I reported after glancing at my GPS. We were just a tenth of a mile away from the summit—how could we possibly turn back? We battled on until we could see the rocky summit cone, envisioning a boulder-hop to the top in a matter of minutes.

What a grave disappointment when we realized that what had looked, from a distance, like a simple boulder field was in fact a jumble of rocks of all sizes, interspersed with stunted spruce trees. How completely deceiving! The rocks weren't close enough together to rock-hop. I stretched my left leg to stand on the first stunted spruce top. It held and I successfully made it to the next rock. When I tried the same maneuver the next time, my left leg disappeared out of sight into a deep spruce trap. It took all my strength to haul myself out of this pit and onto the next rock. Poor Rhonda was having even more difficulty—no spruce tops held her. She fell through into a deep abyss, dangling and stuck, one leg up and one leg down, pack snagging on branches. She flailed and sputtered. Despite this final insult, we had to reach the summit—we could just about touch the rock cairn on the top of Fort! We summoned our reserves of strength and energy to claw, pull, and drag ourselves the final stretch. While it was satisfying to reach this summit, it was not a joyful occasion, with time to celebrate, for all I could think about was that we had to immediately turn around and replicate what we had just done. We were only halfway—that thought was sobering.

I thought about Jeff Rubin, who had bushwhacked solo to Fort Mountain and, despite heavy rain and high winds, persisted toward his goal; he had perished while attempting a bushwhacking descent. After experiencing firsthand Fort Mountain's terrain, it was easy to understand how that could have happened. The water-laden branches of scrub spruces would have quickly saturated him, while poor visibility would have made navigation challenging. He very easily could have become hypothermic and disoriented. If he had not tried to return over North Brother—the only reasonable return route—then he would have bushwhacked down from the saddle. That route avoids the boulder field and the re-climb of North Brother, but would have confronted him with several miles of difficult bushwhacking to the nearest road or trail, in this most remote corner of the New England woods. I felt a kinship with this hiker, who had been in pursuit of the same goal that we had, a fellow member of the Four Thousand Footer Club, striving to join the more select circle of adventurers who attempt the Hundred Highest. He had been so close . . .

"Donna, I have to take at least one picture of you here on Fort!" Rhonda smiled. I felt uneasy behind my cheerful expression—our bushwhack back would be nearly 500 feet up North Brother compared to the 200 feet thrashing up Fort. The new sunset time was 4:20 instead of 5:20. I scanned the landscape from Fort's summit, in hopes of discerning a better route, an opening, some clue. Nothing at all.

"One thing I know," I declared, "we're going farther north across the saddle to detour around those giant boulders. Hopefully we can avoid that mess!"

We descended into the saddle far easier than we'd ascended, by avoiding the hellacious spruce traps and successfully skirting north of the dreaded boulder field. We intersected our footsteps and hoped this would help us make faster progress, but to our dismay the climb was much tougher than the descent. Innumerable times, branches snagged my pack and catapulted me headlong into a mound of snow. My legs were rubbery and weak and I tripped, stumbled, and fell again. We were tired—it was harder to get back up and keep pushing uphill through the spruce trees. *Isn't it about time we made it to the open rock face?* We kept our legs moving and pushed hard until we broke out above tree line.

We allowed ourselves a joyous pause. Soft golden afternoon light on the peaks of South Brother and Coe drew us upward from cairn to cairn to the North Brother signpost—a stark sentinel of artistic perfection. The purity and simplicity of this white world belied a harsh and unforgiving high mountain environment. It was tempting to prolong this reverent moment, but we knew better than to be lulled into complacency by this raw beauty. What a relief to arrive back to a blazed trail—though descending the steep and icy rocks required great care. We reached the col between North and South Brothers in good time and, dropping our packs, tended to our needs and celebrated our achievement. Gorp, dried fruit, and energy bars were all that had sustained us until now—we had not taken a lunch break and, tempting as it was, had resisted the urge to stop for long. We'd declared lunch-on-the-go, sensing danger in a prolonged rest.

"Rhonda, a Mark Twain quote says it all: 'I'm glad I did it, partly because it was well worth it, but chiefly because I shall never ever have to do it again!'"

"That's good," Rhonda said. "I like it." It was particularly satisfying to say *I will never ever have to do that again.* We had bushwhacked to Fort and back, and once was enough. Light remained for another 20 minutes and, in the thick-canopied sections, trail-finding became challenging. I squinted, then opened my eyes wider, to better detect the blazes, feeling the uncomfortable sensation that I was losing my vision. Unfortunately the waxing crescent moon provided no light.

"Do you want to get your headlamp out?" I asked Rhonda.

"No, that will ruin my night vision," she answered with conviction. "I want to put it off as long as possible." I had to agree. Then it was black, the markers no longer visible, and we could barely make out the path. My boots crunched through deep leaves, a sign that I was no longer on the trail. "There it is, over there," offered Rhonda, after hearing me. We carefully made our way down and our marathon day was over. I looked at the clock: 6:04 p.m.

"We'll have to hurry to get back through the gate before seven—I didn't know it was that late. Wait a minute—it can't be six. I forgot to set the clock back." An hour later we found the quiet Appalachian Trail Café and just the right sustenance—warm, replenishing, satisfying fish chowder.

"This might be the toughest bushwhack I've ever done—the most difficult of my New England Hundred Highest." I said. "But they're not all like this!"

"I loved it—I'm always glad to be challenged," Rhonda said. "That's what life is about."

I told her then about Jeff Rubin, who had been completing his hundredth peak in June 1995, and the sadness I felt about this man's fate—how it had prompted me to find out more about him. What I found only made me sadder. He was no rash young man; he was an experienced, fit hiker who had climbed mountains on every continent. He had been a fifty-three-year-old, highly respected Tufts University psychology professor, author of more than twenty books, and father of three children. He'd been a man with great intellectual curiosity and wisdom, an outstanding teacher and mediator, and a caring, generous person. Jeff Rubin had had the rare quality of being able to really listen. To me he was no longer a mere statistic on Baxter State Park's list of fatalities—name/date/cause of death. He was a vivid figure, a hiker of remote peaks, who had unfortunately met a tragic end in the prime of life.

"You waited until we got back safely to tell me this," said Rhonda. "Thank you!"

MARTHA LEB MOLNAR

Coming Home

I'm of average height, weight, and age, but when I hike I feel tall, svelte, and young. Some of my friends are getting facelifts. Some are starting second or third careers. Some are doing both. Instead, I come to the woods, alone. Gliding through them at a brisk pace restores me to a self when the world was fresh and I was full of wonder.

The hikes I like best follow the ancient rounded mountains of the Taconics in southwestern Vermont. Here, there are no soaring heights, shadowy canyons, or roaring rivers. Gentle rises and dips in dense hardwood forests, punctuated by ponds and small streams, define the land. This means I can move swiftly mile after mile, taking huge steps and running jumps. The earth's energy enters through my feet. Each toe finds its finely molded indentation. My knees bend to meet the earth's crust like a finely tuned feat of engineering. My arms swing long like an ape's. My body lengthens as it leaps over rocks and fallen trunks. I notice the flick of a white tail 100 tree trunks away, but don't stop. Miles turn into muscle, hours lengthen into sinews. The freedom of my legs gives freedom to my mind. It takes half of the 4-mile trip to the turnaround before its dartings form into a steady direction. It takes halfway back before all the noise in my head evaporates and my mind is empty, open to this close, forested world. I'm usually alone on this hike. Conversation of any sort—or being forced to adjust my pace to another's—would turn my escape into a mere walk in the woods.

On this October evening though, with the sun only a memory in saffron clouds, I'd like to see another human being, preferably one with a flashlight, a cell phone, and immense forest lore: the man of the woods himself. I started out too late, turned around too late, dawdled too long on the one ridge with distant views. Mostly, I didn't realize how rapidly that high white disk in the sky retreats these days. Useless "if onlys" repeat themselves endlessly. If only I'd waited to do the laundry . . . if only I'd let the answering machine pick up that call . . . if only I'd left earlier, just an hour earlier, if I'd walked faster, eaten faster, turned around earlier. If only . . . I wouldn't be here after sunset, alone, wondering how long before the widely spaced blazes became invisible.

Because I know the trail well, I know that I'm now less than 2 miles from the road. If I can make it to the pond, it'll be easy to follow the trail as it hugs the shore. After that, there'll be a narrow passage for a mile or so through thick stands of white pine, but by then I might hear the road. Still, I'd never been here in the dark, or in any wild place without full camping gear. I'd rather not be here now. My fingers begin to tingle and my nose starts its inevitable drip, a sure sign that the temperature is sinking. I stop to drink the still-hot tea, grateful that I packed it despite the promising day. But why not a flashlight? Part of my "take nothing extra," "keep it simple," "that's the beauty of hiking" principles. Snippets of repetitive conversations play themselves out in my brain, which has by now reverted to its noisy default stage. Pushing on, my pace quickens to an athletic speed-walk.

"Sure you want to go alone?" my husband inquires, again. It's not that he wants to come with me—he gets bored with the same hike after the tenth time—but he's willing to chaperone me.

"Take my phone . . . take a flashlight. . . . what if it rains . . . what if you twist an ankle, what if . . . what if . . ."

He's right and I'm foolish, but I choose not to be pragmatic. I refuse to believe that I'm anything but safe in these benevolent woods. So familiar that individual trees hold memories of themselves in spring flower or autumn disrobing. So known that my body molds itself to the land's contours. Despite the chill in my fingers, my shirt is sticking to my back. I stop. A wet cotton T-shirt will only exacerbate the cold. I sit on a ledge for another sip of tea. With my fingers wrapped around the cup and the rock's warmth coursing down my legs and up my spine, a feeling of confidence returns.

"It's a perfectly gorgeous, calm evening," I reason with myself. "What's the worst that could happen? Just go. Your eyes will adjust to the dark." Fixing the next blaze in my mind, I move into the night.

Assuming the trail is straight since the land appears flat, I gingerly feel my way across the uneven ground, my eyes anxiously searching for the next blaze. When I don't see it after what seems a reasonable distance, I retrace my steps to the ledge. I start out again bearing to the right this time, where there seems to be a straight line of open space through the trees. I move carefully through the opening, but soon feel lost again. Looking up in desperation, I notice the faint white blaze on the tree right in front of me. Finding the next blaze proves more arduous. Following a hill, not big but steep, the trail seems to plummet straight down. I know this cannot be, since trails are carefully designed to take the path of least resistance. But without the forest packed tightly all around, I can't see where that path is. My fingers are tightly clenched in damp palms. My back is stiff with cold or tension or both. My eyes feel distended from the effort of peering into darkness. Breathing rapidly, I give in to panic. I scamper down and back up three times before finding the narrow opening through the resuming forest.

"At this rate, I'll wear myself out long before I get close enough to hear the road, or even reach the pond." Then, "Calm down. Stop panicking. Stay calm," I order my frazzled mind. I repeat the last phrase like a military decree, playing it over and over until it forms itself into a silly little ditty I sing. For a little while I respond to this rhythmic mantra. My feet shuffle along slowly, toes pointed inward to keep from sliding on the slopes. When I get tangled in limbs and blackberry vines, I know I've lost the trail again. I yank at my clothes wildly, shouting obscenities at the bushes. Free at last, I push on, determined to make it to the next blaze. My entire being is now focused on reaching from one blaze to the next. A mere hundred feet define success or failure, maybe even survival. As the night deepens, the tingling begins to reach beyond fingers and toes, up legs and arms. I can't see them but I know my ears are bright red. Meanwhile, the moon promised by the day's perfect sunshine . . . that moon is either a new moon, too tiny to notice in an old forest, or else clouds have come up just after sunset and will keep it shrouded for as long as it matters to me.

"If only I had a flashlight, or a single match . . . or a cell phone!" But when I really consider these objects, which logically should have been in my daypack, I discard them one by one. The phone wouldn't work here. A flashlight wouldn't illuminate a large enough slice of these dense woods. And what would I do with matches? I'm hopelessly incompetent at building a fire that lasts beyond minutes. If I did succeed this one time I'd probably start a conflagration. Continuing to blindly put one foot in front of the other, I worry about my family worrying about me. By now they're probably figuring out how to get to me. I can hear their intense voices. These blend with the great volume of sound that each step on dry leaves, each brush with a branch creates. Together they join the cacophony in my brain. I sniffle and start running, tripping over a log and into a trunk.

I know I'm over the edge when I begin bargaining with fate. "If I get out of here unharmed, I'll take every precaution in the future. I'll never leave with less than 10 pounds in my pack. I'll buy a GPS. I'll leave a trail of glow-in-the-dark inedible crumbs." Soon the bargaining takes on absurd proportions. "If I get out of here unharmed, I won't hike in the woods for

Baby moose.
Photo by Dan Stone

the rest of this year . . ." Then, "not until next fall . . ." Until finally, I agree to never hike alone again, a promise I know even as I say it that I have no intention of keeping.

Occupied with thinking up more outlandish bargaining chips, I step into water, and slosh through it unaware until my boots are filled and caught in deep muck. I scream then, thinking of quicksand. "Stay calm." That's what one's supposed to do in quicksand. Instead I continue to scream and thrash, away, back, forward, anywhere, away from the life-sucking muck. Hauling myself up to a granite boulder, I slowly collapse onto my haunches, my face between my knees, my eyes squeezed tight against my own foolishness. I know that there's no quicksand anywhere within hundreds of miles of this benign landscape. Just as surely, I know that I've lost the trail, which crosses no wetland. Slowly I remove the caked boots and slimy socks, and wrap my feet in the small nylon pack. Uncorking the thermos, I sip at the last of the tea.

Everything I have learned in life, from others, from books, from hard experience, is suddenly useless. I can't see in the dark, and haven't learned how to feel my way. There's nothing to do but wait for rescue. I can surely retain enough body heat to last till then. My head finds a hollow in the trunk behind me where it fits as into a favorite pillow. The coarse bark feels soft and I know it's beautiful in its long, vertical, gray ridges, beautiful in its imperfect symmetry. So is the stony calm all around. The forest and each living thing in it exists in and for itself. I sit, alone, in a heap of exhausted limbs, longing for my own kind.

Closing my eyes, I breathe deeply, and the aroma of millions of drying leaves, of the earth beneath me alive with crawling insects and burrowing mammals, of dew forming itself into droplets, filters through every pore. A large nest sits dimly in the crook of an upper branch above me. I hear the birds shifting in their sleep. A frog splashes into water, and I hear its webbed feet streaking through the shallows. I hear the papery rustle of leaves, each a unique note in the murmuring symphony of the living forest. I hear squirrels' tails wrapping around branches, moths struggling in spider webs, roots pushing relentlessly through the earth. Raising my eyes to the canopy, I see next spring's maple buds clenched like tiny fists. I can count the tree rings in the cut log in front of me. Beneath the craggy boulder on which I sit, I feel the miles of solid bedrock separating me from the boiling core of the earth, sustaining me now with retained warmth and solid presence. I feel the heady spinning of the earth and of my own astonishing presence on this grand planet. I feel the power of it all flowing into me. I could, if I wanted, flow over the land silently, snaking sinuously between the trees, making no disturbance.

Minutes or hours pass. When I open my eyes they're focused on the smooth surface of the cut log. I realize with a start that the clean slice can only mean one thing: I'm sitting right by the trail, now lit by the serene moonlight that has come down unnoticed over the land. I can get up, walk out. So close, I can make it barefoot. So easy, I need not hurry. But I make no move. I want to stay now. My body feels warm and ageless. My brain shivers with joy. I feel like putting down roots myself.

CLUBS AND ORGANIZATIONS

Adirondack Forty-Sixers, www.adk46r.org

Adirondack Mountain Club, www.adk.org

Appalachian Mountain Club, www.outdoors.org

Baxter State Park, www.baxterstateparkauthority.com

Catskill 3500 Club, www.catskill-3500-club.org

Four Thousand Footer Club, www.amc4000footer.org

Green Mountain Club, www.greenmountainclub.org

Leave No Trace (education to minimize recreational impacts), www.LNT.org

Mount Washington Observatory, www.mountwashington.org

New Hampshire Outdoor Council (hikeSafe DVD available), www.nhoutdoorcouncil.org

New York State Department of Environmental Conservation, www.dec.ny.gov

Northeast 111 Club, www.summitpost.org/northeast-115

Sierra Club, www.sierraclub.org

The Waterman Fund (Northeast U.S. alpine stewardship), www.watermanfund.org

White Mountain National Forest, www.hikeSafe.com, www.fs.fed.us/r9/forests/white_mountain

SAFETY GUIDELINES

Ten Essentials for Every Pack in Every Season

Map
Compass
Warm clothing—no cotton
Extra food and water
Headlamp or flashlight
Matches or firestarters
First-aid kit and repair kit
Whistle
Pocketknife
Rain/wind jacket and pants

Hiker Responsibility Code

You are responsible for yourself, so be prepared:

1. *With knowledge and gear.* Learn about equipment, the terrain, conditions, and local weather.

2. *To leave your plans.* Tell someone where you are going, the trail(s) you will hike, when you will return, and your emergency plans.

3. *To stay together.* If you start as a group, hike as a group and end as a group. Pace the hike to the slowest person.

4. *To turn back.* Weather changes quickly in the mountains. Fatigue and unexpected conditions can affect your hike. Know your limitations and when to postpone your hike.

5. *For emergencies.* Even if headed out for a short hike, an injury, severe weather, or a wrong turn could become life-threatening. Know how to rescue yourself.

6. *To share the Hiker Responsibility Code.*

NOTES

1. The Moosilauke Summit Camp was at 4,810 feet; the trail up includes 3,300 feet of climbing. During his four years as a hutman, Rocky carried packboards that weighed an average of 69 pounds; the heaviest was 120 pounds. His duties are recounted in part in "The Home on a Hill," in *Reaching That Peak: 75 Years of the Dartmouth Outing Club,* by David O. Hooke.

2. Built in 1956, the emergency shelter in Edmands Col was an unattractive nuisance. Designed only for emergency use, it became a destination for some people and groups. The area around it became overused and trash accumulated. It was removed in 1982.

3. This account is an excerpt from an Appalachian Trail odyssey from Kinsman Notch on Route 112 to Pinkham Notch. By the third day of hiking, Matt realized that his chronic lower back pain was nearly gone. "I had it for many years. MRIs showed disk degeneration, and I thought this was something I would always have to live with. I even saw a wonderful chiropractor every week. Now I realized that I was no longer in pain!"

4. The old Fabyan Path from the west was later reconstructed by J. Rayner Edmands and renamed the Edmands Path.

5. Later it was determined that Ormsbee had no broken bones.

6. The eight peaks are Bondcliff, Bond, South Twin, Garfield, Lafayette, Lincoln, Liberty, and Flume, with side trails leading to West Bond, Zealand, North Twin, and Galehead.

7. For expert detail on winter camping, see "Enjoying a Frozen World."

8. A slab avalanche breaks at a fracture line instead of at a single point. A large slab can break into many pieces, each of which may be larger than a vehicle, with power great enough to crush buildings and fell large trees. *Winterwise* author John Dunn writes: "Head either directly up or directly down any suspicious slopes—don't traverse them. Snowshoe and ski tracks can act like a giant dotted line to shear off a slab." Hikers and skiers in Baxter State Park should carry avalanche probes and shovels and always evaluate terrain before venturing over it. Susan Kirk (see "Katahdin Ice Climber Meets Lady Luck") has described using a snow pit to evaluate avalanche danger: creating a pit 4-foot deep and 4-foot wide will expose the layers of snow, including any weak layers. If layers come loose as you dig and pull with a shovel, the snow might be weak and prone to slide. For winter safety information in northern New England, visit nhoutdoorcouncil.org.

9. According to a registered nurse, a torn ACL always requires surgery, whereas a torn meniscus might not.

10. At the top of a 25-foot ladder, with no reliable foothold or handhold, the summit of Crane Mountain could be a good location for secure, anchored holds, much like the bolts on the Baxter Peak section of the Appalachian Trail.

11. That would have meant an 8-mile route over the North and South Baldfaces; the AMC *Guide* warns hikers that the open rocks on South Baldface are dangerous when wet or icy.

12. The "blanket" was a space blanket.

13. SOLO stands for Stonehearth Open Learning Opportunities. Founded in New Hampshire, the group designed one of the first wilderness emergency medicine courses in the country.

14. According to the National Weather Service, a catastrophic ice storm and flood, "unprecedented in New England history," struck northern New England and northern New York during the first two weeks of January 1998. Three inches or more of ice accumulated on outdoor surfaces. Seven fatalities were directly attributed to the event.

15. When the temperature is below zero, it is tempting to avoid freezing your fingers and losing body heat by changing gear. Although you might be able to cross a slide without incident most of the time, when accidents occur the consequences can be dire both to yourself and to your rescuers. Dave's snowshoes had old serrated crampons that might not have gripped well on an icy slide. He wasn't convinced that he needed to change into full crampons until I insisted.

16. The AMC *White Mountain Guide* notes: "The steep slabs of the North Slide are difficult, and dangerous in wet or icy conditions." From the gravel outwash of the slide, the route "becomes extremely steep, climbing 1,200 feet in 0.5 miles."

17. Such canisters were affixed to the summit trees of 20 trailless mountains in the Adirondack High Peaks. In 2001, the Forty-Sixer organization agreed to remove them to conform to stricter wilderness regulations. Until 2001, however, most hikers who reached a trailless summit signed in, then wrote down the names of the previous three hikers who had signed the logbook and sent those names, along with their hike description, to Grace Hudowalski, Forty-Sixer historian, who kept records of hiker climbs for nearly 50 years. My book *Women with Altitude* was compiled by research at the New York State Archives, where thousands of these hike records are now stored. Many correspondents have since assumed Grace's role, volunteering for the Office of the Historian.

There are still canisters containing logbooks on 13 trailless peaks over 3,500 feet in the Catskill Forest Preserve, by permission granted in 1999 to the Catskill 3500 Club by the New York State Department of Environmental Conservation. Records of hiker traffic on those trailless peaks are sent to the DEC by the club's canister maintainer, Jim Bouton; logbooks are sent to the club's membership chairman, David White.

18. On a warm January day when David and I hiked to the Zealand Hut, snow bridges were softening over several icy streams. When we walked out two mornings later, the same streams were fully open and flowing too wide to jump over. We sloshed through them, passing many students who were hiking in over 6 miles to the unheated hut, in spite of a predicted snowstorm and forecasts for temperatures near zero. We told them about the open streams and warned that they could not avoid getting soaked, but they replied that they had hut reservations. A wet, cold stay in that hut, under those conditions, could easily have resulted in frostbite or hypothermia. (We were amused to learn that the huts provide each summer guest with three blankets; winter hikers receive no blankets and must carry in their own sleeping bags and food.)

19. Diane Sawyer, author of "Enjoying a Frozen World," recommends *Among the Bears,* by Benjamin Kilham. Through his experiences with raising orphaned bears, Kilham has developed an extensive knowledge and unique understanding of these animals.

20. Six hikers raised an American flag on Mount Liberty after September 11, 2001, as a tribute to those who perished on that date. A committee then established annual memorial hikes, "Flags on the 48," to raise the American flag on each of New Hampshire's forty-eight highest peaks on or near September 11 (www.flagsonthe48.org).

21. Grace Hudowalski was the Adirondack Forty-Sixer historian for 50 years and corresponded with thousands of hikers on a manual typewriter. She urged everyone to write about their adventures. "These are precious experiences," she said, "and if you don't write them down, you won't remember."

22. Stove fuel evaporates rapidly and cools as it evaporates; a spill on bare skin can cause instant frostnip.

23. The AMC's *White Mountain Guide* says: "*Caution:* The extensive areas of open ledge that make Chocorua so attractive also pose a very real danger. Many of the trails have ledges that are dangerous when wet or icy . . ."

GLOSSARY

bivouac, or **bivy**: Camping in the open with no shelter, or improvised shelter.

bivy sack: A light, compact, waterproof bag suitable for emergency shelter.

bushwhack: Off-trail hiking through woods or brush, using map and compass or GPS.

cairn: Pile of rocks to mark a trail.

col: A pass or low point between two adjacent mountains.

crampons: A framework of spikes affixed to the boot sole, often part of a snowshoe, to provide necessary stability on icy or hard-packed surfaces.

cripplebrush: Thick stunted growth at higher elevations.

frostbite: The freezing of body tissue. Frost-nip is the first sign, which appears as white or mottled patches on the skin and occurs quickly if skin is exposed in windy, cold conditions. The skin should return to its normal color after applying gentle pressure; if not, the condition has advanced to frostbite, which is a deeper tissue injury that should not be re-warmed quickly; get to a hospital as soon as possible. If feet become wet, it is essential to change into dry socks and place an insulating plastic bag between dry socks and wet boots. Regardless of how fast you hike, frostbite can easily occur. Place feet on another's mid-body to warm them up.

gorp: "Good Old Raisins and Peanuts," a homemade snack including seeds, candy, other nuts and dried fruit for quick energy.

heat exhaustion: Symptoms are profuse sweating, weakness, nausea, vomiting, headache, lightheadedness, and muscle cramps; stop activity and rehydrate with water or a sports drink. Dangerous *heat stroke* takes place when the skin stops sweating. The condition is accompanied by confusion, lethargy, and possible seizure; emergency medical attention is required.

hypothermia: The most serious danger to hikers, often happening between 30 degrees and 50 degrees Fahrenheit, in rain and wind. Though defined as a drop in core body temperature to 95 degrees, just a 1-degree drop from normal can lead to early hypothermia. It is caused by not eating or drinking sufficiently, being immobilized or in direct contact with cold ground, wearing inadequate or wet clothing in windy, cold conditions, and especially by wearing cotton—which does not dry and clings to the body, drawing out vital heat. Victims experience uncontrollable shivering and become disoriented, lethargic, uncoordinated, and mentally impaired. "To be blunt," writes Peter Crane, "cold makes you stupid—and then all things fall apart quite quickly." If not treated, coma and death can occur rapidly. Remedies include removing wet clothes, providing insulation from the ground, putting the victim in a sleeping bag, covering the head and neck, getting shelter, and supplying quick-energy food and warm non-alcoholic drinks. Carry a survival bag and/or space blanket. Hot packs placed around the neck, armpits, and groin may help, but prevention is the key.

lean-to: Shelter, usually of wood, with a roof and three or four sides, for camping.

lee: The opposite side from the prevailing wind.

peakbagging: Attempting to climb all the peaks on a particular list, such as the Northeast 111, which now includes 115 peaks exceeding 4,000 feet—48 in New Hampshire, 48 in New York, 14 in Maine, and 5 in Vermont. Other popular goals for peakbagging include the hundred highest peaks in a region and "The Grid," which involves hiking each of the highest peaks in every month of the year. Some say that peakbagging is too goal-oriented, while others point out that having a goal inspires the hiker to visit remote peaks and experience a greater variety of wilderness.

posthole: To sink deeply with each step into the snow, a problem usually (though sometimes not completely) remediated by the use of snowshoes.

slide: Steep slope where a landslide has carried away soil and vegetation.

snow blindness: A temporary condition brought on by exposure to the sun's rays reflecting off snow. Wear 100 percent UV sunglasses or goggles.

space blanket: A thin, light blanket made of reflective material to preserve body heat.

spruce hole: A hidden air space, below the snow surface, created by many feet of snow blanketing small spruce trees. These can often be very large, with air pockets under multiple branches.

spur trail: A side path to a point off a main trail.

sunburn: Air is thinner on mountains; practice vigilant application of sunblock.

switchback: Zigzag traverse of a steep slope.

tree line: Elevation above which trees do not grow.

whiteout: Weather phenomenon common in higher elevations, where fog, clouds, and blowing snow can almost totally obscure even nearby landmarks, causing disorientation.

SUGGESTIONS FOR FURTHER READING

Adirondack Mountain Club High Peaks Trails, by Tony Goodwin, Adirondack Mountain Club, 2012.

Backwoods Ethics and *Wilderness Ethics,* by Laura and Guy Waterman, Countryman Press, 2003.

Adirondack Mountain Club Catskill Trails, Carol and David White, eds., Adirondack Mountain Club, 2012.

Forest and Crag, by Laura and Guy Waterman, Appalachian Mountain Club, 2003.

The 4,000-Footers of the White Mountains, by Steven D. Smith and Mike Dickerman, Bondcliff Books, 2008.

Long Trail Guide, Green Mountain Club, 2011.

Maine Mountain Guide, Appalachian Mountain Club, 2012.

White Mountain Guide, by Steven D. Smith, Appalachian Mountain Club, 2012.

Winterwise, by John M. Dunn, Adirondack Mountain Club, 1997.

CONTRIBUTORS

Mary Ellen BaRoss has through-hiked Vermont's Long Trail and the Appalachian Trail. She also completed The Grid—climbing each of the forty-eight White Mountain peaks exceeding 4,000 feet in every month.

Todd Bogardus is a retired conservation officer supervisor for the Law Enforcement Division of the New Hampshire Fish and Game Department, where he served for twenty-four years. During his tenure Lieutenant Bogardus served as the state search and rescue coordinator and the Fish and Game Department's specialized search and rescue team leader, as well as being a director of the New Hampshire Outdoor Council. He was instrumental in the founding and implementation of the hikeSafe program.

Steve Boheim is a New England Hundred Highest member, Adirondack 46er, and Catskill 3500 Club member who organized annual pilgrimages to Baxter State Park for many years.

Donna Brigley has a long list of trails hiked, water bars cleaned, and peaks climbed with family and friends, but cherishes time spent in the wilderness alone.

Melinda Broman was president of the Knickerbocker Chapter of the Adirondack Mountain Club, now merged with the New York Chapter.

Susan Campriello was a reporter for Hudson-Catskill Newspapers.

Rebecca Chapin was formally trained as a geologist and, through nature, discovered an inner calling as an artist, photographer, writer, and explorer.

Peter Crane is curator of the Gladys Brooks Memorial Library, Mount Washington Observatory; a member of Androscoggin Valley Search and Rescue; and serves on the board of the New Hampshire Outdoor Council.

Donna W. Dearborn carries on the legacy of her energetic mother and recreation-director father, who was forever curious about what was around the next bend.

Marjorie LaPan Drake completed the forty-eight White Mountain 4,000-footers in four months, then hiked all the New England Fours. She was a trip leader for the Appalachian Mountain Club.

Johnathan A. Esper is a Winter 116er and pursues his outdoor passions with Wildernesscapes Photography.

John C. Goding left a comfortable job to work as a Peace Corps volunteer on the Thai-Burmese border, is married to Chiraporn, and has a daughter, Julia.

Leonard H. Grubbs ran the Adirondack Forty-Sixers trail maintenance programs for many years, and was an instructor at the Adirondack Mountain Club's Winter Mountaineering School for seven years.

Matt Harris has been in technical theatrical and television production for more than three decades, starting with community theater in Oyster Bay in 1977.

John Hartford taught piano, played the harpsichord, and recorded the Goldberg Variations, which he considered his greatest achievement. He was completing the White Mountain 48 in calendar winter—in spite of cancer surgery that required a feeding tube. John passed away in 2011.

Betty Maury Heald used to think that when she was forty, she'd be "down the tubes!" She and her husband Phil were the first married couple to achieve the Winter 111, at ages fifty-seven and fifty-eight. Betty was the second woman to do so, in 1985—finishing three days after Dot Myer.

Marc Howes has hiked the 115 Northeast 4,000-foot peaks in winter, the hundred highest peaks in New England in winter, all 453 New England 3,000-foot peaks, all peaks with over 2,000 feet of prominence in the Northeast, and nearly every 3,000-footer in the Catskills.

Douglas W. Hunt is an AMC hike leader and co-led AMC's Presidential Range weeklong hut-to-hut traverse for several years. He has completed climbs of the forty-eight White Mountain peaks exceeding 4,000 feet in each month and the sixty-seven 4,000-footers in New England.

Teddy "Cave Dog" Keizer (www.thedogteam.com) has set eight climbing records across the country. He graduated from Brown University as student-body president with degrees in geology, biology, and political science. He is married to Ann "Sugar Dog" Sulzer; they welcomed a son in 2009 and a daughter in 2012.

Michael N. Kelsey is a county legislator and lawyer who teaches at a private college. He also serves as a director at a mental health nonprofit and is a guidebook editor for the Adirondack Mountain Club.

Susan P. Kirk was the fifth woman to complete the 111 Northeast peaks that exceed 4,000 feet in winter. She is a registered nurse.

Kimberly J. LaPorte was raised in Central New York where she lives with her fiancé, Dan, and two sons: Ethan, four, and Danny, one.

Doug Mayer served for seven years on The Waterman Fund board of directors, which supports alpine stewardship throughout the Northeast. He has supervised the Randolph Mountain Club's trail crew for many years and is active in Androscoggin Valley Search and Rescue.

Martha Leb Molnar is a former *New York Times* reporter and a public-relations writer, working from a cabin in Vermont. She recently completed a book about finding land, building a house, and living day to day on a Vermont hilltop.

Timothy Muskat, a poet who has been hiking in the White Mountains all his life, lives with his wife Carla and their two sons, Harrison and Galen, in a small New Hampshire village.

Dot Myer was the first woman to complete the Northeast 111 in winter. She was a Girl Scout leader and trail maintainer for many years.

Anne Norton, bitten by the peakbagging bug, hiked extensively in New England and occasionally in the Adirondack High Peaks.

Benjamin David Potter is an engineer and homeowner in Rhode Island.

Marta Bolton Quilliam is a multiple-round Winter 46er who has helped many people to achieve this coveted goal. She became a correspondent with aspiring 46ers through the Office of the Historian of the Adirondack Forty-Sixers.

Scott "Tuba Man" Rimm-Hewitt graduated from the University of Vermont with a B.A. in music education and completed his Ph.D. after hiking the AT. He has performed in eighteen countries, biked from Portland, Oregon, to Portland, Maine, through-hiked the AT, and run the Boston Marathon with a tuba. A son was welcomed to the family in 2011.

Landon G. Rockwell participated in a two-week study of weather records on Mount Washington and has been a member of the American Alpine Club and the Alpine Club of Canada. He served as hutman at the Mount Moosilauke Summit Camp for four years.

Mats Roing was raised in Alfta, Sweden. After serving as a quartermaster in the Swedish Army, he went to Montana State University in Bozeman.

Ellen McDowell Ruggles is author of *The New England Beach Guide* and works at the University of New Hampshire in Manchester. She is a trip leader for the Appalachian Mountain Club.

Diane Duggento Sawyer and her husband, Tom Sawyer, have climbed all the 14,000-footers in the United States; all the 4,000-footers in England, Wales, and Scotland; the Northeast 115 and the Long Trail in winter; and Mount Kilimanjaro. They also have paddled the 246-mile Suwanee River, biked across the United States, and through-hiked the Appalachian Trail.

Aaron Schoenberg has organized and led hikes for the New York–New Jersey Chapter of the Appalachian Mountain Club and the North Jersey–Ramapo ADK Chapter for nearly forty years.

Roy R. Schweiker is an Appalachian Trail / Long Trail adopter who has visited at least one summit on every date—including February 29. He has climbed over 3,000 different summits.

Arlene Heer Stefanko is an oncology nurse who became hooked on hiking. She and her sister Doreen climbed the forty-six Adirondack High Peaks in winter together.

Keith P. Sullivan led AMC hiking trips for twelve years, was the director of the AMC New Hampshire Mountaineering and Glacier Travel Workshops for five years, and taught winter backpacking and advanced winter wilderness travel for the AMC for ten years.

John Swanson and his wife, Nan Giblin, have together summited all the Northeast mountains over 4,000 feet in winter.

Edith Tucker is a reporter for the *Coös County Democrat*.

Alan Via was the Adirondack Mountain Club's insurance chair and risk manager for twenty-four years. In 2012, ADK published his book, *The Catskill 67: A Hiker's Guide to the Catskill 100 Highest Peaks under 3500 Feet.*

Guy Waterman co-authored, with his wife Laura, *Backwoods Ethics, Wilderness Ethics, Forest and Crag,* and *Yankee Rock and Ice*. They homesteaded in Vermont for nearly thirty years.

Laura Waterman co-authored *Forest and Crag, Wilderness Ethics, Backwoods Ethics,* and *Yankee Rock and Ice* with Guy. They were instructors in the winter mountaineering school operated annually by AMC and ADK. Laura also wrote *Losing the Garden: The Story of a Marriage.* She founded the Waterman Fund, which promotes alpine stewardship in the northeastern United States.

David Scott White has been membership chairman of the Catskill 3500 Club since 2001 and was a director of the Adirondack Mountain Club (ADK) for six years.

Marian Zimmerman completed graduate school at the University of Maine in geology and natural resource conservation and joined the Sisters of Mercy in New York State and Maine.

ABOUT THE EDITOR

Carol Stone White edited *Adirondack Peak Experiences: Mountaineering Adventures, Misadventures, and the Pursuit of "The 46"* (2009) and *Catskill Peak Experiences: Mountaineering Tales of Endurance, Survival, Exploration, and Adventure from the Catskill 3500 Club* (2008), both published by Black Dome Press, and *Women with Altitude: Challenging the Adirondack High Peaks in Winter,* published by North Country Books (2005). With her husband David, she wrote *Catskill Day Hikes for All Seasons,* published by the Adirondack Mountain Club (2002); the couple also edits ADK's comprehensive guidebook *Catskill Trails,* Volume 8 of the Forest Preserve Series, for which they measured 345 miles of trails by surveying wheel. These measurements updated the set of five Catskill Forest Preserve maps published by the New York–New Jersey Trail Conference in 2004. In 2011 they assisted the National Geographic Society in creating a trail map of the Catskill Park.

In 2007, Carol received the Susan B. Anthony Legacy Award at the University of Rochester, along with polar explorer Ann Bancroft and long-distance cold-water swimmer Lynne Cox. They spoke on the theme "Daring the Impossible: Strong Women Take on the World," describing how they draw attention to causes larger than their own ambitions. Visit www.carolwhite.org for further information.

In 2006 she and David completed winter climbs of the forty-eight highest peaks in the White Mountains of New Hampshire; in 1997 they completed winter climbs of the forty-six Adirondack High Peaks; and in 1994 became winter members of the Catskill 3500 Club, whose members climb the thirty-five peaks exceeding 3,500 feet in the Catskill Forest Preserve. Carol served from 2003 to 2007 on the Adirondack 46ers Executive Committee; she also chairs the 3500 Club conservation committee (David is the 3500 Club membership chairman). In 2000 they completed the Northeast 111, climbing all of the peaks that exceed 4,000 feet in New York and New England; they also have climbed eight of the 14,000-foot peaks in Colorado.

They participate in trail maintenance, lead hikes, restore lean-tos, write monthly hiking columns for the *Catskill Mountain Region Guide* and the *Poughkeepsie Journal,* and have led three 4-week hiking classes for the Mohawk Valley Institute for Learning in Retirement. Carol's commentary on how one becomes lost in the forest appeared in a *New York Times* science column by Henry Fountain in August 2009; that month they helped rescue an injured hiker on Mount Marcy, a story in this book.

CREDITS

Excerpts in this book have previously appeared in the following publications and are reprinted with permission.

"Nature Is Unforgiving: Case Studies," by Peter Crane, appeared under the title "The hikeSafe Initiative," in the summer 2007 issue of *Windswept,* a publication of the Mount Washington Observatory. The New Hampshire Fish and Game Department and the White Mountains National Forest are partners and joint owners of the hikeSafe program.

"Winter above Treeline" originally appeared in *Backwoods Ethics* by Laura and Guy Waterman (Boston, MA: Stone Wall Press, 1979). It was later published in *Wilderness Ethics,* also by Laura and Guy Waterman (Woodstock, VT: Countryman Press, 1993 and 2000). It is reprinted here by permission of Laura Waterman and The Countryman Press, www.countrymanpress.com.

"Porky Gulch and Above," by Landon G. Rockwell, first appeared in the *Mount Washington Observatory Bulletin,* summer/fall 1992. It was reprinted in *Along the Way,* Clinton, New York, 1998.

"A Leg Up: Challenges of a Self-Rescue," by Doug Mayer, appeared in AMC's *Appalachia Journal,* December 15, 1990, under the title, "A Leg Up: One Man's Challenge."

"Sub-Zero Weather Incapacitates," by Todd Bogardus, first appeared on www. hikesafe.com in February 2003. The New Hampshire Fish and Game Department and the White Mountains National Forest are partners and joint owners of the hikeSafe program.

"Fall from Saddleback Cliff," by Marian Zimmerman, first appeared in *Women with Altitude: Challenging the Adirondack High Peaks in Winter,* edited by Carol Stone White, 2005. Courtesy of North Country Books, Inc., Utica, New York.

"Injury Miles from Nowhere," by Arlene Heer Stefanko, appeared in *Adirondack Peak Experiences: Mountaineering Adventures, Misadventures, and the Pursuit of "The 46,"* edited by Carol Stone White, published by Black Dome Press. Copyright 2009. Used with permission.

"A Fall from Grace," by Melinda Broman, first appeared in *Adirondac,* a publication of the Adirondack Mountain Club, January/February 1999. It was reprinted in *Adirondack Peak Experiences: Mountaineering Adventures, Misadventures, and the Pursuit of "The 46,"* edited by Carol Stone White, published by Black Dome Press. Copyright 2009. Used with permission.

"Two Lives Saved by Search and Rescue Team," by Edith Tucker, appeared in the

Coös County Democrat, January 10, 2007, Salmon Press Newspapers, Frank Chilinski, publisher.

"Life-Threatening Conditions Cause Fatality," by Todd Bogardus, first appeared on www.hikesafe.com in March 2004. The New Hampshire Fish and Game Department and the White Mountains National Forest are partners and joint owners of the hikeSafe program.

"One Man Dead, One Rescued on Blackhead Mountain," by Susan Campriello, appeared in the *Daily Mail,* Tuesday, March 16, 2010. Reprinted with permission from Hudson-Catskill Newspapers.

"Break on Panther Mountain," by John Swanson, first appeared in *Catskill Canister,* April-June 2002. It was reprinted as "Not Just Another Day in the Woods" in *Catskill Peak Experiences: Mountaineering Tales of Endurance, Survival, Exploration, and Adventure from the Catskill 3500 Club,* edited by Carol Stone White, published by Black Dome Press. Copyright 2008. Used with permission.

"A Nice Day Becomes an Ice Day," by Marta Bolton Quilliam, first appeared in *Women with Altitude: Challenging the Adirondack High Peaks in Winter,* edited by Carol Stone White, 2005. Courtesy of North Country Books, Inc., Utica, New York.

"Descending into the Maelstrom," by Teddy "Cave Dog" Keizer, appears on his Web site, www.thedogteam.com.

Excerpts of "Enjoying a Frozen World," by Diane Duggento Sawyer, includes excerpts from her chapter in *Women with Altitude: Challenging the Adirondack High Peaks in Winter,* edited by Carol Stone White, 2005. Courtesy of North Country Books, Inc., Utica, New York.

"Whiteout and Bivouac on Algonquin Peak," by Dot Myer, first appeared in *Women with Altitude: Challenging the Adirondack High Peaks in Winter,* edited by Carol Stone White, 2005. Courtesy of North Country Books, Inc., Utica, New York.